# PLAYING HARDBALL

BOOKS BY DAVID WHITFORD

Extra Innings: A Season in the Senior League (1991)

A Payroll to Meet: A Story of Greed, Corruption
and Football at SMU (1989)

# DAVID WHITFORD

# Playing Hardball

## The High-Stakes Battle for Baseball's New Franchises

D O U B L E D A Y
New York   London   Toronto   Sydney   Auckland

PUBLISHED BY DOUBLEDAY
a division of Bantam Doubleday Dell Publishing Group, Inc.
1540 Broadway, New York, New York 10036

DOUBLEDAY and the portrayal of an anchor with a dolphin
are trademarks of Doubleday, a division of
Bantam Doubleday Dell Publishing Group, Inc.

Library of Congress Cataloging-in-Publication Data

Whitford, David.
Playing hardball: the high-stakes battle for baseball's new
franchises/David Whitford.
p.   cm.
Includes index.
1. Baseball—Economic aspects—United States. 2. Baseball—United
States—Clubs—Organization and administration. 3. Sports
franchises—United States—Location. 4. National League of
Professional Baseball Clubs. I. Title.
GV880.W45   1993
338.4'7796357'640973—dc20   92-40453
CIP

3   5   7   9   10   8   6   4   2

Once more with love,
for Sara

# Acknowledgments

To write a book about events in Florida and Colorado from a base in Massachusetts, well, you need help, and I was lucky to have lots.

From colleagues, among them: Gordon Edes and Ed Giuliotti of the *Fort Lauderdale Sun-Sentinel*; Dan Le Batard and Scott Price of the *Miami Herald*; Norm Clarke and Tracy Ringolsby of the *Rocky Mountain News*; Barney Hutchinson of the *Boulder Daily Camera*; Teri Thompson of *Westword*; and Irv Moss of the *Denver Post*.

From the many participants in the story who gave me their time, their knowledge, their insight and their trust, especially John Boles, David Dombrowski, John Frew, Gary Hughes, Paul Jacobs, Kevin Knobloch, Steve Matt and Frank Wren. From Margo Malone, archivist of the Florida Marlins; and Diana Stahl, the biggest Orioles' fan that ever worked on the staff of Senator Tim Wirth.

From Don Hinchey, who patiently laid out for me the elements of the Denver story, gave me access to his extraordinary files, and cheerfully answered my questions whenever I called; Lew Cady and all his friends in the Marv Throneberry section; Tom and Patty Jones, who put me up in style in St. Petersburg; Joel Millman and John Rolfe, who shared their resources with a freelancer; Jack Liesner, Carol and Steve Zinati, and Nancy and Ted Davis, who welcomed me to Colorado; and absolutely, Kay Mitchell, who solely on the basis of a flimsy family claim (she's my first cousin, once removed, we think) took me in for weeks on end and then, when I wasn't around, faithfully clipped the Denver newspapers.

But also from Ron Suskind, who helped me see the potential in this project; Ned Leavitt, who encouraged me to go ahead; Rob Robertson, my editor, who always cared as much as I did; Charles Euchner—wise professor, astute critic and ballpark buddy; Al and Del DeSimone, who turned their house upside down to provide me with a place to work; and most of all, for their love and tolerance, Sara and Emma.

# Contents

# PLAYING HARDBALL

# Prologue: At the Doral

HEADQUARTERS for the 1991 baseball winter meetings in Miami Beach was the Fontainebleau Hotel, but Marlins general manager David Dombrowski had to settle for the Doral, a quarter mile up Collins Avenue, because it was the only place he could get a suite. That's part of the reality of working for an expansion team. Fancy set of rooms, though, all done up in wicker and bamboo with a fake fireplace at one end of the living room and not one but two big views, east over the blue-gray Atlantic and south down Biscayne Bay to Miami's bright glass towers. It was here in suite 1730 on Monday afternoon, December 9, with the slanting midwinter rays pouring in the windows, that a dozen Marlins baseball men pulled up chairs around a large coffee table—on top of which were pretzels, soft drinks, jelly beans and a copy of the *Baseball Register*—and set themselves to the task of building a ball club from scratch.

Only a few months before, this would have been an Expos meeting, not a Marlins meeting. In September, Marlins president Carl Barger caught up with Dombrowski—then the Expos' general manager—in Philadelphia, and flew him back to Fort Lauderdale that same night on owner Wayne Huizenga's private jet. The first person Dombrowski hired was another Expo, Gary Hughes, to be his scouting director, followed in short order by Expos John Boles (farm director), Frank Wren (assistant general manager), Whitey Lockman (senior adviser, major league scout), Angel Vasquez (director of Latin American operations) and Orrin Freeman (associate scouting director, international operations), and that's just counting the ones in suite 1730. By the time the commissioner stepped in and put a halt to the raid, the Marlins had come away with fourteen former Expos, comprising almost a third of the Marlins' baseball staff.

That so many Expos moved to the Marlins all at once was partly a case of Dombrowski wanting to surround himself with guys he already knew, which is a baseball tradition at least as old as the seventh-inning stretch. ("If you're going to go to war," says Jeff Wren, Frank's brother, who also made the jump, "it might as well be with your friends.") That said, Dombrowski's friends were evidently well qualified; twice since 1988, Montreal had been named Organization of the Year by *Baseball America* (a predictor, in retrospect, of the young team's strong second-place finish in 1992). Dombrowski wasn't the only GM interested in obtaining their services. So was Bob Gebhard, his expansion opposite in Colorado. And Gebhard, who came from the Twins but used to work in Montreal, managed to get three: Herb Hippauf (national cross-checker), Pat Daugherty (scouting director) and Larry Bearnarth (major league scout).

It turns out Gebhard wanted Frank Wren too, and offered to make him scouting director, which some people would consider a better job than assistant general manager. Wren was tempted. He had been an assistant in the Montreal scouting department for seven years, and so it was the logical next step in his career. Plus it would have been a chance to hook up again with his old mentor. Ten years before, Gebhard had given Wren his first job in coaching (at Jamestown in the New York–Penn League; Pat Daugherty was the manager), and later he opened the door for Wren to move into the front office. Wren even loves to ski. He could have been happy in Colorado.

But to a young, ambitious baseball man aiming to get in at the start of something big, Florida, not Colorado, was the place to be: because of the weather (a little damp perhaps, but at least it doesn't snow); because of the fact that so many ballplayers already live here during the off-season (and presumably would choose to play here, given the choice as free agents); because of the proximity, cultural as well as geographic, to the baseball hotbeds of Puerto Rico, Venezuela and the Dominican Republic (ah, and Cuba, which is bound to open up one day, and when it does!); and because of the pay, don't forget the pay. Dombrowski was making $475,000, reportedly more than any other general manager in baseball except Whitey Herzog. The department heads were all at the "top of the line in the industry," according to Dombrowski, and the major league scouting staff was "the highest-paid in baseball." Even amateur scouts with no prior experience were getting $30,000 to start with the Marlins, 50 percent above the industry norm. And Wren—only 33, and not even a department head—was under contract for two years at a salary of $275,000, or roughly twice as much as the Rockies could come up with. ("If you want to steal somebody away," said a shaken John Antonucci, the Rockies' lead partner, "put another twenty thousand dollars on the table. Don't leave a hundred thousand on the table. That's crazy!")

The pay especially was meaningful—for its own sake as well as for the promise it held. Baseball men are cursed with being experts in a business in which *everyone* is an expert. They're used to being told what to do by fans, players and sportswriters and above all by the rich guys who write their checks. That Huizenga was paying them all top dollar was a happy fact which they chose to interpret as a gesture of respect, a sign that their services were valued, and a clue that Barger, who never knew much about fielding a team (he was a lawyer), and

Huizenga, who knew nothing (he's a football fan), were not only going to allow them to do their jobs, they meant to *encourage* them. And with so much money flowing from the top already, chances were good they would have the resources to do the job right. All of which contributed to the mood of quiet exhilaration in suite 1730.

"The most exciting thing there is is an expansion draft," Dombrowski said, once everybody was settled. "It doesn't get any more exciting than that. It's our franchise, the players that we get. What we do here, what thoughts we have, what original things we can do, will make the difference. Out of the thirty-six players we draft, if we can get six players that otherwise we wouldn't have gotten simply because your judgment is so much better, and because of the extra work you do, those six players can make the difference for a long time.

"The Denver club has the same challenge. They're approaching it, as you know, in a much different fashion than we are. But perhaps in our lifetime there may not be another expansion. So this is our chance to be involved in something unique. Everybody I've talked to in the game says it will be the most exciting thing that you've ever been associated with. The biggest challenge. The most fun."

DOMBROWSKI OCCUPIED the power slot—an armchair in front of the south window, the sun behind his back. Tall and slim, with thick brown hair parted on the side, blue eyes and a weak chin saved by a deep vertical cleft—and wearing an expensive-looking suit of European cut, a lavender shirt and a wide tie with flowers on it—he looked both prosperous and hip, '80s style. Still, he seemed awfully young, younger even than his 35 years. He looked more like a kid fresh out of college getting ready for the fantasy league draft at the office than a baseball man leading other more seasoned baseball men on the biggest adventure of their professional lives.

Dombrowski grew up in Palos Heights, a south suburb of Chicago. His dad is the parts manager at the local Chevrolet dealership. His mom is a secretary at the high school. Smart and athletic, Dombrowski was recruited by Cornell, and played football and baseball his freshman year. But money was tight, and in his sophomore year he transferred to Western Michigan University, which offered him a free ride. There he majored in accounting and set his sights on preparing for the only job he ever wanted: general manager of a major league baseball team.

In December 1977, in the middle of his senior year, Dombrowski approached his parents and asked permission to cash in his childhood savings bonds and fly to Hawaii for the winter meetings, where he hoped to find a job in baseball. "This is really what I want to do," Dombrowski recalls saying (and one can easily imagine what he was like 14 years ago, when he was only 21—buttoned-down, earnest, sober beyond his years). "This is what I would like my life to be," he told his parents, and with some reluctance, they said yes.

Dombrowski trolled the lobby of the Honolulu Hotel in a coat and tie, passing out résumés, working the house phone, introducing himself to everyone he could. ("Some people were willing to meet with me, some people never met with me, some people met with me for a minute.") One day, while he was sitting on a bench outside the front door of the hotel, Roland Hemond, the general manager of the White Sox, walked by. Dombrowski had interviewed Hemond for his college honor's thesis, "The General Manager: The Man in the Middle." It was Hemond who urged him to learn Spanish and major in accounting if he really wanted to get a job in baseball. "I might have something for you," Hemond told him. "Meet me here tomorrow morning at eight."

Dombrowski was doubtful but he kept the appointment. When Hemond showed up, they talked for a few minutes in the lobby. Then Hemond told Dombrowski there were some other people he wanted him to meet and promised to call around two o'clock. Dombrowski spent the rest of the morning on the beach, studying for finals (he'd brought his books on the trip). When he got back to his room, his message light was blinking.

"C'mon up to my room," Hemond said when Dombrowski called.

"I just got off the beach," Dombrowski said. "I'm in my trunks, I've got sand all over me. Can I take a shower and come up later?"

"Everybody's relaxed and casual. Why don't you just come on up the way you are."

After a second round of interviews at Comiskey Park over Christmas vacation, the White Sox offered Dombrowski a job as administrative assistant in the minor leagues and scouting department. But there were two catches: the pay was only $7,000 a year, and he would have to start immediately. Dombrowski's mom was "extremely upset." She wanted him to stay in school, and gave in only after he promised to complete his degree (a promise he eventually fulfilled with correspondence courses). His dad wasn't happy either, but for a different reason. Together they sat down at the kitchen table and worked out exactly what it would cost him to go to work, what with clothes, gas, insurance and a $25-a-week rent to live at home. ("Why do I gotta pay rent?" "Because you're working!") Altogether his projected expenses came to $8,000, more than his pay. "I can't let you start and lose money," his dad said.

The next day, Dombrowski showed his neat list of figures to Mike Veeck, the son of owner Bill Veeck. "Well," Veeck said after he looked it over, "we normally don't like to start people at that high a salary. But because you're the type of guy we like to have in the organization, we'll start you at eight thousand."

It was a small office and Dombrowski did everything. He answered letters, ran the auxiliary scoreboard, timed runners going to first base, and helped drag the tarp over the infield when it rained. As George "Birdie" Tebbetts had done for Hemond when he was a kid starting out in the Milwaukee Braves' organization, so Hemond did now for Dombrowski, sending him out on the road with legendary scout Paul Richards to round out his apprenticeship. Though he had never played professionally, Dombrowski rose swiftly up the organization—to director of player development, then assistant general manager, and finally vice president in charge of baseball operations, a pinnacle he reached before his 30th birthday.

But in 1986, after eight and a half years with the White Sox, Dombrowski was swept out during an organizational house-cleaning by the new club president, Ken Harrelson. Immediately he was hired by the Expos to replace the departing Bob Gebhard as farm director. Two years later, at age 32, he became the youngest general manager in baseball. Sportswriters dubbed him the "Boy Wonder."

But there were signs by the late summer of 1991 that Dombrowski's star was fading in Montreal. After a surprisingly strong finish the year before, the Expos were suddenly in free fall, on their way to a last-place finish 19 games under .500. In June, Dombrowski fired popular manager Buck Rodgers, replacing him with Tom Runnells. Key trades (the other thing they called him was "Dealin' Dave") came back to haunt him; Otis Nixon to the Braves for catcher Jimmy Kremers comes to mind. The roof fell in at Olympic Stadium, literally, forcing the Expos to take to the road for the last month of the season. And some veterans grumbled that Dombrowski was spending too much time in the clubhouse hanging out with the players, which seemed to suggest that maybe the Boy Wonder was losing his grip.

Barger insisted he was surprised when he approached Expos president Claude Brochu at the September owners meeting in Baltimore to ask permission to talk to Dombrowski, and got an immediate green light. He said Dombrowski was his first choice all along; he just didn't think he could get him. Nevertheless, before Barger even spoke to Dombrowski, he offered the job to former Tigers general manager Bill Lajoie. Lajoie all but accepted, but later changed his mind for personal reasons. ("Oh shit," was the first thing Barger said when Lajoie called with the bad news, according to Lajoie.) Dombrowski, on the other hand, never hesitated. He met with Barger for four hours in Barger's room at the Sheraton Society Hill in Philadelphia on September 18, joined Huizenga and Barger for dinner that night in Fort Lauderdale, shook hands afterward on a deal, and appeared before reporters at Joe Robbie Stadium the next morning.

Whenever he was asked during those first few months,

Dombrowski invariably described the job of building an expansion team as a "dream come true." Hughes, the scouting director, used exactly the same line. So did Gebhard in Colorado, and Daugherty too, and no doubt plenty of other baseball men on both expansion teams whose words just never got written down. Maybe part of the reason was that among the myths that sustain baseball, one of the most powerful is the myth of renewal. It has to do with starting fresh each spring; with the feeling that accompanies the day when the newspaper prints the standings for the first time, and every team is in first place; with the old autumn saw "Wait till next year!"; with winter hot-stove speculations; with hope. To be a part of building any ball club is to participate in that myth of renewal. But to build an expansion club goes back even further, to creation, to a time of pure imagining. To be a part of building an expansion team is to live for an extended time, dreamily, in spring.

NEVER BEFORE had two expansion teams been given so much time to prepare. Peter Bavasi, the original president and general manager of the Blue Jays, remembers how he arrived in Toronto in the late summer of 1976, four months before the draft and nine months away from opening day. "I always thought it an appropriate gestation period for an infant franchise," he says, "to be delivered some nine months after inception." By comparison, Dombrowski and Gebhard each had a full year to get ready for the draft.

On the other hand, they had a bigger job. In the past, expansion was strictly a one-league affair; when the Blue Jays and the Mariners joined the American League, AL teams divided the expansion-fee pot and AL teams supplied all the players for the draft. Now the National League was expanding. But with the cost of a franchise risen to a staggering $95 million (compared with $7 million in '77), and no further expansion contemplated anytime soon, AL owners fought for, and won, a cut of the proceeds, albeit an unequal one. As part of the deal, the Rockies and the Marlins would be able to choose players from both leagues, according to a formula designed to lessen somewhat the exposure of the AL.

The draft would work like this: To begin, all the existing teams in both leagues protect 15 players from throughout their organizations. Then the Rockies and the Marlins alternate selections until one player each has been chosen from all 26 teams. In round two, the NL teams protect three more players, the AL teams protect four, and the Rockies and the Marlins pick again. The last round begins the same way, but it ends as soon as all 12 NL teams, but only eight AL teams, have sacrificed one more player each. By then, every NL organization will have lost, in theory, its 16th most valuable player, its 20th and its 24th; and every AL club, its 16th, its 21st and possibly its 26th.

Gebhard, with fewer resources than Dombrowski, was going to have to rely primarily on Larry Bearnarth, the former Montreal pitching coach. Bearnarth was new to scouting— he'd never even used a radar gun—but to him alone in the Rockies' organization had fallen the task of scouting the big leagues full-time. The rest of the scouts were expected to focus their attention on the amateur draft until June, at which point the more experienced among them would be assigned professional coverage from the big leagues down through class A. It was a makeshift approach, obviously budget-driven, and a clear sign that money was tight in Colorado.

Dombrowski was luckier than Gebhard. Huizenga not only came up with the money to pay him and everybody else in the organization top dollar. He also gave him practically free rein to spend what he thought he had to spend in order to win. So Dombrowski had gone out and hired five top-flight professional scouts: Whitey Lockman, Cookie Rojas from the Angels, John Young from the Rangers, Ken Kravec from the Royals and Scott Reid from the Cubs. From this day forward, all of them had but one job—to make sure the Marlins were ready for the draft on November 17, 1992.

Lockman's assignment, as Dombrowski explained it now, was the same as Bearnarth's. To scout the big leagues full-time beginning in spring training and compile a preferential list; basically 1–650, although that doesn't take into account players who move between the minors and the majors during the season. "Ken, Cookie, Scott, John," Dombrowski said, nodding at each in turn, "you will each be given a division and will be responsible for every club—AA, AAA and major league—in those organizations. That's your division, your players, your responsibility. Your *guys*. What we're going to ask you to do is prepare a priority list within your organizations, 1–24 in the National League and 1–26 in the American league."

Apart from Lockman, 65, who wore loose-fitting pants and a blazer, and whose hair had gone soft and white, all the Marlins' scouts seemed cut from the same mold; fortysomething, hair firmly in place (going gray but not all the way there), at home in tight-fitting slacks and pastel polo shirts open at the neck. Unlike Dombrowski, the scouts were all former big league players. Lockman, a 15-year veteran, was the one leading off second base at the Polo Grounds on October 3, 1951, when Bobby Thomson hit the home run known as "the shot heard round the world" that capped the Giants' legendary comeback; he went on to manage the Cubs in the early 1970s. Rojas played for 16 years, was an all-star in both leagues, and managed the Angels in 1988. Kravec, at 40 the youngest of the five scouts, pitched eight years for the White Sox and the Cubs. Reid was up briefly with the Phillies in 1969 and '70. Young retired from the Tigers in 1971 with a .500 career batting average—two hits in four at-bats.

"John," Dombrowski said, turning to Young, "you take the American League West." Young, who lives in Diamond Bar, California, grunted accommodatingly. AL or NL, it made no difference to him, as long he got a western division.

"Scott, let me just ask you, between the two leagues, which one do you feel more comfortable with, National or American?"

"Probably the National League is better," Reid said. "I'm very familiar with the American League but most of that information we've already got. There ought to be a way for me to pass it on."

"That's a good point," Dombrowski said. "So you'll take the National League West? Okay, and, um, Ken, why don't you take the American League East. And, Cookie, you take the National League East. Whitey, you've got the major leagues.

"Couple of things. Your schedule is your own, however you want to set it up. Just keep me informed. The kicker to that is please don't wait to cover the minor league clubs till the end. I've talked to general managers who've been involved in this. They all say the clubs out there are going to do whatever they can to hide players. They'll have guys who will all of a sudden disappear with injuries the second half of the year, or they'll move them from AA to A in June because they figure that's when we're going to start covering them, like we normally do. You guys are the best scouts in the business. I'm counting on you being able to dwarf other clubs as far as their knowledge of the minor leagues goes. That's where we're going to steal players. So please, start covering the minor league clubs early."

By minor leagues, Dombrowski meant class AA and above. Most of the players in A ball would be ineligible for the draft. But not all, especially this year, and especially if clubs engaged in the kind of player shuffling Dombrowski had been warned about. And so to make sure the Marlins saw everybody, Dombrowski had come up with a new category of scouts he called master scouts, who'd be responsible for covering the A leagues. Already he'd hired Birdie Tebbetts from the Orioles, Lou Fitzgerald from the Braves and Eddie Bockman from the Phillies, all of them legends among baseball men, and all of them well into their 70s.

"Some of these guys judgmentally may not be quite at the top of their games," Dombrowski said, "but I think when it comes to recognizing the players we're talking about, they'll be helpful. They'll be responsible for talking to you, and letting you know if there's anybody that's really a quality prospect that's draft-eligible. Some of them are up in age and their memories may not be quite as good. It may be up to you to prod them on what they have."

By now it was after four-thirty in the afternoon. Ties were being loosened, shoes were coming off. Away to the south and west, the sun was slipping behind the Miami skyline, casting the room in shadow. Dan Lunetta, the minor league administrator, stood up to turn on a light and knocked over a soft-drink can. "That's it," someone said, "the first error committed by a member of the Florida Marlins!"

"PEOPLE ARE GOING to continually ask: what's our philosophy?" Dombrowski said after a ten-minute break. He sat with his legs crossed. Most of the scouts sat with both feet on the ground. "I've been asked that a thousand times already and you're going to be asked it too. Standard pat answer: we're taking the Best Player Available. Are you gonna take young players? Are you gonna take old players? Are you gonna take a mixture? We're going to take"—and this time everyone chimed in—"*the Best Player Available*. Good. They might get tired of the response, but keep giving it to them. Because we don't want to tip our hands. When the Rockies are sitting there and they're deciding, 'Do we protect a veteran guy or a young guy?' we don't want them to think that they know what we're going to do. Because then we'll have made their decision for them. It might only be one player, or it might be two players, but those are the one or two players that we'll want to get. So let's not tip our hands."

"I really think that you can't overemphasize that," said Hughes, who was sitting next to Wren on the couch. "They're going to ask, 'Well, what if Jose Canseco and Mark McGwire and Will Clark . . . ?' We're going to take *the Best Player Available*. Eventually they'll respect you for that answer. We'll even make up T-shirts if you want."

"Now, one of the things that we'll have to ask ourselves," said Dombrowski, "and I don't know the answer right now, but when we get to the third round, maybe the second round, are we taking the best player available or filling needs? Probably because of free agency we'll be able to take the best player available. But we may at some time have to switch over to a need. We have said that we're not going to dip into free agency next year in a major way. But let's say Barry Larkin's sitting out there, and Barry Larkin says, 'I want to play in Florida,' and our other total payroll is eight million dollars, and this guy's in the prime of his career, he'll be playing for

ten years. Shoot, maybe we sign the guy and give up our number-one draft pick for the next year because he's going to be a
guy that can anchor our ball club for years to come. Most likely
guys like Barry Larkin aren't going to want to play here,
they're going to want to play on clubs that have a chance to
win. We're more apt to get the guy like Andre Dawson—thirty-
five or thirty-six or thirty-seven years old, saying, 'That's
where I want to play.' And then we have to say, 'Well, gee,
we're not willing to pay a guy four million dollars for two
years, when by the time we get a chance to be competitive, he's
not going to be with us anymore.' One thing we can do, we
can control where our payroll is going in the future. We're not
tied to an Andres Galarraga, for example. We don't have those
difficulties. We can plan where we want to go.

"There's going to be a lot of guys out there next year, and a
lot of clubs are going to be at their max payroll, and there may
be some bargains. There may be some filler players that we
can sign—maybe someone who can be an everyday player for
us for a year or two while we let some young guy develop, or
maybe a guy that fulfills a utility role at a bargain-basement
price that later on we can trade. You're going to judge them all
by their ability, but let's face it, some positions have more
value than others. Catchers are hard to find. In the expansion
draft, there's a lot of value attached to catchers. Or else a guy
like Davey Martinez—in the last year of his contract, a five-
plus guy, going into free agency, a two-million-dollar-a-year
player. You might as well say this guy's not us. But there are a
lot of clubs that are interested in him and you might get a
pretty good prospect for him. He has value out there. So that's
where value is going to be really important."

Dombrowski was dancing. What he wanted his scouts to understand was that there will undoubtedly be players the Marlins will draft for no other reason than to trade them. The
rules discourage this by trying to make sure that no one other
than the expansion teams sees the protected lists. Otherwise
the Marlins might be tempted to prearrange a deal for Andre
Dawson, for example, after the Cubs left Dawson unprotected
knowing full well the Marlins had no interest in him. The risk

the Marlins take is that they wind up with an expensive player they don't want. Which is why the deal has to be worked out in advance. Which is against the rules. Which is why Dombrowski was dancing.

"The more you guys can find out about what Denver might do, the better," Dombrowski continued. "They're not going to have the coverage that we're going to have. For example, you might find out that Bob Gebhard, being from Minnesota, likes the Minnesota players. So maybe we decide that we want to take Minnesota players because they don't really have the coverage on the rest of the league. I would doubt that Denver is going to take a lot of guys who are breaking-ball hitters, even if the guy can hit the ball out of the park. They can look for guys who are DHs. We have to take care of ourselves first and foremost but we've got to be aware of what Denver's doing.

"We're going to need a manager. If you get a chance to watch a manager, and are impressed by him, please let me know. Make an effort to have breakfast or lunch with him and get to know him a little better. Right now I've sat down and made a preliminary list—fifty guys—and I don't know who's going to be available. There might be somebody out there that you have a real good feel on and I don't know anything about."

"David," said John Boles, "can I ask a question?"

"Sure"

"This may be way off base. Is there any thought on your part that we might get a manager, an interim manager, until the guy we want becomes available?"

"There's been some thought about that. One of the things we're going to have to decide, if we don't get *la crème de la crème,* are we going to decide to take a young manager, a first-rate quality guy, and surround him with perhaps some veteran coaches, and see that guy grow? Or do we take a veteran guy, and let him manage the club for a little while, and have a young guy on his staff or at the minor league level that we might be grooming to take his place?"

Next, Frank Wren explained the grading system. "The top category is 'Excellent,' " he said, "which is a franchise player, and there may be only one or two of those guys. The second group is 'Good,' which still could be an all-star type of player, but is not that franchise type of player. And then 'Average' is an everyday player or a starter or whatever, but he's never going to be an all-star. You know, Spike Owen, a guy like that. 'Fringe' is a role player—ninth or tenth pitcher, fringe left-hander, something like that. And then 'Organizational' is an emergency major league guy, at least AAA-competent."

The categories were the same as those used by the major league scouts in Montreal, to which were added a second set of rankings applicable only to the expansion draft—high interest, medium interest, low interest or no interest. Again, Dawson might still be an "Excellent" player, but the Marlins would have no interest in drafting him. "You're talking about what you project a guy to be," Dombrowski put in. "So if you're talking about a prospect as compared with a major league player, you have to consider where you think his future value's going to be. That's not unlike the June free-agent draft."

On into the early evening they talked. About Joe Robbie Stadium (grass field, normal dimensions, high humidity, probably a pitcher's park); about the importance of scouting switch hitters from both sides of the plate; about the need to distinguish between throwing arms in the outfield (the average right fielder's arm is stronger than the average left fielder's); about spring training ("I don't put much stock in spring judgments"); and about travel arrangements ("Call the Greek, he'll take care of you"). Then Wren went over the list of supplies they'd all be receiving: an American League *Red Book*, a National League *Green Book*, a copy of the *Baseball Register*, subscriptions to *Baseball America*, *The Sporting News*, and *Baseball Weekly*, a scout's pass to every ballpark, organizational rosters, major and minor league schedules, a laptop computer and a radar gun.

Finally, Dombrowski unfolded his legs, looked around the room, and asked if there were any more questions. The men smiled and shrugged their shoulders. It had been a long meeting. Now it was time for dinner, and after that a group excursion to Joe Robbie Stadium on this Monday night to watch the Dolphins play.

"Everybody here should plan on being in Fort Lauderdale after the end of the season and basically commit the next five, six weeks until the draft," Dombrowski said in closing. "We're going to be busy."

# 1

## Playing Hardball

*Baseball is something that happens 162 times a year. So you have 162 times each year for the city to be a little happy or a little sad together. Economic impact may well be hocus-pocus. "We'll now have a multiplying factor of six! Wait a minute, let's make that eight!" Who knows? But the fun of it is where the real impact is, I think. It's a matter of fun. We'll have more fun.*

—LEW CADY, creative director
Broyles/Allebaugh/Davis, Englewood, Colorado

FOR A BASEBALL MAN, summer is the busy season. Even before he retired, Bob Howsam found time every winter to go to Arizona, but summers he was always in Denver or St. Louis or Cincinnati, working hard. Now that he's retired, Howsam and his wife, Janet, come to Glenwood Springs, Colorado, during the warm months—for the mountain air, for the view across the canyon from their patio, and for the healing, hot-spring waters. At 73, Howsam has wavy white hair he combs high off his forehead, a pink face and rock-hard Popeye fore-arms that go all the way back to his days as a Navy delivery and test pilot during World War II and before that to when he was a pretty good semipro ballplayer down in La Jara, Colorado.

As a young man, he had the good fortune to marry a girl who was smart and pretty and also the daughter of Edwin C. Johnson. Like so many other Coloradans of a certain genera-tion, Johnson came West on a stretcher, near death with tu-berculosis. He took a work cure on a mountain homestead way out in northwestern Colorado. When he got his health back he moved to town, to Craig, where he ran a flour mill and taught school and eventually got himself elected to the legislature. In 1931 he was elected lieutenant governor, and after that gover-nor, and after that United States senator. He served 34 years in public office and was never once defeated, a Democrat in a Republican state. "He loved his state," says the son-in-law. "He loved his country. He was a self-made man, a strong man. They used to say he'd cut his throat and the other person would bleed to death."

After the war, young Bob left the family honey farm in southern Colorado and went to Washington with his father-in-law as chief aide. "I wanted to find out if I was interested in politics," he says. Not very, it turned out. But luckily the gov-ernor (that's what the people always called him in Colorado, even after he went to Washington) had another passion be-sides politics and that was baseball. Johnson helped resuscitate the old class A Western League following the demise of the wartime Victory League, and for that they named him honor-ary president. So in 1947, Johnson asked Howsam if he wanted to go back to Denver as executive secretary of the new league. What was supposed to be a six-month assignment be-came for Howsam the first step in a lifelong journey. And a first step, it turns out, toward the day when major league base-ball would break out of its ten-city northeastern kingdom, and in successive waves expand west and south across the continent and even into Canada, and land at last, nearly half a century later, in Denver.

HOWSAM DIDN'T LAST LONG in the league office. The very next year, together with his father and his brother, he bought a controlling interest in the Denver Bears and moved them out of old Merchants Stadium and into a new lighted ballpark dug out of a dump at the corner of 20th and Federal and paid for with $250,000 in bonds floated by the governor himself. Bears Stadium was a modern marvel. Fans drove their cars right up to the adjacent parking lot, then walked down the berm to their seats. The outfield opened on a view of the growing Denver skyline. There was nothing else like it in the Western League. In 1949, the first full season in the new stadium, the Bears drew 463,039 fans, a minor league record. "It was one of the few things in town," Howsam says, "and it was great."

In those days the Bears pulled in fans from all up and down the Front Range, and from the tiny farming communities on the plains east of Denver. On town nights, fans supplied their own pregame entertainment. The folks from Yuma, Colorado, used to bring jackrabbits, which were let loose on the infield for the players to chase down. Howsam was an innovator. He experimented with speeding up the game by having his pitchers warm up on the sidelines before the inning was over. He advertised all-beef hot dogs. He once commissioned a Denver bakery to come up with a powder that smelled like bread baking in the oven, something he could spray around the ballpark before the gates opened to stimulate concession sales. ("They couldn't do it," Howsam says sadly.) He designed a hideous-looking thing called a strike-zone uniform, all white between the knees and the armpits but otherwise navy blue, which was supposed to help the umpires call balls and strikes; umpires loved them, players hated them. Years before Charlie Finley ever thought of it, Howsam tried out yellow-colored baseballs for higher visibility, and multicolored bases. Unlike Finley,

Howsam always dressed the Bears in black shoes, on the theory that as long as the ball was white, it should be the only white object on the field, in order to make it easier for the fans to follow the action.

Weather was sometimes a challenge. When it snowed, Howsam hired fraternity boys from the University of Denver to roll big snowballs all night until the field was cleared. Then if the infield dirt was still wet he'd cover it with wood shavings, soak it with gasoline, and set it on fire. One day he burned 600 gallons. April was the worst month, totally unpredictable, which is not to say May was never a problem. Once the Bears were snowed out three straight days at the end of May. October can be beautiful in Colorado, but Howsam remembers a day in October when 17 inches of snow fell and snapped the branches off the trees. On the other hand, he says, there were Februaries when he could have held spring training right there in Denver, and Christmas days when the warm winter wind called by its Indian name, "chinook," meaning snow eater, came blasting up the Front Range all the way from Mexico, and Howsam played catch with his son in shirt sleeves in the park next to his house.

IN 1952, the landscape of major league baseball still looked exactly as it had in 1902. The same two leagues, the same eight teams per league, and the same ten cities represented (three teams in New York; two each in Philadelphia, Boston, Chicago and St. Louis; and one each in Detroit, Cincinnati, Cleveland, Pittsburgh and Washington, D.C.). But pressure was building, what with incomes rising across the country and population centers shifting, and in 1953 the Boston Braves became the first team to upset the status quo of half a century by abandoning the market they shared with the Red Sox and relocating to Milwaukee. One year later the Browns surrendered St. Louis to the Cardinals and moved to Baltimore. And the year after that the A's handed Philadelphia to the Phillies and headed for Kansas City, in what was the big leagues' first foray beyond the Mississippi. The A's move in particular had repercussions in Denver, for it left the Kansas City Blues'

American Association franchise without a home. Howsam
bought the club, the Yankees' top farm team, and moved it to
Denver, and in 1955 the Bears were reborn as a class AAA
team.

The only reason Howsam made the jump to AAA was to
satisfy the fans in Denver, who maybe weren't ready for the
big leagues yet but figured they were better than a class A
town. It was a mistake, he now feels. His costs went up, attendance stayed flat, and at about the same time the world of
minor league baseball changed forever. "National TV came
right on in and smothered us," says Howsam. In a scenario
played out across the country, the Bears at the ballpark suddenly had to compete with the Yankees on television, and of
course they could not. Even the blackout rule, which pre-
vented head-to-head competition and was supposed to benefit
the minor leagues, worked against Howsam because of the
time-zone factor. Often the Yankees game would just be heading into the seventh inning or so by the time the Bears game
got underway in Denver, forcing the televised game off the
air. Fans were livid, and blamed the Bears. Howsam went so
far as to try to get a local exemption to the rule, just to get the
fans off his back.

Attendance declined; revenues suffered. Howsam took to
selling off his ballplayers just to survive. One year he made
$100,000 that way and still lost money. Trying to think of a
way to make television work for him instead of against him, he
looked into something called Phonevision from Zenith, actually a primitive version of pay-per-view. Howsam dreamed of
one day sending Bears games to subscribers up and down the
Front Range. He even flew to Chicago to view a demonstra-
tion at the Drake Hotel—they broadcasted *Pride of the Yankees*
on the system—but nothing more ever came of it.

Gradually Howsam was coming around to the idea that if he
couldn't beat major league baseball, maybe he could figure out
a way to join it. And it was in that context one summer evening in 1958, after a Bears game, that Howsam and his father-
in-law sat talking together in Howsam's car outside the governor's apartment on Grant Street between 11th and 12th, mull-
ing over the possibility of forming a third major league.

Starting a new league was a revolutionary idea, but not a new one. A couple of years earlier there'd been some talk in California of upgrading the Pacific Coast League, a movement that fizzled once the Dodgers and the Giants moved west. What got Howsam started was a speculative magazine article he had read on expansion by Branch Rickey. Howsam knew Rickey pretty well. They'd met for the first time back in '47, when Rickey was still in Brooklyn and Howsam was executive secretary of the Western League. In 1951, after Rickey moved to Pittsburgh, the Bears became a Pirate farm club (a terrific arrangement for the Bears, who got some good players out of the deal, except that Howsam had to learn to live with Rickey's eccentricities; Rickey liked to call at 6 A.M. Eastern time, to hell with time zones).

So there they were on Grant Street, Howsam behind the wheel, the governor in the passenger seat, coat off, wearing his red suspenders. "My father-in-law and I sat out there and we talked about Denver's opportunity," says Howsam. "What we were trying to do, frankly, was to find things for our stadium. Because of TV moving in on us, and really cutting our attendance down, we had to try to find a way to be able to continue to have baseball in Denver, and really compete with TV. I told him about this article of Mr. Rickey's. We agreed that the thing to do was to call Mr. Rickey and visit with him, which I did."

Howsam met with Rickey—by then 77 years old and retired from baseball—at the home of Rickey's daughter in Columbus, Ohio. Both men agreed that baseball was in no hurry to expand, that there were nevertheless cities capable of supporting teams, and that a new league made sense. The upshot of that first exploratory meeting was the formation in July 1959 of the Continental League, with charter franchises in Denver, Houston, Minneapolis–St. Paul, New York and Toronto, and Branch Rickey as commissioner. Later, franchises were added in Atlanta, Buffalo and Dallas–Fort Worth. Rickey went so far as to set up a class D minor league in North Carolina, which would have become the league's proprietary farm system; players were signed, games were played. The plan, according to Howsam, was for the Continental League to start play as a class AAA league in 1961 (the cities they selected were all AAA cities anyway), then graduate to full major league status after three years.

Major league baseball was wary of the upstart Continental League but did not actively oppose it, at least not at first. Part of the reason was that the established leagues had grown complacent. The last new league to challenge baseball's monopoly had been the Federal League in 1913, and it folded after three years. Still, it's unlikely that the Continental League would have gotten as far as it did were it not for the fact that baseball was in the midst of one of its periodic grillings by Congress. U.S. Representative Emanuel Celler of Brooklyn, chairman of the House Judiciary Committee, was holding hearings at the time on baseball's antitrust exemption. And Senator Estes Kefauver of Tennessee, chairman of the Senate Antitrust and Monopoly Committee, had recently introduced legislation to break up baseball's stranglehold on its labor force. Now was not the time to squash a potential competitor.

Instead, baseball co-opted the Continental League, agreeing in the summer of 1960 to expand by two teams in each league, and hinting at further expansion down the road. In 1961 the American League placed new franchises in Los Angeles and Washington, the latter to replace Calvin Griffith's Senators, who moved to Minneapolis and became the Twins. And in 1962 the National League took in the Continental League's two strongest cities, adding teams in Houston and New York. "They told us that as they expanded, they would take all the cities in," says Howsam. And for a while it looked like they would, one way or another. Atlanta got theirs after the Braves left Milwaukee in 1966. Dallas–Fort Worth got the Rangers, formerly the Washington Senators, in 1972. And in 1977, the last time baseball expanded, Toronto got the Blue Jays. But years later, with Buffalo and Denver still waiting, Howsam went back through his files to try to find a written reference to what he remembers as baseball's firm promise to one day satisfy all the Continental League cities. He was unsuccessful. "I never could find it," Howsam says, "and as I think back, I don't think baseball would have ever put something like that in writing."

The demise of the Continental League nearly destroyed Howsam. In order to meet the new league's minimum requirement of 35,000 seats, he added a grandstand in right field; now he found himself owing three-quarters of a million dollars to the Gerald Phipps construction company for seats he couldn't fill. At the same time he was saddled with another new acquisition, a football team, the Denver Broncos of the new American Football League, whose inaugural 1960 season was a flop. "I had two balls in the hand and I wasn't a wealthy person," says Howsam. "Baseball was my livelihood."

Eventually Howsam had to put the Bears and the Broncos up for sale, and in May 1961 both teams were taken over by a consortium led by one Gerald Phipps, the man who built the new grandstand. Howsam was crushed. On the night he lost control of the Bears, the story goes, Denver sportswriter Frank Haraway found him sitting all alone with his tears in the dark of the empty stadium. Howsam confirms the story. What was going through his mind?

"That I hadn't got the job done," he says 30 years later. "If I had planned it differently I could have done it, but your heart sometimes overshadows your head, and that was wrong. Denver had been so good to us in baseball, and I wanted to do it for Denver. At that time it was the greatest disappointment that ever happened."

Old Bears Stadium is still where it always was at the corner of 20th and Federal, but you can't really see it anymore. That's because it's buried under four levels of new stands that have been added over the years, raising capacity to more than 76,000. And it has a new name, one that's more familiar to football fans than to baseball fans: Mile High Stadium. For in the years following Howsam's sale of both teams, the Broncos eclipsed the Bears as Denver's main sports attraction. Phipps, a wealthy man to begin with, became even more wealthy thanks to the spectacular rise in value of NFL franchises. And Howsam was left to wonder what might have been.

But while Howsam may have missed his one big shot at becoming rich, there were compensating pleasures. In 1964 he got back into baseball as general manager of the St. Louis Cardinals, thanks to a recommendation from Rickey. And from there he went on to Cincinnati, where he was responsible for assembling the great Reds teams of the 1970s that came to be known as the Big Red Machine. "I couldn't have had it better," says Howsam.

And neither should he feel that he let Denver down. Were it not for the Continental League, there's no telling how long the door to expansion might have remained closed. Now it was open, and through that door lay Denver's eventual reward.

IN 1974, two Denver baseball boosters, Larry Varnell and Jim Burris, packed a scale model of Mile High Stadium into the back of Burris's station wagon and drove to New Orleans to attend the baseball winter meetings. Burris was the general manager of the Bears and had once been commissioner of the American Association, so he was hardly a stranger at such a gathering. Neither was Varnell, whose job as public affairs director at Denver's Central Bank left him with plenty of time for the job he really enjoyed, chairman of the Denver Chamber of Commerce sports committee. Varnell signed with the Cardinals out of high school in 1939, the same year as Stan Musial. "He went on to the Hall of Fame," Varnell likes to say, "and I went on to oblivion." During the war Varnell managed the Navy ball club at Pearl Harbor, an episode he remembers longingly as "really the highlight of my life." Bob Lemon played second base. (It was there, says Varnell, that Billy Herman turned Lemon into a pitcher, although Lou Boudreau would later get all the credit; Lemon went on to win 20 games seven times for the Indians and is in the Hall of Fame.) Varnell's toughest decision was who to play at shortstop, Pee Wee Reese or Phil Rizzuto; Rizzuto wound up at third.

Varnell and Burris were self-appointed baseball ambassadors. They had no real backing or else they would have flown to New Orleans instead of driven. Their mission as they understood it was simply to spread the good word about the Queen City and its continuing desire for big league baseball. Toward that end they set up a hospitality suite where baseball men could drink for free and check out the stadium model and get to know Larry and Jim. Back then, had somebody walked into their suite and offered to sell them a team, they wouldn't have known what to do. When baseball expanded in 1969, Denver had been passed over in large part for want of a qualified buyer. Five years later, the ownership question was still unresolved. The way Varnell remembers: "We were just talking about hopefully, since we didn't have a local owner, finding a city that was not doing well—and there were a lot of them then—that would be interested in moving to Denver, which was virgin territory because of its geographical location."

Nothing ever came of that trip to the winter meetings in 1974, at least nothing that can be measured. But within a couple of years Denver's status as a potential major league city took a giant step forward with the emergence of a bona fide big league buyer, billionaire Marvin Davis. The son of a boxer turned dressmaker turned oilman, Davis skipped the first two stages and went directly into oil, scoring big successes early in life as a Rocky Mountain wildcatter. The persistent energy shortages of the 1970s fueled a decade-long boom in the Colorado economy—the same as was happening in Texas and Saudi Arabia—and locally no one profited more than Davis. "Marvin Davis is either very incisive and clairvoyant or else he's the luckiest guy in the world," says Varnell, who came to know him well. "When oil was the big thing in Denver, everything he touched, he bought it at the right time and sold it right at the peak. Everything he touched."

As early as 1976, Davis tried unsuccessfully to buy the White Sox. A year later he went after the Orioles, and failed again. But Davis was keen on buying and he kept on trying. "One year I went to the winter meetings," Varnell recalls, "and he says, 'You find the team, I'll write the check.' " Fans in Denver began to like their chances. It seemed only a matter of time before the wildcatter scored his next big hit.

In late 1977, Davis reached an agreement in principle with
Charlie Finley to buy the Oakland A's and move them to Denver for the '78 season. Finley's A's had dominated the game in
the early '70s, winning five straight division titles sandwiched
around three World Series championships. They had won
their last AL West pennant in 1975, year one of the free-
agency era. Since Finley was not about to pay his stars what
they were worth in the open market, he tried to sell them all
before they had a chance to become free agents. Commissioner Bowie Kuhn, acting in "the best interests of baseball,"
voided most of the deals. But by 1977, playing without Catfish
Hunter, Vida Blue, Reggie Jackson, Rollie Fingers, Ken Holtzman and Joe Rudi, the A's dropped to last place. Now Finley
was anxious to sell.

But there were sticking points, beginning with the A's long-
term lease at Oakland–Alameda County Coliseum, which did
not expire for another ten years. A buyout was discussed, and
later a compromise arrangement whereby the Giants would
play half their games at Candlestick Park and half on the other
side of the bay (one obstacle was the insistence by Oakland
interests that the team change its name to the Bay Area Giants). In the end, though, the lease issues were overshadowed
by Finley's divorce, which tied up all his assets (including the
A's) and ruled out a deal in time for opening day. Denver
adman Lew Cady, a passionate fan despite never having had a
big league team of his own to root for, remembers seeing
printed schedules in books and magazines that spring with the
listing "Denver or Oakland A's," it was that close.

From then until the spring of 1980, rumors of an imminent
deal involving Davis and Finley's A's cropped up so many
times that casual fans in other parts of the country probably
assumed that Denver already had a team. In October 1978
news broke of a possible three-way deal, in which Davis would
buy the White Sox and Comiskey Park, Finley would move the
A's to Chicago, and Davis would lease Comiskey Park to Finley. In December, after American League owners (anxious
themselves to be rid of Finley) offered to put up $4 million to
help Finley buy his way out of the lease in Oakland, a straight-

up transaction between Finley and Davis again seemed likely (UPI reported it as fact), but that too collapsed. A year later Finley and Davis got together yet again, and probably this time the deal would have gone through. But before the details could be worked out, Al Davis announced his plan to move the NFL Raiders from Oakland to Los Angeles. Faced with losing both the A's and the Raiders, Coliseum authorities took steps to reopen Finley's lease buyout arrangement. And with that, a thoroughly frustrated Davis broke off talks in the spring of 1980, ending (for the time being) the bitter courtship between Denver and the A's.

"Marvin Davis is a very tough negotiator and dealer," says Varnell. "He's a high-stakes player. A winner. What happened with the A's was something which he was not accustomed to, and which he did not like. Finally he said, 'I'm tired of being kicked around and I'm through with it.'"

WHILE DENVER was preoccupied with chasing down the A's, baseball had gone ahead and expanded for the third time in its history, adding Toronto and Seattle to the American League in 1977. Seattle was a special case, having lost the ex-pansion Pilots after just one year to Milwaukee, where they became the Brewers in 1970; by awarding Seattle a replace-ment franchise, baseball sidestepped a $32.5 million lawsuit and avoided yet another potential showdown over antitrust. Toronto was a special case too, but for a different reason. To-ronto was the last of the available mega-markets in the United States and Canada. The American League almost had to ask itself, "Can we afford *not* to go into Toronto? Because if we don't, the other league will."

But after that the pressure was off. Between 1961 and 1977, ten teams—the equivalent of a whole new league and then some—had been added to the major leagues. The old ten-city kingdom connected by the points of the northeastern rail grid, which had survived well into the '50s, was by the late '70s a multinational empire with outposts in 24 cities coast to coast. And while for the first time an imbalance existed between the major leagues—14 teams in the AL, only 12 in the NL—the

National League showed no inclination to rectify it, at least right away. Plenty of cities still wanted teams, but most, like Denver, were frankly second-tier; capable of supporting a franchise, no doubt, but hardly a market that screamed out to be filled.

IN 1983, a young Mexican-American lawyer named Federico Pena was elected mayor of Denver under circumstances no politician would choose. The year Pena took office turned out to be the last year of the oil boom. By 1984, fast-dropping energy prices were eating away at profits from low-margin Rocky Mountain leases. When the federal government decided to back out of a massive project to extract oil from shale in northwestern Colorado, the impact was felt throughout the region. Denver, as much as Houston or Dallas, was left with a staggering surplus of downtown office space. High-tech industries faltered, housing prices plummeted, and the rapid growth in Colorado's population—30 percent in the decade of the '70s—abruptly ceased.

The recession helped define a new set of priorities for the liberal Democratic mayor. "When your city is basically dying," says Pena, "which our city was, you need to make investments to get that economy going again and turn things around." Until Pena was nominated as Secretary of Transportation by President-elect Clinton, he would conduct occasional early-morning office hours over coffee at a bed-and-breakfast on 17th Street, within walking distance of Denver's financial and political centers. Dressed for business in a dark suit and a white shirt, his thick black hair parted neatly on one side and his earnest face framed by a pair of oversized horn-rimmed glasses, he looks not much older today than when he was first elected mayor eight years ago at age 36.

"Now, in that context," he continues, "you've got homelessness, you've got drug problems, you've got gang problems, you've got record foreclosures, record bankruptcies of corporations, a high unemployment rate which is above the national average. It was my judgment that the way you try to salvage that situation is you've got to diversify the economic base, you've got to stimulate economic development, you've got to attract new industry, etc., to at least keep the ship afloat, so the ship doesn't sink. When you're in a deficit situation, you can't go out and spend ten million dollars taking care of the homeless, because you don't have it. You're laying off people, you're closing city services, you're shutting down. Once you have the resources, then you can go out and do those other things. Unfortunately that's the economic dilemma that most mayors in this country face today."

During his two terms in office (he chose not to seek a third term in 1991), Pena backed a full lineup of publicly subsidized development projects: the mall at Cherry Creek, which Pena says brought new retailers to the Denver market; the $110 million convention center, which opened in 1990; the $2.7 billion airport now being laid out on the prairie 25 miles east of Denver and scheduled to open in October 1993; and finally the new baseball stadium, itself part of the larger effort to attract a major league baseball team, which Pena has no trouble justifying in largely economic terms.

"One, we believed that it was a good investment for our economy," Pena says, "that it would help diversify our economic base, and bring new revenue into the city. Secondly, we believed it was one way of further putting Denver on the map nationally and internationally. I think if you're going to compete in the global marketplace you've got to step up to the plate, so to speak, in many areas, and one is you have to have all the major sports teams in your city. And thirdly, this is just a great sports town, and as a kid who grew up without major league baseball but who loved baseball and played baseball, I think a lot of kids in this state would love to be able to go watch major league players, and right now they don't have that experience."

Early in Pena's first term, a study commissioned by the Denver Chamber of Commerce concluded that baseball would be worth $75 million annually to the Denver economy. It's true that partisan economic-impact studies of the kind put out by the Denver Chamber of Commerce are notoriously unreliable; independent economists will tell you that too often they rely on bogus assumptions and inflated expectations. But such studies aren't intended for economists, they're intended for voters. Tom Ferguson, former president of the Beacon Council, which promotes economic development in Dade County, Florida, explains:

"I think that every city that was competing for baseball was trying to show the community, 'Look what baseball's going to do.' Everyone promotes that because typically in most communities you're asking the taxpayer to subsidize the stadium or an expansion. And the fact is, there's a lot of money spent in professional sports. But when you get right down to it, I mean, sure, there's impact in baseball, but now that it's all over with, one has to ask the question, 'Well, if you didn't spend your eight dollars on that baseball ticket, wouldn't you have spent it somewhere else?' Chances are you'd have probably spent it elsewhere in the marketplace. . . . It's internal marketing. It's all to sell the local community on making an expenditure."

To the extent that the community gets sold, politicians almost have to respond. Baseball becomes a battleground in the intercity war for economic survival, a chance to score big, or else be humiliated. And pretty soon cities are chasing ball clubs the same way they chase factories and corporate headquarters —with incentives, concessions and aggressive lobbying. Denver, led by Mayor Pena, eagerly joined the fray. As recently as 1974, just sending Varnell and Burris down to New Orleans to get friendly with the boys at the winter meetings had seemed an appropriate way to promote Denver. Not anymore. During his first year in office, Pena created the Denver Baseball Commission, a blue-ribbon panel with a paid staff, a permanent office and a $75,000 seed grant from AT&T. (Within 18 months, the DBC would pull in $1.2 million in cash and in-kind corporate contributions.) The DBC got rolling in the spring of '84 with something called the Denver Baseball Symposium, which brought the two league presidents and a dozen other baseball executives to Denver for a tour of the city and a lavish banquet. The night before the banquet, a promotion billed "Challenge the Majors" attracted 32,926 fans to a Bears game at Mile High Stadium, more than attended any of the major league games played that night elsewhere around the country. "You can see how we were trying to market it," says Don Hinchey, a former commission member. "We've got a stadium, we've got the fan enthusiasm, we've got civic support, and we've got corporate support."

The DBC sent a full delegation to the 1984 winter meetings in Houston and rented a booth at the trade show. Buffalo was there too, along with Washington (all its people wearing red-and-yellow windbreakers), St. Petersburg (bright green blazers) and Indianapolis. Somewhere, veteran baseball executive Cedric Tallis was quietly lobbying on behalf of Tampa, which at the time was still in competition with St. Petersburg. Baseball had recently announced plans to conduct a "feasibility study" on expansion, so this was an opportunity for all the cities to flex their PR muscles. And it was a chance to meet Peter Ueberroth, the new commissioner, who had replaced Bowie Kuhn in midseason. Kuhn had not been popular in Denver. Many still held him partly responsible for the fiasco with the A's and Marvin Davis. Ueberroth was an unknown, but when he consented to meet privately with representatives from all the potential expansion cities, the members of the DBC delegation were hopeful.

The meeting took place in a conference room at the downtown Hyatt. Ueberroth sat alone at the head of the table. There were not enough seats for everyone, and those who arrived late had to stand in the back. The attitude of the participants was extraordinarily deferential, "almost as if we had been granted an audience with the Pope," Hinchey recalls. Members of the press were barred. (The only person in the room not connected with an expansion hopeful was Ron Labinski, an architect with HOK Sport, the stadium designers, whose presence was discovered during introductions; Ueberroth allowed Labinski to stay.)

Ueberroth began with a warning—"If one word of the content of this meeting gets out . . ."—which seemed silly, in retrospect, because almost nothing of substance was said. Ueberroth did all the talking and was careful not to make any promises. Only at the very end, when it was clear the meeting was going nowhere, did Steve Katich, the young, towheaded executive director of the DBC, raise his hand and hazard a question.

"Everyone was being nice," says Katich, now a Denver consultant, "and I was certainly being very nice, but I said, 'Commissioner, it would really be of tremendous benefit—I think I speak for all of us when I say it would really be of tremendous benefit—if you could outline some sort of timetable for this. It would make it easier because we've been working hard in our communities to try to generate support.'"

Whatever Katich was expecting from Ueberroth, it wasn't what he got. "Maybe I was naive," he says. For back then Katich still assumed that big league baseball, and the cities hoping to become a part of big league baseball, were on the same side. Now he knows better. "It was a perfectly legitimate and candid answer from a person who is representing a group of people who do not want to expand," Katich says now with the wisdom born of experience.

For Ueberroth threw Katich a hard, flat look. "Why should I?" End of meeting.

BASEBALL HAD LITTLE to gain from expansion and much to lose. To the owners' way of thinking, more teams only meant more competition for star players (and higher salaries in the end), less big-draw games played between traditional rivals, smaller pieces of the TV pie all around, a decrease in the value of their holdings (resulting from an increase in the supply of available franchises), and a general diminution in the quality of play. Roy Eisenhardt, who bought the A's from Charlie Finley, once told Katich—half jokingly, one assumes—"If we're going to make baseball a purely money deal based on the value of franchises, we should just put all the franchises on the East Coast and West Coast and a team in Chicago and call it a day."

On the other hand, the owners didn't mind flirting, especially if it led to improvements in conditions back home. For as cities geared up for expansion, they couldn't help but make themselves increasingly attractive candidates for relocation. That was something the owners were able to exploit, in much the same way that factory owners use the threat of relocation to extract concessions on wages and taxes. Pressure was building, expansion was coming, everybody recognized that. But the longer the owners could hold out, the more they stood to gain. A timetable for expansion? Why, indeed.

An early case study in how to profit from expansion fever without ever expanding (or even relocating) was about to play itself out. In the spring of 1985, shortly after the winter meetings in Houston, Tampa businessman Frank Morsani reportedly cut a deal with Eisenhardt to buy the A's for $37 million. Morsani had reason to be optimistic. In 1984 he had purchased a 42 percent stake in the Twins from Calvin Griffith, and immediately announced plans to move the team to Florida. But when the other owners objected, Morsani turned around and sold to Carl Pohlad, who kept the Twins in Minnesota. Afterward, Commissioner Kuhn praised Morsani, going so far as to say he deserved "future considerations" (a promise with which fans in Tampa Bay would soon become bitterly accustomed). But Morsani wasn't the only one interested in buying the A's. So was Marvin Davis, still, and by August rumors were flying that the A's were finally on their way to Denver. Eisenhardt all along denied he was trying to sell the A's to anybody. On the other hand, he told everybody who would listen that the A's were losing money and were unhappy with their lease arrangement in Oakland. Oakland, understandably, was nervous. In the end, after an all-night negotiating session with Oakland mayor Lionel Wilson, Eisenhardt emerged with a favorable new lease and a $10 million loan. The A's stayed in Oakland.

Back in Denver, the DBC was pressing ahead. The Cubs and the Mariners stopped by on the way home from Arizona that spring and played a pair of exhibition games at Mile High Stadium. More than 76,000 fans showed up, and each team left town with $130,000. "If I were asked to vote today," a delighted George Argyros, owner of the Mariners, told local reporters, "I'd have to give Denver the absolutely highest priority." That got everybody fired up. "People really believed that it was going to happen anytime," says Hinchey.

And then, nothing. Zero. Until one day early in October when a letter arrived at the DBC office at Mile High Stadium, signed by deputy commissioner Ed Durso. "I have enclosed for your use," the letter began, "an outline containing a listing of criteria developed by the Long Range Planning Committee for evaluating prospective sites for the establishment of a Major League Baseball franchise."

"This created a stir," says Hinchey. "This is quite a wish list." The highlights: baseball wants a local owner; baseball wants the local owner to be an individual rather than a corporation, have a net worth of "$100 million or more," and be willing to commit his entire net worth to baseball; baseball wants a baseball-only stadium with natural grass, luxury boxes, a state-of-the-art video scoreboard and "satellite receive/send capability"; baseball wants a compliant local government, one that understands it must "minimize or eliminate political pressures . . . and tax disincentives"; and baseball wants a minimum 10,000 season tickets for the first five years, guaranteed.

"The committee would like to have an opportunity to meet with you on November 7 or 8 in New York City to discuss your interests in light of the material we have provided . . . ," Durso went on. "I look forward to your reply."

"IT WAS WEIRD," says Steve Kaplan, the former city attorney under Mayor Pena, now with a private firm in Denver. "It wasn't clear what it was really all about. You knew that they weren't ready to expand, but you also knew you had to go do it." Adding to the confusion in Denver's case was an extraordinary offer from the San Francisco Giants, which surfaced only days before the scheduled meeting in New York.

In 1976, Bob Lurie had rescued the Giants at a time when the team seemed about to fold or leave town. But by 1985 he was already fed up with cold, windy Candlestick Park. Plans were in the works for a privately financed stadium to be built on the San Francisco waterfront, but Lurie was impatient. In early October, he put the Giants up for sale. Then toward the end of the month he switched tactics, sending Giants president Al Rosen and vice president Corey Busch to Denver for a secret meeting with Pena, Kaplan and Tom Nussbaum, Pena's chief aide. Claiming they had no interest in leaving San Francisco permanently, Rosen and Busch asked Pena if Denver would be willing to let the Giants play in Mile High for two or three years, or until a new stadium was ready for them back home.

Pena knew full well he was being used. "It's a plan that has a number of complexities," he told the *Denver Post*. "I'm very cautious about frustrating the people of Denver and Colorado." On the other hand, what better way to prove to baseball that Denver was capable of supporting a big league franchise? Pena signaled Denver's willingness to go ahead.

Once San Francisco mayor Dianne Feinstein caught wind of the plan, she threatened to sue. "There is no way the Giants are going to Denver," Feinstein said on the same day Pena and the rest of the Denver delegation traveled to New York. "If Denver is participating in these talks with the Giants, it's committing a tort and opening itself to major liability." That put a damper on the growing excitement in Denver, but overall the incident served to raise Denver's standing going into the meeting with baseball's Long Range Planning Committee. As Pena said, "The fact that no other city was approached [by the Giants] indicates that Denver is the number-one city for a team."

A total of 13 cities accepted baseball's invitation. The ground rules were strict, seemingly arbitrary, and they kept changing. Denver prepared a video, only to be told at the last minute that videos were not allowed. Each city was allotted exactly 55 minutes; "That includes your introductions and your schmoozing and then your actual presentation," says Hinchey. Six on Thursday and six on Friday (baseball insisted on hearing St. Petersburg and Tampa together). They drew lots, and Denver came up No. 2 on Thursday morning, right after Columbus, Ohio.

Columbus was the longest of long shots, but that didn't stop Mayor Dana Rinehart from puffing out his chest as he emerged from the conference room at baseball's law firm, Willkie, Farr & Gallagher, and strode past the waiting members of the Denver delegation. It was rumored that Pirates owner Dan Galbreath, who was from Columbus, was shepherding his hometown through the process. The Denver people knew full well that their city was a far more attractive candidate for expansion than the third-largest metropolitan area in a state that already had two teams—the Indians and the Reds. But they also knew that they had no close ties to anyone in the baseball establishment; worse, they suspected they were already on the outs with Commissioner Ueberroth. "Ueberroth's daughter went to school at Boulder and everyone thought he would be a big fan," says Kaplan. "But Ueberroth didn't like Denver. He didn't like the mayor. I don't know if it was partisan politics, ethnic politics, something personal, that he didn't see an owner he could relate to—I don't know what it was."

In any case, Ueberroth certainly made no effort to put the Denver people at their ease. The first thing he said to the mayor and his entourage after their 2,000-mile trip to New York was that he was not going to introduce anybody on his side of the table; if they wanted to know their names, he suggested they consult the nameplates. Then he told them they would not be welcome at the winter meetings this year, that anything they had to say, they should say right now. Not that Denver was being singled out; the same went for all the expansion hopefuls. "Their attendance [at the winter meetings] would be counterproductive," Ueberroth explained afterward to the press. "Totally counterproductive to their interests."

Steve Katich of the DBC took two minutes to introduce everyone from Denver, then turned the meeting over to the mayor. Pena started off by saying he was "sympathetic" to the concerns of Major League Baseball, which was to say he had read the list of expansion criteria and was willing to play ball. He spoke of his hopes for a "partnership" between the team and Denver's private sector, of his willingness to show "flexibility" in lease arrangements, and finally of his commitment to "fairness" in all his dealings with baseball.

Next up was Dean Bonham, Katich's assistant at the DBC, whose tough job it was to talk about Mile High Stadium. Baseball was looking for a baseball-only stadium; they'd made that clear. Bonham could and did explain that Mile High was originally built for baseball. While he acknowledged that in its present form it wasn't quite up to major league standards, he spoke of the city's commitment to pay for improvements, and ticked off what was already in the works—new dugouts, tunnels and locker rooms, expanded media facilities, a better warning track and extra parking. On the other hand, nothing Bonham said spoke to the issue that lay at the heart of the baseball-only requirement. It wasn't about aesthetics or suitability; it was about control. Who controlled the scheduling, the revenue from luxury boxes, the stadium advertising? The unavoidable answer to all those questions was the Broncos.

Kaplan spoke next. He made a point of saying that the Broncos were supportive of big league baseball coming to Denver, and that they "recognized that some accommodations would have to be made." Still, it was plain to everyone that until Denver built a stadium, it had a problem in baseball's eyes, especially in view of what other cities were apparently willing to do. Columbus, for one, had just told the committee that it would be pleased to build a new stadium, and before the day was over, Miami and Vancouver would make the same promise. "All of us felt," says Kaplan now, "that if baseball said to us, 'You have to build a stadium,' we could then put together a package to do that. But we were not going to go to baseball and say, 'Oh yeah, we'll build you a stadium.' People in the community felt that we didn't need a stadium, and baseball sure as hell didn't need a stadium. How that issue had to be handled was pretty delicate."

The final person to speak on Denver's behalf was John Dikeou (du-KEW), a downtown real estate magnate who had bought the Denver Bears at the 1984 winter meetings and changed their name to the Zephyrs. Dikeou was one of two potential team buyers from Denver. Marvin Davis was still in the picture but he had chosen not to accompany the Denver delegation to New York, perhaps because he sensed it would be futile. The decision to include Dikeou in the presentation had been a difficult one for the DBC. For one, he was a political adversary of the mayor. "It is my pleasure to introduce

John Dikeou," Pena had said only moments before, but that was nonsense, and everybody on the Denver side of the room knew it. But there was more to it than political bickering. Dikeou is a loner, the eldest son of a Greek immigrant father who sold popcorn on the streets of Denver before he started buying up downtown real estate. Over time, the Dikeou brothers had added to their father's holdings, to the point where the family fortune reportedly topped $200 million, the bulk of it in undeveloped property.

Most people in Denver were surprised when Dikeou announced his interest in buying a major league team. He abhors publicity, does not talk to the press, and is plainly uncomfortable in the spotlight. "Not very Malcolm Forbes-like in the way he presents himself or his empire to the world," says Lew Cady, who helped Dikeou create the AD campaign for the Zephyrs. Dikeou launched the Zephyrs in 1983 as a vehicle for pursuing an expansion team—"the team that has nothing . . . yet," named for the California Zephyr, which pulls into Union Station at 9:40 every morning on its way from Chicago to Oakland. And a year later he bought the Denver Bears and changed their name to the Zephyrs, a move that angered long-time Bears fans.

Denver's baseball aristocracy—the crowd who ran the sports committee at the Denver Chamber of Commerce and belonged to the Denver Athletic Club—were never really comfortable with Dikeou. To them, he was always "the outsider," and among themselves they talked about "John's inability to blend in with the establishment." Most, such as one longtime member of the Denver Athletic Club who doesn't want to be identified, were sorry to see Dikeou eclipse Marvin Davis as Denver's owner-in-waiting. "I think the other owners would have embraced [Davis]," he says, "because first of all, and I guess this is not something you normally say, a lot of them go to the same church, and he was close to [former Yankees and Indians executive] Gabe Paul and a lot of those people. And secondly they knew that he could afford to be in that group and hold his own, and I think they appreciate that. Marvin would have been a very welcome member of that small group."

And Dikeou?

Silence for a long minute, then: "Uh, not for the record, but no. John Dikeou is reserved. Some people say almost reclusive. Certainly introverted. John Dikeou would not have fit into that group in my opinion, and I think that's really the consensus."

But here Dikeou was anyway, standing before Ueberroth, the two league presidents and nine major league owners, telling them all about the Zephyrs and taking pains to reassure them of his ability to pay the price.

During the question-and-answer session that followed, Charles Bronfman of the Expos asked straight out if Denver was willing to build a new ballpark; he was told that no decision had yet been made. John Madigan of the Cubs wanted to know about the number of parking spots at Mile High Stadium; 10,000, he was told, of which half are publicly owned. Peter Hardy of the Blue Jays wondered whether, if Denver ever did build a new stadium, it would have to be domed; no, because the Bears and the Zephyrs had been rained out or snowed out on average only six times a year. John McMullen of the Astros asked for details of the city's contract with the Broncos, and wanted to know if Denver would be willing to do the same for baseball; Kaplan responded, "It would be different, but we'd find a way to work it out." Jerry Reinsdorf of the White Sox asked how many people lived in and around Denver, he'd heard it was 3.5 million; not quite, said Pena, actually 1.8 million. Madigan asked how the Zephyrs were doing at the gate; around 300,000 last year, Dikeou said, somewhat apologetically. Katich piped in with the theory that competition from televised big league baseball was probably a factor, but Bronfman quickly reminded him that television was a factor everywhere these days, thanks to cable superstations. Everybody wanted to know about taxes that might affect baseball, and Kaplan had to admit that Denver collected not only a seat tax but also a room tax, which led to frowns all around. Finally, Peter Hardy looked at Dikeou and asked him what attracted him to major league baseball.

"It's been a longtime dream of mine," Dikeou answered.

But was he buying the team as an investment?

Yes, Dikeou said. He and his brothers were not in business to lose money.

"What other businesses are you in?" John Madigan asked.

Real estate, Dikeou answered. Also oil and gas and other investments.

To which a chorus of owners responded, "You'll need them!"

MIAMI, which followed Denver, was generally thought to have improved its chances, thanks to a strong showing by Dolphins owner Joe Robbie. The Tampa Bay Baseball Group (Morsani's outfit) surprised everyone—including St. Petersburg, which was in the room with them at the time—by announcing it had already signed a four-year television-rights contract worth $21.3 million, contingent on a franchise being awarded to Tampa. Afterward, St. Petersburg feigned indifference. ("So what?" John Lake of Suncoast Baseball Limited told the *Rocky Mountain News*. "I've got a [TV] guy standing in the wings just as ready as they are.") But apparently the bitter cross-bay rivals had fallen to bickering even in the midst of their joint presentation. "We did tell [both groups] one thing quite clearly," Ueberroth said to reporters during remarks at the conclusion of two days of presentations. "There's no possibility in the foreseeable future—in the year I-don't-know-how-many-thousand—that we'll consider two franchises in that area."

Still, the consensus among handicappers even then was that one way or another, in one city or another, Florida was likely to get a team. Washington was a leading candidate too, its standing bolstered by the persistent rumor that former commissioner Bowie Kuhn was solidly in D.C.'s corner. Indianapolis, which at one time was proposing to play baseball in the Hoosier Dome, only to discover later that it wasn't big enough, managed to salvage its chances by promising to build another stadium just for baseball. Phoenix came on strong with a grandiose development plan—one which, it turns out, was destined never to get off the ground. New Orleans mayor Ernest

Morial suggested that if baseball wasn't ready to give his city a franchise of its own, then New Orleans was willing to serve as permanent host to the World Series. The New Jersey Sports and Exhibition Authority, which developed the Meadowlands sports complex across the Hudson River from New York City, presented baseball with an overwhelming offer, promising not only a new stadium but also two million paid admissions guaranteed. "They got into guaranteeing substantial revenue," Ueberroth said afterward, apparently as amazed as he was pleased. "That gets people to sit up and pay attention."

And Denver? Word was, Denver had not helped its chances, in part because of the owners' dissatisfaction with Dikeou but also because of the stadium issue. Afterward, Pena would remember how Ueberroth had interrupted a line of questioning from one of the owners about stadiums, and assured Pena, "You would be foolish to build a stadium before you have a team." But it was obvious that as long as there were other cities who were quite willing to appear foolish, Denver was at a competitive disadvantage.

In the end, the two days of presentations left the members of the Denver delegation with a vaguely unpleasant aftertaste. Even the farewell wine-and-cheese party baseball put on for the cities was seen by Katich, at least, as something "ridiculous, another sign of the seriousness of the whole affair, or lack thereof."

"There was this dance going on," says Kaplan, "between trying to go through the motions of dealing with expansion, and not being serious about it, and communities had to respond. But I think there was a sense that it wasn't going to happen right away, a sense that it was really early in the process, that it was going to take a lot longer than we had hoped." Ueberroth was no help at all. "Is [expansion] on the agenda [at the winter meetings]?" he said, repeating a question from a reporter. "Absolutely, certainly. But does it mean there will be a decision . . . one way or another? I would not say that."

So were the meetings important? another reporter asked. "Yes," Ueberroth responded without hesitation. He spoke first of the problems with the way expansion had been handled in the past, clouded as it was by legal and political issues. "Baseball has not controlled its own destiny," he said. "Now I think it has taken a step toward doing that." And then he said this: "It's very, very healthy. When the owners see some of the efforts some of these cities are [making] to attract a team and make it financially viable in their community, they are going to go home and scratch their heads."

Somewhere, Jerry Reinsdorf was beginning to feel an itch.

THE '85 PRESENTATIONS stirred up interest in expansion around the country, which baseball did its best to ignore. Any hope of something happening in 1986 died that spring. And as time went on it became increasingly clear, as Kaplan had suspected, that nothing was going to happen, not now and not anytime soon. DBC director Katich had let himself hope that the trip to New York was the start of something big; he realized now it was the end.

"We were so close to it," says Katich, "that we thought that what we were doing was really important, when the fact of the matter is, people in major league baseball didn't give a shit about whether or not we got baseball. They didn't care about expansion, the issue was not important to them. I said I would give a hundred bucks to the first reporter that calls me up and says they've got a major league baseball owner who will go on the record saying he supports expansion now. There wasn't a single one. They would all talk about: 'We all recognize that expansion is inevitable, we recognize that we're going to need to do it at some point in time.' Originally, when I first got involved, it was: 'We need to find a replacement for Bowie Kuhn, we need to get the new TV package negotiated, and we need to get the collective bargaining agreement negotiated.' After the New York meetings it was off the table. My read of it was the owners said to Ueberroth, 'Okay, you've done your thing. Now let us tell you what reality is. Reality is, we have no intention of expanding right now.' "

In January 1986, citing promising developments on the stadium front, Giants owner Bob Lurie announced he was staying put, ending Denver's slim hopes of landing even a short-term tenant for Mile High Stadium. In April, plans for another two-game exhibition series—this one involving the Yankees and the Blue Jays—were buried under a foot of snow, disappointing 40,000 ticket holders and sending DBC officials scrambling into damage-control mode. "Everybody gets rain or snow," Katich told the *Denver Post,* speaking on a cordless telephone while he knocked snow off the trees in his backyard. "Toronto, Montreal, Philadelphia, Boston. It happens to everybody."

By the middle of 1986, Pena and the DBC had decided to shift gears. Until now, the focus had always been on making Denver an attractive candidate for expansion, which meant going through channels, playing the PR game with the owners, dealing with the commissioner—following the rules. But obviously it wasn't working. "We weren't going to wait for expansion," says Pena. "I mean, after we got burned once—we thought we were going to have expansion under Ueberroth and it didn't happen—we said, 'We better go out and steal a team.' So that's what we were trying to do. Not steal one, but negotiate with those owners that indicated they wanted to leave markets where they were losing money."

Pena put Kaplan, the city attorney, on the case. Besides the Giants and the A's, Kaplan held talks with the White Sox and the Mariners during the mid-1980s, all the while keeping close tabs on what was happening with the Indians and the Pirates. "We made a decision to deal with every one of these in a very straightforward way, professionally," Kaplan says. "The idea was to let people know we were ready to do business, that it was a good economic deal for the team and the community." Marvin Davis, meanwhile, was said to be talking to the Padres, and there were rumors connecting John Dikeou with the Orioles. To those like Larry Varnell who were watching from the sidelines, it was one long tease. "It seemed that every time a major league club wanted some concessions from the city it was operating in, and they were having difficulties with their negotiations, they'd just tell them, 'Okay, if you don't give us what we want, we'll move to Denver,' " says Varnell. "That happened at least a half dozen times."

According to Kaplan, the talks involving the Giants and the White Sox "were probably the most serious." After the Giants made it clear they meant to stay put, attention focused on Chicago, where Reinsdorf was plainly unhappy with 77-year-old Comiskey Park and pressing hard for a new deal. "Chicago was determined to have a new stadium," says Kaplan. "They wanted to stay, but would not without a new stadium. One way or another they were determined to get one." In June, Reinsdorf and co-owner Eddie Einhorn traveled secretly to Denver, where they met with Pena and toured Mile High Stadium. "We like what we're hearing," is the way one participant summarizes Reinsdorf's remarks at the conclusion of that meeting. "We'll send back our money guys." On July 8, White Sox vice president Howard Pizer and controller Terry Savarise did in fact visit Denver. On that same day, Reinsdorf announced that the White Sox planned to be out of Comiskey Park by 1990, and confirmed that they were talking to other cities.

Very quickly, though, the focus was shifting to St. Petersburg, where city officials were edging ever closer to a bold plan to build a $110 million domed stadium at taxpayer expense—on spec. Championed by St. Petersburg assistant city manager Rick Dodge, the dome was conceived as a way to force the expansion issue, or else provide an irresistible option for any team that wanted to move. Even Major League Baseball was taken aback by the huge risk St. Petersburg was contemplating, and took steps to absolve itself of responsibility. On July 16, on the eve of the vote by the city council, St. Petersburg mayor Edward Cole received an extraordinary telegram from Commissioner Ueberroth.

"You have before the citizens of St. Petersburg important decisions regarding the construction of a new stadium," it began. "On behalf of Major League Baseball, I want to reaffirm to you that no assurances can be given with respect to the establishment of a Major League Baseball franchise in St. Petersburg. Indeed . . . St. Petersburg is not among the top candidates. We do not want there to be any misunderstanding of baseball's position. . . ."

Eight days later, the city council voted 6–3 to go ahead anyway. And on November 22, 1986, more than 9,000 delirious supporters, many of them carrying tiny plastic shovels with "I Dig the Stadium" printed on the blade, gathered in an empty lot just west of downtown St. Petersburg to break ground for the Florida Suncoast Dome.

While the dome was rising, the White Sox continued their dance with the city of Chicago. Denver was no longer in the picture, but for a while it looked like the White Sox were ready to move to a new domed stadium to be built in suburban Addison. Then in the spring of 1988, rumors surfaced that the White Sox were negotiating once again with St. Petersburg, and were close to coming to terms on a 30-year lease. In the end, it took a midnight session of the Illinois legislature, during which funds were approved for a new stadium, to keep the White Sox in Chicago. A few more ticks of the clock and they were St. Petersburg-bound.

"We had an executed contract," says Dodge. "They were coming. I was sitting here in my office in the last hours going over the press release. Yes, we drove the Illinois legislature to act. But if they hadn't acted, where would the White Sox be playing? They would be playing right here in Florida, right here in our facility. It's a game of leverage and those that are competing on the outside have none, except to offer their wares in the most attractive way."

In Denver, baseball backers watched closely the events unfolding on the other side of the continent. One plain lesson to be learned from St. Petersburg was that you don't build a stadium before you have a team to play in it. Fine. On the other hand, Dodge was right; the only reason St. Petersburg was in the game until the last inning, and very nearly came away with a surprise win, was the stadium. There was a lesson there too. Until recently, the Denver Baseball Commission had always been reluctant to talk about a new stadium, on the theory that Mile High was more than adequate, and of course it was. But lately the DBC was coming around to the position that the only way to compete with the likes of St. Petersburg and Buffalo (which had recently completed a new downtown ballpark of its own) was to match them offer for offer. If that meant spending millions on a new stadium, so be it. And so began the third stage in Denver's quest for baseball. Once it had been judged appropriate to send a couple of glad-handers down to the winter meetings to soften up the sellers. Later the mayor stepped in and made baseball a government priority. Now comes the recognition that schmoozing and lobbying are not enough, that the only way to win is with a staggering investment of public funds.

IT WAS IN THE FALL of 1988 that Neil Macey attended a city council meeting and heard the Denver Baseball Commission report on its progress toward building a new stadium. Macey is a real estate broker, a political activist and a baseball fan. As a teenager living in Chicago, he worked as an usher in Comiskey Park. "I really enjoyed baseball as I was growing up," says Macey, "and I have a six-year-old son, Todd, and I thought: Wouldn't it be great if he had it too? And wouldn't it be great if the metropolitan area had it." Macey is also a close friend and political ally of John Dikeou. "I'm in commercial real estate and he owns a lot of downtown property. We work together a lot." Dikeou was the only potential franchise buyer left in town, Marvin Davis having lately sold his big house in southeast Denver and moved to Beverly Hills. Macey knew that if a stadium ever got built, and Denver won a franchise, his friend would likely be the chief beneficiary.

The other thing that's important to know about Macey is that, as an ally of Dikeou and a fellow Republican, he was a natural opponent of Pena and, by extension, Pena's hand-picked DBC. Macey went to that meeting of the city council prepared to be disappointed. "Basically," says Macey, "Paul Swalm, who was then on the council, asked the three who made the presentation what progress they had made toward getting the stadium built. And they said, 'Well, none really, we're gonna do it with public-private cooperation'—that's the buzzword. And Paul said, 'Well, what private developers are willing to contribute land or money toward this deal?' And [mayoral aide Ron] Stracha said, 'There's nobody that we've talked to yet that's willing to do that.' Bottom line, that's what happened. You left the meeting with the impression that they had absolutely no way to get the stadium built. They weren't making any progress at all. They didn't have a clue what to do."

Macey saw an opportunity. "There were a lot of issues that were starting to come to the fore at that point in time," he says. "A major capital improvements project for the city of Denver, which eventually passed, like four hundred million dollars, it was a truckload of money. The library, which was a hundred million. The RTD [Regional Transit District] was talking about having a light-rail sales tax. The convention center was already done. The airport was coming on board. There were so many things on the plate that Denver really couldn't afford to come forward with a stadium itself. And in terms of putting the issue on the ballot, which is something that happens around here quite a bit now, someone had done a poll for them and it showed that in the city of Denver it would fail two to one if it were put up for a vote.

"Then in November of 1988, we had a cultural-facilities-tax election, which basically imposed a one-tenth of one percent sales tax on the entire metro area—all of Denver and parts of five other counties—to be used to pay for cultural facilities, the symphony and the zoo and all of those things. Basically, it didn't add that many more new cultural facilities; it just shifted most of the burden from Denver to the entire metro area. And it passed with seventy-five percent of the vote in each of the six counties. Now, you can't get seventy-five percent of the people to agree that trees are green. So I was totally impressed, which gave me the idea that if seventy-five percent of the people will vote for that, you could get fifty-one percent of the people to vote for baseball. So I basically wrote the legislation to set up the district and had my attorney draft it for me."

Macey is speaking from the one-man offices of Greater Denver Properties, Inc., Neil Macey president, at the Denver Tech Center on Interstate 25 south of Denver. What a visitor notices is the virtuous blond hair, the bright eyes and above all the irony lurking behind the smile. "Well, first I went to John

Dikeou and showed it to him. He thought it was a great idea, and he said to me that he thought I should run it through the legislature. I said, 'John, real estate's not as good as it used to be. I have to get paid to do this.' So he agreed to pay me to lobby the bill through."

Macey called several legislators he knew, but no one wanted to touch it. By consensus, the timing was all wrong. Then someone suggested Kathi Williams, a three-term Republican from suburban Aurora. "So I cold-called her," Macey says. "I had never met her before. And I was about halfway through the explanation of how the bill would work and she says, 'I'll sponsor it, come on over, and we'll get it written.' This was the very end of December."

In January 1989, on the eve of the legislative session, Macey and Williams paid a courtesy call on Mayor Pena. Kaplan was there, the city attorney; and Katich, the head of the DBC; and a handful of other local officials who'd been a part of Denver's quest for baseball going on six years. "They all made their semi-negative comments," Macey remembers, "and then [Pena] said, 'Neil'—and Federico and I have collided on the convention center and a couple of other things—he said, 'Neil, frankly I strongly recommend that you don't introduce this legislation. It will never pass and will hurt our chances of getting baseball. If you have to do something, I strongly recommend that you wait another year.' He was totally against it.

"I said, 'Federico, we're going to do it anyway.'

"And so we went and did it. And once the ball started rolling up there, they didn't stand in the way. Once they realized that it was going forward, they got involved and they helped."

All kinds of political dynamics were at play here: Democrats vs. Republicans, Pena vs. Macey, the DBC vs. Dikeou, the governor vs. the legislature. To create a multicounty stadium district would be to strip power from the mayor and the DBC by taking control of the process away from Denver and distributing it among six counties. Macey wanted originally to can the DBC and replace it with a six-member stadium district board, with two members appointed by the speaker of the House, two by the president of the Senate and three by the governor. But

Roy Romer, the newly elected Democratic governor of Colorado, said no way.

"The governor," says Williams, "would send his lobbyist down every day and say, 'Kathi, if you don't give the governor all the appointments, he's gonna veto the bill.' Once I had enough momentum on the bill, I said, 'You tell Roy if he wants to veto baseball, be my guest. He can be the governor that vetoes baseball.' Well, he called me at home—this was a Sunday morning—and he said, 'Let's discuss the problems we have. Would you come and meet with me in my office this afternoon?' "

Romer argued that unless he alone made the appointments, Dikeou was bound to end up on the board, and that was a conflict of interest. For if the stadium ever got built, and Dikeou bought the team, he'd wind up negotiating the lease with himself. "When we talked about the conflict of interest," says Williams, "we talked about the difference between promoting baseball on the one hand, and watching out for the taxpayers' best interest on the other, and that's why we decided to have a baseball commission and a stadium authority."

Out of that meeting came an important amendment to the legislation. On one side would be the Colorado Baseball Commission, an 18-member statewide board, to which Dikeou was ultimately appointed chairman (by the legislature) and Macey, executive director; the CBC, like the DBC it replaced, was essentially a lobbying outfit, free to go after baseball with all the enthusiasm it could muster. On the other side was the stadium district board, made up of seven public servants appointed by the governor and charged with building a stadium and negotiating terms with the eventual tenant.

"It was a compromise," sums up John Frew, a former aide to Colorado senator Tim Wirth, now a lawyer with Fairfield and Woods, which advises the stadium district. "There's a real anti-Denver bias in the legislature, which led to some non-Denver legislators putting together an idea that said basically, 'Let's take this away from Denver.' They said Denver had been sitting on its hands for years. They had a point. I'm not saying it's right, I'm not saying it's wrong, but they did have a point.

That generated excitement in the legislature to the point where the state took over the process. Two bodies, one the whole state, the other just the six counties around Denver. But it was made explicitly clear—it couldn't have been made clearer—that Steve Katich was not to be on either body. This was a 'Fuck you, Denver' deal, and it passed."

HB1351 was approved by the Colorado legislature on May 9, 1989. It contained the following declaration:

> The general assembly hereby finds, determines and declares that the location of a major league baseball franchise in the state of Colorado would be a source of recreational entertainment for the residents of the state; that a major league baseball franchise would stimulate economic development throughout the state resulting in increased tourism, the creation and maintenance of new jobs, and the attraction and retention of sports and entertainment events; that in order to be considered for the location of a major league baseball franchise, it is essential that the mechanism exist for financing and constructing a major league baseball stadium in the Denver metropolitan area; and that the creation of a major league baseball stadium district will promote the health, safety and welfare of the residents of the state.

But how to pay for all that? According to Macey, the legislation never would have made it past the House Finance Committee were it not for language inserted at the time calling for a goal of 25 percent in private funds to build the stadium. "Then we got over to the Senate," says Macey, "and they wanted to make it 50 percent mandatory, and Kathi and I convinced them to settle for a 50 percent goal." And so the final version states: "The district shall make every reasonable effort to obtain funding for a target amount of at least fifty percent of the total costs incurred."

Passage of the bill in the legislature was only the first step. Step two was a referendum asking voters to allocate the necessary funds by approving in advance a special sales tax of one-tenth of 1 percent, contingent on the awarding of a franchise. If passed, Denver would be able to offer baseball an ironclad promise of a new stadium, without having to build the stadium first. The referendum was scheduled for the August 1990 primary.

Why a primary, rather than a general election? "There wasn't much happening in the primary," says Frew. "So the question is: 'Do you want to hide it and take chances on a larger turnout on what amounts basically to a tax-increase proposal? Or do you want to roll the dice, highlight it, and stick it in the primary?' " Supporters of the new stadium took some polls, did some focus groups, and decided they could live with the crowd that turns out for primaries—older and more conservative than those who vote in general elections, but also less numerous. The goal was to identify enough stadium backers and get them to the polls to make the difference. One way they did this was by circulating petitions at Zephyrs games, then comparing the names with the list of registered voters; anyone who didn't match got a call reminding him or her to register and vote.

In July 1990, one month before the primary, the district came out with a plan of finance for the proposed stadium. "The plan of finance said we're not going to get fifty percent privatization but we're at least going to get thirty percent," says Macey. "That's what we sold to the voters." Lee White, the Denver investment banker who wrote the plan, says his "biggest accomplishment" was to make sure that financing issues weren't a political question. "When it was introduced in July of 1990," says White, "everybody looked at it and said huh, that makes sense, and then it was hardly debated at all. It wasn't a big political issue here whether or not the plan of finance was a feasible one or whether it was appropriate or anything. It was a nonissue in the vote, which was exactly what we wanted it to be."

Pena, the stadium district, and the Colorado Baseball Commission all campaigned hard, leaning heavily on the economic-impact argument. A new study commissioned by the district put the economic impact at $93 million now, up from $75 million in 1983. "It's a pure business deal," Pena said at the time. "That's the only way I can do it. If I didn't think it was a moneymaker for the city, I would question using public dollars for that. There are some things that we do and some things that we don't do, and that's one of them that I concluded was a good investment."

But not even White—the investment banker who wrote the plan of finance—believes that. "It's my view that from a very strict accounting basis of the taxpayer dollars spent vs. the taxes generated, even on a secondary basis, baseball is a marginal investment of the public's tax dollars," says White, a view corroborated by most independent economists. "In some cases if the team is successful, you can construct a scenario where the taxpayers will get paid back the dollars that have been invested, and if it's a poorly performing team, then they won't. I personally think the team will be successful, and successful enough to repay most, if not all of the public investment over a period of time; its rate of return from a strict accounting viewpoint will be adequate but marginally so. And to some extent, funding recreational opportunities out of the tax base is an important investment but not one of the most important investments. Education and health care in my mind personally are more important. But given the relatively small amount of tax dollars that were being asked, given the rapid repayment of the bonds, given the long-term social and psychic benefits, this is a good investment for the community, it can be justified."

Kaplan: "Some people argued that it was an economic development activity. I always took the view that this was not what this was about. I always took the view that this was about fun, about quality of life, building a community that had a lot of diversity, a lot of activities. Baseball is a part of that, the symphony is a part of it, art museums are a part of it. It's part of building a whole community, and it's fun. Which is a separate question from priorities, whether the hundred-plus millions of public dollars spent on the stadium is appropriately spent. You can ask that about a lot of things. For good or bad, that's the tradition of sports facilities, generally speaking, in the United States."

Pena: "Whether we like it or not, there are some things that people are going to support, other things that people are not willing to support. If we went to the six-county area and asked that they increase the sales tax by a tenth of a percent to build shelter facilities for the homeless, would it pass? I don't know, I really don't know."

In the end, the stadium backers spent $400,000 on the campaign, not to mention another $200,000 worth of free publicity and in-kind contributions. With all that, plus the fact that there was almost no organized opposition, it's not surprising that the initiative passed, 54 percent to 46 percent. Finally Denver had what it never had before—the promise of a new stadium. And just in time. For by the summer of 1990, after more than a decade of happy talk and empty promises, expansion was about to become a reality.

# 2

## The Senator and the Commissioner

THE FIRST TIME the senator and the commissioner met face to face was at a tennis tournament in Scottsdale, Arizona, in early January 1987—something called the Senators' Cup, a charity go-around starring senators and CEOs, the politicos versus the corporate honchos. Among those in town for a weekend of sun and sport at the John Gardner Tennis Camp (all for a good cause) was Tim Wirth, the brand-new senator from Colorado.

Wirth had long been seen as a comer on the national stage. He was six feet five, athletic, strikingly handsome, a charismatic Democrat with mainstream appeal. He had overcome a hardscrabble childhood in Denver, including the death of his father when he was three years old, to win scholarships to Exeter and Harvard, ultimately earning a doctorate in education at Stanford. At age 35 he was elected to Congress as part of the so-called class of '74, unseating a four-term Republican incumbent in Colorado's 2nd Congressional District thanks to Watergate and a boost from the newly enfranchised 18-year-olds. In the House he had joined a group of young, reform-minded Democrats who called themselves neoliberals, tempering the old-time liberal religion with a dose of pragmatism. Wirth was out front with the progressives on the environment and defense (against the B-1 bomber, the MX missile, and Star Wars) but apt to take a hard line on social programs and the federal deficit (pro Gramm-Rudman)—a "terrifically versatile politician," in the words of Kevin Knobloch, his former legislative director. Meaning he could please almost anyone.

Wirth was reelected four times, surviving the anti-Carter backlash in 1980, and in 1986, when Gary Hart announced he was leaving the Senate to run for President, Wirth stepped up to take his place. It had been a bruising, hard-fought contest, decided finally by 17,000 votes out of more than a million cast, but Wirth prevailed. And now here he was in Arizona, only days after having been sworn in at the Capitol, making one of his first public appearances as a U.S. senator, a powerful man playing at the top of his game.

Peter Ueberroth was not quite a senator, yet. On the other hand, the California travel agent turned grand pooh-bah of the 1984 Olympics turned baseball commissioner had already been mentioned so many times as a likely Republican candidate that lately the pundits were saying he could conceivably bypass the Senate altogether and run for President in 1988. For now, though, Ueberroth had his hands full rescuing the National Pastime from financial suicide. A delicate, complex task, to be sure, but Ueberroth was up to it.

Ueberroth had succeeded Bowie Kuhn as commissioner in 1985, the same year the owners voluntarily opened their books to try to prove to the world just how much money they were losing. The owners claimed some $58 million a year in red ink, or more than $2 million per team; the players union disagreed, arguing that, accounting tricks aside, the figures really revealed significant industry-wide profits. Throughout the late summer and fall of 1985, in a series of quietly dramatic closed-door meetings, Ueberroth had somehow managed to make plain to the owners that by recklessly bidding against one another for players (the average salary by then had surpassed $400,000, up some 700 percent in the first decade of free agency), they were only hurting themselves. "Well," Ueberroth was quoted by *The Wall Street Journal* as having told the owners during the World Series in St. Louis, "you are smart businessmen. You all agree we have a problem. Go solve it."

Ueberroth denies having said any such thing, but the point is, the owners got the point. That winter was the season of baseball's great collusion. Of the 62 players who declared themselves free agents, only five switched teams; of those five, not one was pursued by his previous employer. The owners' sudden loss of appetite for high-priced talent was noted with deep suspicion by the Players Association. The union filed a grievance, charging the owners with violating Article VIII of the Basic Agreement then in force, which forbade clubs from acting "in concert" with other clubs to rig the free-agent market. In time, baseball's arbitrator would rule in favor of the players, finding the owners guilty of collusion three times and, as of January 1991, awarding $280 million in damages.

But the long-term consequences of the conspiracy were not something the owners worried much about in the early part of 1987; they were too thrilled with the immediate results. Baseball had just completed its first acknowledged moneymaking season in eight years. Attendance was at a record level. And the owners' determination to hold the line on salaries, now in its second year, showed no sign of weakening. Thursday, January 8, 1987, the day before festivities got underway in Scottsdale, was also the day eight of baseball's biggest names—including Bob Boone, Andre Dawson, Bob Horner, Lance Parrish and Tim Raines—were hung out to dry. The so-called January 8 Eight, all of them free agents, chose to ignore the deadline for re-signing with their old teams in hopes of finally scaring up some serious offers from other clubs. Except for Parrish, who later signed with the Phillies at below market value, those offers would never materialize.

All of which reflected stunningly on Ueberroth. Here he was, a newcomer to baseball, still getting settled in the job, and already he had succeeded in persuading 26 of the most competitive, contentious and egotistical millionaires from two countries to sing the same song. Patty Patano, a longtime Ueberroth employee, said of her boss in Kenneth Reich's *Secrets of the Organizing Committee,* a chronicle of the '84 Olympic Games, "Control is his life force . . . his whole life is run on that basis." Well, so far, so good. At this moment, Ueberroth was unquestionably in control of his game.

But maybe not for long. "Everyone was being nice to each other," is the way Wirth remembers the mood of the gathering that weekend in Scottsdale. And it was in that spirit that Wirth approached Ueberroth, and after the usual pleasantries were exchanged, came right to the point.

"You know, what we ought to do is set up a way in which Major League Baseball and the Senate could talk to each other about expansion," the senator said to the commissioner. "I figure it's time for you guys to expand. You seem to do this every ten or twelve years. It's about time."

The commissioner smiled. He was good at that, completely believable; it was a big part of why so many people thought he had a future in politics. Probably, though, he hoped like hell the senator wasn't serious.

SOON AFTER RETURNING to Washington, Wirth wrote a letter to Ueberroth. The tone was cordial, the content routine, the sort of thing Wirth did on behalf of constituents all the time. In this case, he simply wanted the commissioner to know that when it came time for baseball to expand, Denver was ready. He talked up the Colorado economy, made note of the fan support enjoyed by the Broncos, put in the good word. Wirth wasn't forcing the issue, so from Ueberroth's perspective, it was nothing to worry about.

But unbeknownst to Ueberroth, Wirth also asked Bob Drake, a longtime adviser and his political director during the Senate campaign, to scope out the expansion issue and see if there wasn't some way for him to get involved. It was Drake who suggested the idea of sponsoring an effort in the Senate, which is what led to the appearance early in the fall of 1987 of a Wirth-gram on the subject. Wirth-gram was office slang for the senator's periodic memos to his staff. Written in the senator's own hand, chock-full of directives and ideas, an unsolicited Wirth-gram was something half welcomed and half dreaded by the (un)lucky recipient. This one, addressed to Knobloch, raised for the first time the possibility of organizing an informal committee comprised of senators from every state that had a city thought to be a serious candidate for expansion. The upshot, on November 4, 1987, was a festive Capitol Hill press conference—complete with bats, caps (with city names) and corny metaphors—to announce the formation of the Senate Task Force on the Expansion of Major League Baseball. The goal: six new major league teams by the year 2000.

Why a task force? Committees, subcommittees, select committees and special committees are all formal bodies requiring congressional enactment. That leaves caucuses and task forces. Caucus suggests talk, task force suggests action. Task force it was.

What will historians make of this task force one hundred years from now? That on the eve of the third millennium, in the richest, most powerful country on earth, where nevertheless the federal government was operating $2.4 trillion in the red; where seven and a half million able, willing citizens were unable to find work, hundreds of thousands were living on the streets, and one out of ten families was feeding itself with food stamps; where every year thousands were dying of AIDS, and thousands more were being gunned down in the streets; when there was global warming to worry about, plus the hole in the ozone layer, not to mention the S&L bailout; that in such a place and at such a time, 15 of the people's highest representatives (14 U.S. senators and the delegate from the District of Columbia—all of them men, naturally—chose to take a stand on . . . what? The injustice suffered by people deprived of the pleasure of going to baseball games.

"This is so fucking far down the list," admits Donald Fehr,

president of the Players Association, "that you feel guilty about taking up somebody's time on it. It cannot conceivably, by the wildest stretch of anyone's imagination, be a congressional priority."

"The driving force behind this task force is the baseball fever we each see in our home states," Wirth said candidly at the press conference, adding, "Fans are calling and writing to members of Congress, seeking our help." Senators get calls and letters from people asking them for help all the time, on every kind of issue. Part of what made this expansion thing particularly agreeable to so many of them—from Democrat Howard Metzenbaum of Ohio on the left to Republican Dan Quayle, the junior senator from Indiana, on the right—was pretty obvious: you could not lose, everybody was for it. "From the standpoint of home-state constituencies," Knobloch explains, "there was not a real downside to this."

That said, it's probably not fair to dismiss the work of the task force as pure puff politics. Part of Congress's job is to regulate industry, big and small, which is why there is not only a Senate Banking Committee and a House Agriculture Committee but also a Congressional Footwear Caucus. Major League Baseball today is a $1.5 billion industry. If you buy the economic-impact argument from the baseball boosters, then it probably does make sense from a public-policy standpoint for Congress to step in and break up the expansion logjam; it becomes a development issue, a way to create jobs. But even if you don't buy all that stuff the Chamber of Commerce types churn out, there are other reasons why someone (Fehr included, although he'd rather not admit it) might choose to take the issue seriously. For as long as baseball is free to operate as an unregulated cartel, as long as it can sustain a high level of unsatisfied demand for its product, as long as cities have no choice but to compete suicidally with one another to try to attract and later hold on to franchises, then baseball wins and everybody else loses, in a hundred different ways: stadiums are built with tax dollars, roads and other components of the infrastructure are improved for private gain at community expense, and revenue streams are diverted from the public purse into owners' pockets. "By controlling the supply," says Knobloch, summing up, "they're creating situations where the taxpayer is coughing up dough."

THE BASEBALL MONOPOLY is a quirk, an accident of history. Its origins date back to the chaotic early days of the professional game, when ballplayers freely sold and resold their services to the highest bidder. That meant that rosters were always changing, which admittedly was a problem: for the fans, whose loyalty was abused; for the integrity of the game (in the summer of 1875, A. G. Spalding and three teammates on the Boston Red Stockings secretly signed contracts to play for the rival Chicago White Stockings the following season); and above all for the owners. The owners probably could have solved everybody's problem fairly and unambiguously from the start, had they been willing to pay the price. They were not. Instead they devised what came to be known as the reserve clause, a fluid, interlocking system of agreements—some written, others simply understood—the point of which was always to deny players the right to bargain with anyone other than their original employer. Specifically, the reserve clause gave owners an absolute right to renew a player's contract when it expired, at which point the player had no choice but to sign a new contract containing the same clause; by signing, the player sealed his own fate. For the owners, the benefits were immense: a stable work force, a consistent product and low wages. For the players, though, it was tyranny.

From the beginning, disgruntled players and rival leagues challenged the reserve clause. And more often than not, when such disputes found their way into court, judges hit the reserve clause with stinging comments. In 1914, a New York State Supreme Court judge, ruling in the case of Chicago White Sox first baseman Hal Chase, who jumped to the Buffalo Buffeds of the old Federal League, described the conditions under which ballplayers worked as "quasi peonage" and "contrary to the spirit of the Constitution of the United States." But while the courts were at times reluctant to enforce the reserve clause, baseball's own methods of enforcement—

notably, the blacklist—were left untouched. So the players were not helped by all the litigation; it was not until 1975 that baseball arbitrator Peter Seitz, acting outside the courts on authority derived solely from a union contract, finally overturned key elements of the reserve clause and opened the way to free agency. Meanwhile, the owners enjoyed complete dominion over the players.

The crucial case was known as *Federal Baseball Club of Baltimore* v. *National League of Professional Baseball Clubs,* brought by the owners of the failed Baltimore Terrapins following the collapse of the Federal League in 1915. The plaintiffs argued that the reserve clause and its companion, blacklisting, were violations of antitrust law. A lower-court jury agreed, awarding $254,000 in damages, but the ruling was reversed on appeal. The case reached the U.S. Supreme Court in 1922. There the legendary Justice Oliver Wendell Holmes, writing on behalf of a unanimous Court, upheld the lower court's reversal on what would seem to be untenable grounds; that "exhibitions of base ball . . . are purely state affairs," and therefore outside the purview of the Sherman Antitrust Act of 1890, which regulates commerce only among states or with foreign nations. Holmes allowed "the fact that in order to give the exhibitions the League must induce free persons to cross state lines." But he maintained that "the transport is a mere incident, not the essential thing. That to which it is incident, the exhibition, although made for money would not be called trade or commerce in the commonly accepted use of those words." In other words, baseball is a game, not a business.

That baseball entered on a golden age of prosperity beginning in the 1920s was due largely to two factors: Babe Ruth and *Federal Baseball,* which had begun its progress through the courts during Ruth's rookie season. The difference is that Ruth retired in 1935, while *Federal Baseball* still goes to bat for the owners every day. Twice since the 1922 decision fresh challenges to baseball's antitrust exemption have made it all the way back to the Supreme Court, only to be shot down on the authority of *Federal Baseball.* In 1953, the Court reaffirmed for the club in *Toolson* v. *New York Yankees,* a case involving a minor leaguer, George Toolson, who was placed on the ineligible list for refusing to accept a demotion. "We think that if there are evils in this field which now warrant application to it of the antitrust laws it should be by legislation," the Court declared. In 1972 the Court heard *Flood* v. *Kuhn,* in which outfielder Curt Flood of the St. Louis Cardinals challenged the club's right to trade him against his will. Once again, the Court deferred to precedent, then tossed the ball back to the legislative branch. "If there is any inconsistency or illogic in all this," wrote Justice Harry Blackmun, "it is an inconsistency and illogic of long standing that is to be remedied by the Congress and not this Court."

Congress has from time to time accepted the Court's invitation to scrutinize baseball's antitrust exemption. Since 1951, when Emanuel Celler's Subcommittee on the Study of Monopoly Power began to look at baseball, there have been all manner of hearings, inquiries and special investigations. In 1958, Mickey Mantle, Casey Stengel and Ted Williams were called to Capitol Hill to testify during the All-Star break. In 1960, the full Senate actually voted on a measure sponsored by Estes Kefauver of Tennessee that would have broken the baseball monopoly and freed the way for the Continental League; the bill was defeated, 73–12. In short, there's been plenty of talk over the years, but not much action.

And so baseball's antitrust exemption stands, despite frequent stirrings from Congress; despite a consensus among judges and lawmakers that it is probably inappropriate; and despite the fact that every other professional sports league, including the NFL, has to play by antitrust rules. Now, it may be true that thanks to free agency, salary arbitration and the five-and-ten rule (which gives veteran players the right to veto unwanted trades), antitrust has lost some of its urgency, at least for the players. But not all. "There is no collusion if there are antitrust laws," Fehr states flatly, "because if there had been we would have owned them when it was over. Treble damages with what we were doing, you're talking about a billion dollars. [Antitrust] expands your options enormously." Apart from labor issues, antitrust remains an underlying issue in just about everything else baseball touches, from the sale of television rights (baseball enforces a local monopoly in each territory) to decisions about when and where to shift franchises (baseball decides, not the team that wants to move) to expansion.

The point is, baseball has lived with its antitrust exemption, comfortably, for more than 50 years, and it would just as soon keep it. So when a senator invites a commissioner to Washington to talk about expansion, the commissioner may grumble—"Congress has no more right to tell us where to put a franchise than to tell McDonald's to put one on Fourth and Main," which is the basic attitude of baseball, according to one insider —but the commissioner goes.

INCREDIBLY, Ueberroth skipped the first meeting of the task force at the Capitol on November 6, sending deputy commissioner Ed Durso in his stead. It was a good, clean snub, a sure sign that he meant to play hardball (the strategy, according to a former adviser to the commissioner, was to "save Peter for later, go feel them out, see what they're doing"). Durso confined his remarks to procedural matters, running down the rules by which expansion would take place if and when baseball should decide to go forward, all the while managing to avoid saying anything of substance. Baseball was "sympathetic" to expansion, Durso told the roomful of senators, but not committed.

It was obvious that Wirth, for one, was not used to dealing with anybody's number two. He kept referring to Durso as Ueberroth's "AA," or administrative assistant, which is the title normally given to the senior aide on a congressional staff. Tom Korologos, a heavyweight Republican lobbyist who, besides serving as baseball's ambassador on Capitol Hill, occasionally coaches Supreme Court nominees for their confirmation hearings, sat next to Durso throughout the meeting, and interrupted frequently in order to set Wirth straight. "He's chief operating officer of Major League Baseball," Korologos kept insisting. "It's not the same thing."

Ueberroth could stall, but sooner or later he would have to

respond. On December 15, a full six weeks after the task force went public, he finally consented to a face-to-face meeting with the senators in Washington. Ueberroth insisted on certain conditions—no staff, no notes, no press—which made for hard negotiations in the days leading up. It was finally agreed that since Korologos was to accompany Ueberroth, the senators were entitled to one staff member as well; not one each, but one for the whole committee, who turned out to be Knobloch. The setting was a cramped second-floor room on the Senate side of the Capitol. Knobloch, who made the arrangements, would have preferred something larger. On the other hand, the only real consideration was that the meeting take place in the Capitol itself, rather than in an office building somewhere else on the Hill—more convenient for the senators, perhaps more intimidating for the commissioner—so Knobloch took what he could get.

If Ueberroth was in any way awed to find himself in the halls of power, seated opposite a phalanx of U.S. senators, he gave no sign. When the door closed, it was Ueberroth who tapped his spoon against his water glass to shush the murmur, who then pushed back his chair, stood up, and said, according to the vivid recollection of one who was there, "Do you want me to give you a line of crap? Or do you want the truth?"

Now, most senators enjoy a good brawl, but only up to a point. Immediately they jumped on Ueberroth with all they had. The thing is, they're all used to winning, to seeing the other guy back down. Ueberroth refused to budge, which was shocking. Not that Wirth or anyone else on his side expected to take care of expansion in a single day; this was going to take time, that was understood. But a senator comes to expect a measure of civility, if not deference, from those he comes in contact with. Here was Ueberroth treating all of them the same way he treated his owners, which was no different than the way he treated his staff during the '84 Olympics—with imperiousness bordering on contempt—and he got away with it.

At one point, someone raised the possibility of putting a spokesman for the task force on the agenda at the next owners meeting. "Okay, fine," Ueberroth reportedly said. "C'mon. Screw up expansion forever if you do that. Just once." Later it would be whispered—though Knobloch denies it—that by the end of the meeting, senators were raising their hands like schoolchildren, waiting until Ueberroth called on them to speak. "He intimidated those guys," says a former Ueberroth adviser. "It was a clash, but they caved."

The message the commissioner delivered that day was essentially . . . no. No commitment, no timetable, no promises. "Don't be threatening us," he told the senators. "It's not going to get anybody anywhere. If you want to be productive, I'll work with you. If you want to be political about it, we won't get anything accomplished." By the end of the meeting, Ueberroth had succeeded in alienating more than a dozen U.S. senators. But he didn't stop there. As soon as the meeting broke up, Ueberroth strode along with everybody else to the podium in the Senate television press gallery, where he held forth in front of the cameras. The commissioner had said earlier he wasn't going to do that, so the senators were surprised. Miffed, too. Access to the microphones in the press gallery is the exclusive privilege of those whose authority is derived from Article I, Section 3, of the Constitution. Which, it goes without saying, does not happen to include commissioners of sports leagues.

"You had a bunch of United States senators," says Fehr, who got the rundown from participants later, "that sort of naively believed that if they contacted the commissioner of baseball, they would get a cooperative response. They hadn't yet reached the point where they understood that the only thing these people pay attention to is getting hit over the head with a two-by-four. It didn't surprise me at all. It stunned a lot of *them*—the audacity of it, I think, as much as anything else. They thought they were important people and Ueberroth told them they weren't."

Exactly how little had been accomplished was made clear three weeks later in a letter Senator Wirth mailed to Ueberroth on behalf of the task force. In it, Wirth thanked him for his "commitment to discussing with the team owners the development of a timetable for deciding whether Major League Baseball will expand, and for implementing any subsequent expansion." In other words, thank you for promising to talk about when it is you plan to talk about whether or not you might ever expand.

It was nothing, and the senator knew it.

IN THE MONTHS that followed the cave-in on the Hill, the commissioner did his best to ignore the senators and their task force. As far as Ueberroth was concerned, they had had their meeting, he had told them what was what, and that was that. Problem solved. When he got another letter from Wirth on March 9, 1988, reminding him that it had been ten weeks since they last spoke, and wondering if he had anything new to report, Ueberroth sat on it for three weeks before responding. "I remain optimistic," he finally wrote back, "that there will be steady progress on this matter culminating in the not-too-distant future on a definitive expansion program for Major League Baseball." Kiss off, Senator.

The task force needed a boost, which Fehr of the Players Association was more than happy to supply. Expansion, while not at the top of Fehr's wish list, was up there—more teams, more jobs, more bidders for free agents, simple as that. Toward that end, Fehr had commissioned a suitability-for-baseball study of the top two dozen markets in North America, and would soon embark on a multi-city tour to make known the results and try to whip up interest wherever it was flagging. Also, Fehr was looking ahead two years, when it would be time to negotiate a new Basic Agreement with the owners. He worried that if expansion was not resolved by then, it might become a bargaining chip. Fehr wanted expansion, sure, but he wanted a lot of other things too. Better to let the Senate take care of expansion, if possible, so that he could go into negotiations with one big wish already crossed off his list.

Wirth was intrigued but also wary when the task force starting getting overtures from Fehr. "I was never really a hundred percent sure what his agenda was," Wirth says, "but I knew my agenda was to get expansion, and I didn't want to do much with Fehr that was going to alienate too many owners to the point where they would feel that the task force was lined up with Fehr." Being a politician, Wirth could count. He knew that expansion required approval by a three-quarters majority of the owners (the commissioner might promise, but in the end it was the owners' call), which left Wirth with little room to maneuver. While he was all for "raising the temperature," as he put it, he preferred to go gently. Alienate one too many owners—"I didn't want to go beyond twenty-five percent, see what I mean?"—and the ball game would be over.

Fehr met with the task force on Thursday, April 14, 1988, and was a big hit, exactly what the senators needed after being shut out by Ueberroth. "Don came in and really pumped them up," says Knobloch.

Specifically, it was Fehr who forced the issue of baseball's antitrust exemption and convinced the lawmakers to confront baseball with it directly. "The essential problem you're dealing with with expansion," argues Fehr, "is the desire by the owners to maintain an artificial scarcity of franchises. They do that for two reasons, one of which is, it pushes up the value of existing franchises. And the other reason is, it leaves X number of metropolitan areas out there that will attempt to induce a team to move, and those inducements provide the background against which concessions from the existing municipality are insured. . . . What I'm doing is, I'm going down to the Congress and I'm saying, 'All of these leading-light citizens (the owners), all of whom are all over the Capitol all the time for all kinds of other reasons, and all of whom contribute all kinds of money to everybody and their brother's campaigns, they're really a bunch of schmucks, and they're acting in a fundamentally inappropriate manner, and you gotta go get 'em.'"

Up until that point, the owners had blithely assumed that antitrust was like the bogeyman—scary, sure, but make-believe. After Fehr's pep talk, the bogeyman was suddenly a little more real. "Baseball had better get its act together," Senator John Warner (R-Va.) told reporters after the meeting with

Fehr broke up, "because if Congress gets into the batter's box, we'll hit the ball and we have no idea where it will go."

Warner spoke on behalf of a task force whose numbers were growing along with its conviction. By now there were 19 senators (a lot, any way you look at it), plus special delegate Walter Fauntroy (D-D.C.), former big league pitcher turned representative Jim Bunning (R-Ky.) and Canadian senator R. J. Perrault, who flew in from Ottawa whenever there was a meeting. And for anyone running down the list of members, two names jumped out: Howard Metzenbaum of Ohio, there on behalf of long-shot Columbus but also chairman of the Antitrust, Monopoly and Business Rights Subcommittee of the Senate Judiciary Committee; and Dennis DeConcini of Arizona, the ranking Democrat behind Metzenbaum on that committee. For better or worse, the temperature was rising, and baseball was beginning to feel it.

Three days after Warner's pointed remarks appeared in newspapers all over North America, Ueberroth told *USA Today*, "I have never responded to threats and I don't think I'll start now." So maybe it was just a coincidence that when Wirth wrote to Ueberroth yet again, this time he received an immediate reply. Ueberroth was apologetic, he simply could not accommodate the task force before the upcoming owners meeting in San Francisco, as Wirth had requested. Perhaps they could agree on a "mutually acceptable" date later in June? Wirth got right back to Ueberroth with a list of available slots, aides worked out the details, and on June 22, a somewhat subdued commissioner returned to Washington for a second session with the task force.

The supporters of an expansion team for Washington, D.C., put on a show that day. There were signs up for Ueberroth to see all along the route from National Airport to the Capitol. Banners hung from office buildings. The media turned out in force, half a dozen television cameras and several dozen reporters from all over the country—a bigger presence than veteran staffers were used to seeing for anything short of a national emergency. To accommodate them, Knobloch reserved a larger space this time, an Appropriations Committee room on the first floor, Senate side, a grand room with lots of marble and a big chandelier. The plan, made partly to avoid a repetition of the press-gallery embarrassment, was to meet in private, then open the doors and allow the reporters in for questions and the obligatory photo op.

What followed, according to one participant, was "a dramatic sea change in conduct and cordiality" from the last time the two parties had met. Even so, there were tense moments. Six months had passed. During that time power had shifted to the point where something like a balance could be said to exist. Sensing the possibility of real progress, the senators went on the offensive. No more teasing, they demanded, no more stringing us along. Cities everywhere are spending serious money—on promotions, on season-ticket drives, even on stadiums—without knowing when or if baseball will go ahead and expand. Exactly what are your plans?

Ueberroth refused to be pinned down. Basically, he said that cities would be stupid to commit themselves to expensive projects—such as building stadiums—until baseball made up its mind, which it had not. This was not what the senators wanted to hear. It contradicted every signal baseball had been putting out for years—from the publication of expansion criteria back in 1985 to Ueberroth's assurance to Wirth three months earlier that expansion was coming in the "not-too-distant future"—and it made them angry. Voices were raised, and for a while the meeting threatened to get out of hand.

There were those on the task force who tended to be more vocal than others, for particular reasons of their own—among them, Democrat Al Gore of Tennessee, still a presidential candidate when he joined the task force, and the two embattled senators from Arizona, Republican John McCain and Democrat DeConcini. As members of the so-called Keating Five, McCain and DeConcini were perhaps guilty of indulging in a little old-time camouflage politics, grandstanding for baseball as a way of diverting attention from the S&L scandal. Surely it was no accident that the constituency most harmed by Charles Keating was by and large the same constituency pushing hardest for expansion in Arizona: northern retirees who grew up with baseball.

In the eyes of some of his colleagues, Wirth was too timid. It was time to get tough, to bludgeon baseball with this antitrust thing, if that's what it took, and get on with the game. "Some of those guys were really rolling that [antitrust] ball down the middle of the table," Wirth recalls. But Wirth always resisted. By nature, his were the politics of inclusion, of consensus building, of seeking the common ground. And because he was chairman, the task force increasingly took on his personality. Once a producer from *Nightline* called, hoping to schedule Wirth for a segment on expansion, but Wirth wasn't interested. His sense all along was that it was best to avoid doing anything that might harden baseball's position and delay expansion even further. *Nightline* eventually gave up.

On this day, Wirth did everything he could to temper emotions and prevent a meltdown. At the same time, he and everyone else on the task force knew that there was no way they could allow Ueberroth to simply walk away again without making some kind of promise. As the meeting wore on, the crowd of reporters massing in the hallway just outside the door grew to the point where its impatient murmuring could be plainly heard by everyone inside the room. "Which made for an interesting dynamic," says Knobloch. For soon the door would open, the newshounds with their cameras and their microphones would come tumbling in, and the senators would have to toss them a bone. Progress was critical.

In the end, what they got was a firm commitment by the commissioner to a follow-up meeting between Labor Day and October 1. Not much, but at least the senators could claim that the train was rolling. Even if no one was quite sure yet where it was going, or how fast.

THE COMMISSIONER had one last surprise in store for the task force. And this one, when it came, almost knocked the train off the tracks.

In late summer Ueberroth informed Wirth privately that he meant to step down as commissioner as soon as a replacement could be found. This was startling news, all the more so because at the last meeting the senators had made a point of asking Ueberroth about his future, and he had reassured them. His contract did not expire until December 31, 1989—still almost a year and a half away—and he had hinted strongly that he planned to stay on even longer, if need be, in order to wrap up negotiations for a new national television contract and a new Basic Agreement with the Players Association. The senators could only conclude that they had been intentionally misled.

That fall, the owners chose A. Bartlett Giamatti, president of the National League and former president of Yale, to succeed Ueberroth, effective opening day, 1989. Thinking there might still be time, Wirth contacted Ueberroth anyway, reminding him of his promise to meet with the task force in September. But the commissioner's office informed Wirth that the transition had already begun and that Giamatti was now taking the lead on expansion.

"The Task Force has made some progress in the last ten months in raising the profile of the expansion issue, opening communication lines with Major League Baseball, and making known the concerns of potential expansion cities . . . ," Wirth summed up in a letter to Senator Perrault in late October. "Yet, with the accelerated switch in baseball commissioners, we find ourselves, in some respects, starting again from the beginning."

THE NEW YEAR of 1989 brought changes all around, not only a new commissioner but new members of the task force as well: the two senators from California, Republican Pete Wilson and Democrat Alan Cranston, signed on on behalf of Sacramento (no matter that California already had five major league teams); Florida Republican Connie Mack, grandson of *the* Connie Mack, replaced Lawton Chiles in the Senate and hence on the task force; and Republican Dan Coats of Indiana won appointment to the seat abandoned by now Vice President Dan Quayle (Quayle is remembered by staffers as an "active member" of the task force who "wasn't shy about speaking up") and so inherited the cause of Indianapolis.

The resignation of Ueberroth was seen as a setback by the expansion forces, if only because baseball's actions have always been so unpredictable, and access to its inner circle so jealously protected, that personal relationships are valued above all. No one got along with Ueberroth, it's true, but the members of the task force thought that at least they were beginning to understand him. The same qualities that made him impossible to deal with—his arrogance, his willfulness, his absolute adherence to his own agenda—suggested that once he did come around, the owners would follow in short order.

But Wirth had reason to be hopeful about the appointment of Giamatti. Both men had been guests a short while before at an intimate dinner party at the Jefferson Hotel, attended also by Treasury Secretary Nicholas Brady and Republican senator John Heinz of Pennsylvania, and hosted by Eli Jacobs, who was then in the process of buying the Baltimore Orioles. Jacobs arranged for Wirth to sit next to Giamatti, and the two hit it off right away. So that when Giamatti responded to Wirth's invitation to meet with the task force, saying he would be "pleased to continue the dialogue" begun under his predecessor, the pleasure seemed genuine.

What followed only emphasized the initial good feeling. The signals Wirth kept getting, beginning with the meeting of the full task force and the commissioner-elect at the Capitol in February and confirmed throughout that spring in private conversations, told him that far from being another ogre on expansion, Giamatti could well turn out to be an ally. "Bart was absolutely charming," Wirth remembers. "He was terrific. He was willing to do anything. He said, 'You guys want to have meetings, fine. You want to have press conferences, fine. You want to have hearings, fine. Whatever you want to do.' Giamatti wanted expansion. He said right away he wanted it to occur. And I think what he wanted to do was use us to [give him the] ability to talk about this sort of thing with all of these owners."

As it turned out, the task force did not have to "start again from the beginning," as Wirth had feared. Ueberroth, while maddeningly vague on specifics, had nevertheless for years spoken encouragingly about expansion. Whatever his agenda, the sum effect of his posturing raised hopes everywhere, and so added to the pressure on the owners to act. Now comes Giamatti, himself inclined to go ahead with expansion, and the pressure builds even more. At some point something had to give, if only because the last thing the owners wanted was an all-out fight with the fans and their representatives in Washington. The only thing certain about a fight, they knew, was that even if the owners won the battle, they would lose the war.

The *business* of baseball has thrived for as long as it has by drawing on a vast reservoir of goodwill toward the *game* of baseball—which is a dirty trick, granted, but it happens all the time in America. Former Commissioner Fay Vincent once tried to pooh-pooh the millions of dollars the cable network ESPN has lost on baseball by pointing out "there are only so many tractor pulls" you can televise. The commissioner's sarcasm drew an approving chuckle from the audience, which was made up of owners, executives and sportswriters attending baseball's winter meetings. The truth is, such condescension is justifiable. Does anyone seriously doubt that, on the scale of diversions, baseball occupies an infinitely higher plane than tractor pulls (or hockey, for that matter)?

Baseball may have started out long ago as just another game, but very quickly it got all mixed up with beauty and memory and longing, with the cadence of the seasons, the smell of grass in spring, youth and everything about it, the American Dream, glory, loss and death. Baseball is a poem sung by generations of poets, annotated by intellectuals, exploited by admen ("Baseball, hot dogs, apple pie and Chevrolet!") and celebrated finally by all of us. "If baseball is a narrative," wrote the lyrical scholar Giamatti, "an epic of exile and return, a vast communal poem about separation, loss, and the hope for reunion—if baseball is a Romance Epic—it is finally told by the audience. It is the Romance Epic of homecoming America sings to itself."

But hold the chorus while we cut to the bone. Baseball is also a commodity; a product that someone figured out long ago can be packaged and displayed behind walls so that people will pay to see it; and in that respect, a close cousin to tractor pulls and carnival sideshows starring the world's fattest teenager. Every baseball executive knows this as well as he knows the odor of his own underarms, and occasionally the rest of us catch a whiff. Former New York Mets president Frank Cashen was entertaining a group of Harvard Business School graduates at the ballpark one day during the go-go '80s when he explained to them the difference between fans and customers. A fan is anybody who follows the Mets. A customer is someone who buys a ticket. It follows that fans are irrelevant and customers count, especially big (corporate) customers who buy blocks of season tickets.

No fan wants to be reminded that baseball is a business. It's distracting, it breaks the spell. Anyone who has stuck by the game through the '60s, '70s and '80s understands this, having been forced to come to terms with domes, multipurpose stadiums, plastic playing surfaces, the DH rule, multimillion-dollar salaries, million-dollar *average* salaries, strikes (the other kind), lockouts and World Series night games—all of which spring from greed. That so many still care—major league baseball drew a near-record 55.8 million fans in 1992—speaks to the beauty of the game and its power to enchant us.

The owners respect the power of tradition, they really do. Some of them even understand it. All of them recognize that it is money in their pockets. It translates into popular sympathy for management in labor disputes, widespread disgust with player salaries and finally a willingness on the part of ordinary citizens to shore up the baseball business with generous subsidies, if that's what it takes. It forms the basis of what might be called the cultural-impact argument (which is usually made in tandem with the economic-impact argument): that baseball, as much as a symphony orchestra, an opera company or an art museum, is a star in the cultural constellation, part of what makes a great American city. Which is not an argument that can be made for tractor pulls.

In the end, what spooked the owners most about the ongo-
ing work of the task force was not antitrust, though antitrust
certainly was a factor. And it wasn't just the thought of not
being on good terms with power—"The guys have other
things going," one insider explains, "are you gonna piss off
[House Ways and Means Committee chairman Dan] Ros-
tenkowski?"—though that was scary too. The fact is that if the
owners had the will, they probably could have held out longer,
and eventually they might have won. But at what cost?

What if Senator Metzenbaum were to have been asked by
his colleagues on the task force to convene a special session of
his Antitrust Subcommittee in order to reexamine baseball's
exemption? Or worse yet, if the task force were to have taken
its hearings on the road, giving fans in cities like Buffalo, Denver and St. Petersburg a public forum in which to vent their
anger? "Those options existed," says Knobloch. "You have
some extremely creative U.S. senators who are superb at representing their home states. Probably at some point, had they
felt strung along and misled, they would have headed in that
direction."

From the owners' point of view, expansion was a bad idea,
they didn't like it at all, there was no way any of them were
going to realize any long-term benefits from the deal. (Although, as Philadelphia Phillies owner Bill Giles allows, "you
do get a pretty good piece of change. Up front, anyway." One
hundred ninety million dollars, to be exact, or $12.3 million
per National League owner, which couldn't have come at a
better time—the collusion settlement cost each team $10.8 mil-
lion.)

On the other hand, they realized that they were up against a
"political force," in the words of one highly placed baseball
executive, "which [had] reached sort of a critical mass and
[could] not be ignored." Nearly two years of nonstop pressure
from what one owner, Bill Giles, refers to condescendingly as
"the scene in Washington" finally convinced a majority of the
owners that there was little to be gained by postponing the
inevitable. Not if it meant a future filled with subpoenas and
raucous public hearings and damning testimony from politi-

cians, economists and ordinary fans. At stake was an intangible asset of immense value to the owners—our collective goodwill —and in the end that was something they were loath to risk.

"What would have been brought to the public's awareness," says John Frew, Wirth's former administrative assistant, "is that here are some very, very wealthy owners who hold up cities for hundred-million-dollar stadiums and don't care about anybody else. I believe baseball looked at that and saw that it was not in the best interests of baseball."

ON AUGUST 2, 1989, four months and a day after taking office, Giamatti flew down to Washington at the invitation of the task force. On the surface, the mood was one of hopefulness and congeniality. Most of the senators were favorably disposed anyway toward the plump, bearded Renaissance scholar, whose abundant charm and obvious love of the game distinguished him sharply from Ueberroth. That Giamatti seemed on first glance to be a less obstinate opponent than Ueberroth, if not exactly a pushover, only endeared him to them all the more. To the senators, the new commissioner looked like someone they could muscle.

Again the task force met privately, this time in the Mansfield Room, which is not the grandest room in the U.S. Capitol but may be the most distinguished, with its rich paneling, its marble fireplace and its life-size oil painting of former Senate Majority Leader Mike Mansfield (which dwarfs a much smaller portrait of George Washington). The Mansfield Room is where current Majority Leader George Mitchell hosts his regular Tuesday luncheon for all the Democratic senators, and consequently is where much of the real work of the Senate gets done. It has an aura of history about it, and power, and might have overwhelmed someone who didn't happen to be the former president of an ancient Ivy League university. Giamatti, for his part, glancing around as he settled in his chair, would have felt like he was back in New Haven.

Giamatti's appearance on Capitol Hill came on the heels of significant developments elsewhere. Earlier that summer, at their quarterly meeting in Kansas City, the owners had taken what looked like a huge step toward satisfying the task force, agreeing to expand by two teams in the National League according to a timetable to be announced within three months of signing a new Basic Agreement with the players union. This was the long-awaited "timetable for a timetable," which Wirth had sought for almost two years. But there were problems with it, and the senators had questions that wanted answering.

First, they suspected they were no closer now than they had ever been to knowing exactly when expansion would occur. Assuming that talks with the players union could be wrapped up before the current contract expired at the end of the year (by no means a safe assumption), then they would get their timetable by early spring. But what the timetable would call for—whether expansion in one year, or two, or five—was left completely up to the owners. Second, there was simply no way two teams would ever satisfy 19 senators. The goal of the task force had always been six teams—two in the American League and four in the National League, for a total of four eight-team divisions. Maybe Florida's senators, Bob Graham and Connie Mack, could live with two (no matter what, Florida was certain to get at least one) but no one else could. Al Gore of Tennessee and John McCain of Arizona—both of whom, by the way, represented cities which were no better than marginal candidates (Memphis and Phoenix)—jumped on the commissioner almost as soon as the door closed, pushing hard for more teams. Gore especially was "obnoxious," or so he appeared to one Senate staffer, "to the point where he was beating up on Giamatti."

As it turns out, the notion of satisfying the task force completely by going ahead with six new teams was "not so crazy," according to a source in the commissioner's office. "I thought seriously about that," says a former adviser to Giamatti, "and even at one point had a discussion with Bart about actually doing that. I said, you know, 'Just do it—just think about it, anyway. Doing it all at once, you'd remove the issue for fifteen years. There would be a tremendous amount of money involved for baseball. You'd be a hero in Washington and in these cities. And if you did it spaced out enough, it would be planned.' "

Those were the arguments in favor. On the other side, there was doubt in a lot of people's minds whether six new cities capable of supporting a major league franchise even existed. And clearly, it was to baseball's advantage to promote division within the task force, especially where it already existed. One baseball executive goes so far as to say, "I never was really worried about the Senate task force when it was obvious they weren't pushing for a team in Washington. There were just inherent conflicts among all of them as to where these teams would go. 'I want the team in Florida, I want the team in Denver, I want the team in California, I want the team in New York, I want the team in Tennessee, I want the team in Ohio.' When they looked around the table they all knew that ultimately they all weren't going to be winners. If they had all banded together and said, 'We want a team in Washington, D.C.,' I think that would have been a much more potent political force."

But what worried Giamatti most about the idea of a huge, all-at-once expansion, according to one of his advisers, was what effect suddenly increasing the work force by more than 20 percent would have on the quality of play. By all accounts, the commissioner sincerely believed that too much expansion too fast would dilute the talent pool and tarnish the brilliance of the game. The senators were skeptical. For years, so-called baseball purists (usually purists who already had a hometown team) had been making the same point, and perhaps they were right. But lately, with expansion fever growing, the owners had begun taking up the cry, and to hear them join now with the purists, it was as if the DH and AstroTurf had never happened. Giamatti wasn't an owner, but today he was here as their representative. And so the senators pressed him hard, to the point where he was compelled to defend himself.

To begin, Giamatti noted that baseball was a sport "unlike any other." He went on about the farm system, about the need to develop talent over a period of many years, about the process of bringing players along. Adding even two new teams, he argued, much less six, would drain the pipeline, with implications for quality of play throughout the major leagues. "This isn't like basketball, where you can take somebody off the courts in high school and make that person a professional ball-player," Giamatti said. And then he added, "Baseball requires different neurological skills."

Heads cocked, eyebrows lifted. A half instant later the whole room was in an uproar. That the commissioner would speak of "neurological skills," and with reference to baseball, which is 70 percent white, and basketball, which is 75 percent black, was simply astounding. Still fresh in everyone's mind was Dodger general manager Al Campanis's remark to Ted Koppel on *Nightline* that blacks "lack the necessities" to become major league managers; it had cost Campanis his job and brought about a long-overdue reexamination of racism in the National Pastime. Up to this point, the senators had been rough on Giamatti. Now they went ballistic.

"I didn't learn economics at Harvard or Yale or someplace like that," shouted McCain, a graduate of the Naval Academy. "But the way I count it there is plenty of talent and there are plenty of cities that can support a major league team!"

One after another the senators climbed up on their soap boxes, some of them carrying on in a way that "would have pissed most men off," according to Frew. But Giamatti was unfazed. He sat quietly through all their tirades, paid polite attention, held his peace, and all the while kept the corners of his mouth turned up just enough to indicate that he was not offended. And only when they had finished, and he had been invited to respond, did he state gently but firmly, so that there was no possibility of his being misunderstood by anyone, "I believe that we will expand by two teams. Soon. But two does not equal six."

And then he took a deep drag on his cigarette—Giamatti was a chain-smoker, it bothered him not at all that he was the only person in the room who had dared to light up—and blew smoke in all their faces.

Congressional aides, while generally appreciative of political theater, tend also to be cynical. Basically, they've seen it all.

And yet those few who were lucky enough to have witnessed in person Giamatti's stunning performance before the task force on that late summer day in the nation's capital are thrilled even now when they recall it.

"He was masterful!" says one.

"He basically said, 'Fuck you,' " remembers another. "But he did it with class and style. He just had them in knots!"

"Giamatti was just, you know, the blows! He just put on the Vaseline and they were just sliding right off of him!"

It was beginning to dawn on the senators that perhaps they had underestimated this guy. Giamatti was a charmer, granted, but at bottom he was every bit as tough and unyielding as Ueberroth. And as the senators went from being angry to frustrated to sorely exasperated, it was only a matter of time before somebody (probably it was McCain, although in any case others immediately chimed in) uttered the "A" word.

Giamatti could have let it pass, but he didn't. For almost two years, ever since the task force had come along, baseball had lived with the imminent threat—sometimes veiled, sometimes explicit—of Congress taking away its antitrust exemption. The way Giamatti pounced now, it was as if he had been waiting for just such a chance to finally confront the issue head-on. He began by playing down its importance, asserting that as far as relations with the players went, it was practically a nonissue. So why keep it? Giamatti asked rhetorically. For one very good reason: without it, teams would be free to move wherever they wanted, anytime they felt like it, and baseball would be powerless to stop them. Such movement, he suggested to the senators, was not in the best interests of their constituents.

Giamatti's rebuttal was the fruit of intense internal discussions played out over many months about how best to respond to the task force's threat. To some—like the National League owner who dismisses the whole antitrust issue as "overblown" and says flatly, "I don't think Congress would ever overthrow the antitrust exemption that baseball has"—the threat was never real. He and others have felt all along that if it ever came to a vote, there were enough legislators from states that already had teams who could be counted on not to tinker with the status quo. But Giamatti went one step further. He tried to prove that the antitrust exemption worked for small-market cities that still wanted teams too; indeed, it was their only hope.

A consultant to the commissioner's office explains the theory behind baseball's thinking: "Okay, so they get a club. And after the first year or two, they fail. The club doesn't perform, attendance falls off, and the glamour and the glory of the first year—'My goodness, isn't this wonderful, we have baseball in my hometown!'—fades, and the only person that can save the club from moving is the commissioner. The owner would move immediately. You see how fast Steinbrenner would have moved to New Jersey, you see how fast Cleveland would have moved, you see how fast the Pirates would have moved in those bad years. Every senator that comes up with the antitrust thing, I say to him, 'Senator Metzenbaum,' or 'Senator Whoever-you-are, fine, when they move the Indians or they move the Pirates, when they move whoever they are that's threatening this, please don't call the commissioner, because he has no authority now to keep that ball club there.' He's the one that stopped the Indians from moving to St. Petersburg in the first place. He's the one that stopped the Seattle move this time. They always threaten [removal of the exemption], and we are concerned. I would never say to the commissioner, 'Kiss it off.' But in the end we can beat that."

Ueberroth might have said exactly that to the task force. Giamatti, as was his nature, chose to cast the argument in nobler terms.

"What's better for America?" he asked the roomful of senators, punctuating his pauses with thick streams of blue smoke. "Who's better able to service America, baseball or you guys? I would submit to you we are. Because if you have your way and lift the antitrust exemption, then the only way you'll get your teams is through relocation, not expansion, I'll guarantee you that. And relocation means blackmail, highway robbery, the Baltimore Colts leaving in the middle of the night. It becomes very, very costly, to the point where smaller markets have no chance of getting a team.

"The position of baseball is that we will allow a team to relocate only when a city gives up on it. It's your choice."

"He picked off half the senators with that line," says Frew admiringly. "He divided the room."

EXACTLY 30 days after Giamatti's dramatic appearance on Capitol Hill, on September 1, 1989, the Friday before Labor Day, at approximately three o'clock in the afternoon, officer Richard Krauss of the Edgartown, Massachusetts, police department responded to an emergency call at the Giamatti family's summer home on Martha's Vineyard. Krauss, who was cruising only a block away when the call came through, was met at the door by Paul Giamatti, the commissioner's 22-year-old son, and shown to the bedroom. There he found the elder Giamatti lying in bed, his wife, Toni, administering mouth-to-mouth resuscitation. He was "in full cardiac arrest," Krauss would say later. "There was no breathing and no pulse."

Giamatti was taken by ambulance to Martha's Vineyard Hospital in the community of Oak Bluffs, where doctors tried for more than an hour to revive him. At 4:32 P.M., Angelo Bartlett Giamatti, age 51, was pronounced dead.

To the extent that Giamatti will be remembered more for the four months he was commissioner of baseball than for the eight years he was president of Yale, it will be because of Pete Rose. Rose was already under investigation for gambling when Giamatti took office. But it was Giamatti who received special investigator John Dowd's final report, and Giamatti who, the week before he died, banned him for life. Giamatti's sure handling of the Rose affair was widely seen as confirmation of his fitness for office, dramatic proof that the quiet professor had the guts after all to stare down the game's greatest hitter, and do what had to be done.

Which by then came as no great surprise to the members of the Senate task force on expansion. For clearly Giamatti was the big winner in that showdown as well. By refusing to sidestep the antitrust issue, Giamatti called the Senate's bluff, and so splintered the task force's biggest stick. After Giamatti, the senators on the whole realized that there was only one way forward, and that was to shut up about antitrust and play by baseball's rules; meaning expansion by two teams, not six, and on baseball's timetable, not theirs.

As late as October 1989, in a letter to the new commissioner, Fay Vincent, Wirth was still talking tough. "It is our concern," he reiterated by way of staking out a position with his new adversary, "that expansion of the leagues in the 1990s not be limited to only the two National League teams announced in June. To that end, we have initiated a review of legislative options that might move the process forward."

But in fact no such options were ever seriously discussed. On June 14, 1990—within 90 days, as promised, of having signed a new Basic Agreement with the Players Association— Vincent unveiled baseball's long-awaited expansion timetable. All prospective owners would be invited to make a presentation before the National League expansion committee sometime before September 30; the committee would then announce a "short list" of finalists by December 31 of that year; and the committee promised to pass along its recommendations for approval by the rest of the owners no later than September 30, 1991.

Not six recommendations, by the way, just two. But the task force took what it could get, and hasn't been heard from since. "Giamatti had held out an olive leaf that basically said, 'Look, play your cards right, you're gonna get two teams,'" says Frew. "And from that point on, I think that was the way Tim and the other senators viewed their chances."

AS IT HAPPENED, baseball came in well under its self-imposed deadline, all but settling on Denver and Miami by the early summer of 1991, and wrapping things up for good on Friday, July 5. Two months later, Commissioner Vincent traveled to Denver for a celebratory banquet in honor of the new team that would call itself the Colorado Rockies, and it was there that the commissioner finally gave the senator his due.

"I think the citizens of Colorado should know that if it hadn't been for Tim Wirth and his task force there probably wouldn't have been any expansion," Vincent said then. "The political pressure played a significant role in the process."

Vincent's praise begs the question: What role, if any, did Wirth play in baseball's decision to award a franchise to *Denver,* as opposed to all the other cities that would have liked to have one? Was baseball, perhaps, rewarding Wirth for being such a good sport, for not forcing the antitrust issue, indeed for helping to keep the likes of McCain, DeConcini and Gore in line? Not many would believe that, other than to note—perhaps significantly, perhaps not—that neither Phoenix nor Memphis made it so far as the final six. But really, it's far-fetched, if for no other reason than it requires us to believe that the owners are capable of acting out of loyalty, when instead all indications are that what they really respond to is force. And force, it turns out, is what the soft-spoken senator from Colorado was able to marshal, and to a far greater degree than any of his colleagues.

On March 1, 1990, Wirth mailed a letter to Commissioner Vincent on generic stationery ("Congress of the United States"), promoting Denver as the ideal expansion city. "A Denver club would not only represent Denver and Colorado," Wirth wrote, "but [the] entire . . . Western Plains and Rocky Mountain region." Nice message, but what really packed a wallop was what followed. The letter was co-signed by Wirth and Republican representative Dan Schaefer of Colorado's 6th Congressional District, and attached to it were three pages filled with more names. The first two contained signatures of U.S. representatives from states all over the West (plus Mike Oxley of Ohio, Carl Pursell of Michigan, Clyde Holloway of Louisiana and Dean Gallo of New Jersey thrown in for good measure). Forty-one names in all, totaling almost 10 percent of the House.

Impressive, but then seats in the House are apportioned by population, whereas in the Senate it's two seats per state, regardless of size. Page three was the clincher, signed by at least one senator from all the states that border Colorado, plus North Dakota, South Dakota and Idaho (the only exception being Arizona; Phoenix still had competing hopes of its own).

Eighteen names in all, 19 counting Wirth, *nearly 20 percent of the Senate,* and all of them united behind Denver.

What better way for baseball to make the Senate task force go away than to give the senator from Colorado and all his Senate allies exactly what they wanted?

# 3

# The Lawyer, the Lease, the Partnership and the Public Servant

*Ha Ha—Ha Ha! It's a great lease. I gotta hand it to those people who negotiated it, it's a hell of a lease, boy! In fact, it's unbelievable.*
—Carl Barger, President of Marlins
on the Rockies' Coors Field lease

"I'VE BEEN to a lot of meetings," says the lawyer, Paul Jacobs, "and this one was *bizarre*."

The whole thing was supposed to be hush-hush, although by midmorning the lobby of the Denver Westin was thick with reporters. The participants met upstairs in room 401—the Daniels room, according to the brass plate on the door—a narrow, hotel-ugly conference room with pink walls and sliding-glass doors that faced a concrete terrace. The place was packed. At the head of an oblong, cloth-covered conference table sat Roy Romer, the silver-haired Democratic governor of the state of Colorado. Every other seat around the table was taken, and so were all the chairs along the walls, and plenty of people were left standing. The reason for the overflow was simple. Not everyone in the room had been invited. A lot of them, having heard what was going on, just decided to show up.

Today was Friday, only three days after the big election on Tuesday, August 14, 1990, when local voters agreed to a tax increase to build a new baseball stadium in Denver. The vote capped a summer-long campaign by stadium backers that had cost more than $400,000, most of it put up by the Greater Denver Chamber of Commerce. In the days leading up, supporters passed out 50,000 boxes of Cracker Jack (each with a baseball surprise), packed the 16th Street mall to sing "Take Me Out to the Ball Game" (while local radio stations played along on the air), and collected a mile's worth of signed "booster coupons," which they mailed to "baseball officials" in New York. In spite of all that, plus the enthusiastic support of Governor Romer, Denver mayor Federico Pena and Colorado senator Tim Wirth, not to mention the absence of any real organized opposition, victory was far from certain. For one thing, the timing was all wrong, what with the Rocky Mountain economy still reeling from the effects of slumping energy prices. Besides, where in America were there voters these days willing to support a new tax for anything? Stadium votes in Phoenix and San Francisco had lately gone down to defeat. Right up until election eve, polls were predicting the same result in Denver.

Incredibly, the voters said yes. And by a convincing margin, 54 percent to 46 percent, thanks to strong support from the suburbs (if it was up to Denver County alone, the answer would have been no). Specifically, what the citizens of the six-county Denver Metropolitan Major League Baseball Stadium District agreed to was this: a one-tenth of 1 percent sales tax increase (a penny on a ten-dollar purchase) for as long as it took (up to 20 years) to raise $100 million, or 70 percent of the cost of the new stadium. Private money, plus the income from

rent, parking, concessions and the rest, would make up the
$40 million difference. Unlike the crazies in St. Petersburg,
who built their stadium on spec, Denverites made sure the
deal was contingent on landing a major league team. But a
team needs a buyer—in this case, a buyer capable of staring
down a $95 million price tag—and that was the rub.

Up until last month, everybody figured John Dikeou, owner
of the class AAA Denver Zephyrs, would be that buyer.
Dikeou's primary reason for creating the Zephyrs back in 1983
was to lay the groundwork for one day becoming the owner of
a major league team. By the time Dikeou bought the Denver
Bears and changed their name to the Zephyrs, he already had
a big league uniform (blue for the sky, green for the grass), a
logo (a baseball with Z-shaped stitching) and a slogan ("The
team that has nothing . . . yet"). For years, Denver baseball
fans had imagined the future by conjuring up a headline that
read "Z's Clobber A's."

But Dikeou, who runs what remains of his downtown real
estate empire out of an unassuming storefront at the corner of
18th and Welton, was struggling lately. Early in July, it had
surfaced that he was being sued for $7 million by creditors,
proof that he was finally wobbling under the weight of collaps-
ing property values and soaring vacancy rates in the de-
pressed Denver market. Shortly thereafter, Dikeou dropped
out of the baseball picture altogether, leaving Denver suddenly without a moneyman.

For three decades, ever since Bob Howsam's near-miss with
the Continental League in 1961, Denver had been doing everything in its power to prove itself worthy of major league
baseball. Year after year, fans packed Mile High Stadium, civic
boosters flirted with the owners, politicians offered up concessions, and millionaires jostled for the privilege of buying.
More than any other city in North America, Denver profes-
sionalized the art of franchise seeking. But now with expansion finally on the agenda, and with the funds in place to build
a beautiful new stadium, the only thing missing was the one
crucial ingredient—a buyer.

"I was pretty dispirited at that time," recalls Lee White, the

Denver investment banker who put together the plan of finance for the new stadium. "Here we were three weeks from the election with a ninety-five-million-dollar expansion fee and no owner candidate. I was pessimistic, even if the vote were to pass, because I didn't see an ownership group coming together, nor did I know anybody who had the cash to do it locally."

Time was running out. In exactly two weeks, the completed expansion application, together with a check for $100,000, was due at the National League office in New York. That meant the governor had 14 days—starting now, starting from scratch—in which to locate a buyer. Either that, or be held politically responsible for blowing Denver's best shot ever at breaking into the big leagues. That was the purpose of today's meeting. Which was why the governor didn't mind that the room was overcrowded, not at all. On the contrary, anyone who looked half serious was more than welcome. The situation was that desperate.

PAUL JACOBS had arrived early enough to secure three seats near the head of the conference table for himself and the two other members of his party, Steve Ehrhart and Mike Nicklous. They made an unlikely trio: Jacobs, fifty, the East Coast transplant, tall and lanky, with sleepy eyes, a salt-and-pepper goatee and an air about him of intellectual superiority; Ehrhart, forty-three, the ex-jock golden boy from Colorado College by way of nearby Lakewood, on the chunky side now but poised as ever, possessed of a flawless hair helmet; and Nicklous, fortysomething, the slick New York promoter, plump and balding and quick with a grin.

The occasion that had brought them together was an informal meeting, a few weeks before, of the handful of lawyers at Jacobs's firm—Holme, Roberts & Owen—who had an interest in sports. With Dikeou out of the picture, Jacobs thought he saw an opportunity for the firm to step into the void and, in effect, create a new client. "Dikeou isn't going to do this thing," he had argued then. "I don't think there's anybody in

Denver who's going to lead it. There's an opportunity here for somebody to pull together this group and make it happen."

Jacobs, whose specialty was real estate law, knew something about lining up investors; he estimates he has put together more than 40 acquisition syndicates in the 24 years since he graduated from law school at the University of Denver. Lately, too, he had dabbled part-time in sports. He had a hand in drawing up the latest Denver Nuggets lease at McNichols Sports Arena, and had done Ehrhart's contract for him when he took over as president, general manager and part owner of the USFL's Memphis Showboats in 1984, which was how they met. It so happened that one of the other lawyers at the meeting, Dan Hoffman, had known Ehrhart even longer, going back to Ehrhart's days as a sports attorney in Boulder. Jacobs and Hoffman agreed that Ehrhart's contacts might be useful, and as soon as the meeting broke up, the two went upstairs to Hoffman's office and placed a call to the World Basketball League in Memphis, of which Ehrhart was then commissioner. Now, Ehrhart was far from being capable of buying a baseball team; he was a lawyer, he didn't have that kind of money. But he was intrigued and he knew people with lots of money. Ehrhart talked to Jacobs at length, and later agreed to put him in touch with Nicklous, the owner of the Kansas City Royals' class AA farm team, the Memphis Chicks.

On Monday, the day before the stadium vote, Jacobs spoke to Dick Robinson of Robinson dairy (also the chairman of the Chamber of Commerce), who had been appointed by Governor Romer to head up a blue-ribbon search committee. Robinson told Jacobs then that if the measure should pass, there would be a meeting for all potential team buyers on Friday morning at the Westin, 10:15 sharp. Thursday night, Ehrhart and Nicklous flew in from Memphis, checked into the Westin, and met Jacobs for dinner in the Augusta dining room. It was the first time Jacobs and Nicklous had ever laid eyes on one another.

Now here they were together again the morning after in a room full to overflowing with sports-baron wannabes, some of them familiar to Jacobs (cable TV moguls Bob Magness and

Gene Schneider, Rob Klugman from Coors, Jerry McMorris from NW Transport), some of them not (who was the blond kid in white shoes?), anxiously waiting to hear what the governor had to say.

First off, the governor introduced Steve Kurtz, a partner in the suburban Englewood accounting firm of Shenkin, Kurtz, Baker & Co. Back in 1988, about the same time the Senate task force was beginning to act up, Romer had asked Kurtz to run some revenue and expense projections for a hypothetical major league team doing business in the Denver market. Kurtz had consulted with baseball executives in Milwaukee, Kansas City and Texas. He had talked about trends in media rights with Bill Daniels, the Denver entrepreneur regarded as "the father of cable television." He had constantly updated his numbers, most recently taking into account both the outrageous $95 million franchise fee and the ball-buster decision by baseball to deny the expansion teams a cut of the national TV money their first year, effectively adding $14 million to the purchase price. And he had boiled his message down to this:

"You need at least a hundred million in equity," he told the prospective buyers. "You need somewhere between thirty million and forty million in bank credit. And you need a stadium lease that's going to give you *all* revenue sources. *All* revenue sources. No rent. If you have that, then you have a chance of making baseball work in Denver."

All the revenue? No rent? Had this been an open meeting, and were it not made up entirely of people who stood to profit from a sweetheart stadium lease, surely someone would have pointed out that what Kurtz was proposing flatly contradicted the plan of finance put before the voters only 72 hours before. As far as the taxpayers were concerned, the deal was supposed to be a 70-30 public-private split, with revenue from the stadium augmenting the sales tax as a means of paying off the public debt. Now here was Kurtz saying forget that, it won't work, the only way baseball survives in Denver is if the team keeps all the money, every penny.

Basically, he said, they were talking about a $120 million deal—$95 million for the franchise fee, plus another $20 million or so in start-up costs. Of that, he told them, baseball demanded a starting equity position of 60 percent (which came to only $75 million; Kurtz's prudent advice was to shoot for $100 million). On the revenue side, there was no question that in Denver ticket sales would be the single largest source. Kurtz's best guess was based on two million fans per season paying an average $8.25 per ticket, or about $16 million. Local media—free TV, cable and radio—he tagged at $5 million to $6 million; a long way from the Yankees' $50 million but better than Seattle's $2 million. As for stadium advertising, parking and luxury boxes, he said those would never amount to much as long as the team was playing at Mile High Stadium, the home of the NFL Broncos. But once the new ballpark was ready, Kurtz expected big gains across the board; depending, once again, on the lease.

As for expenses, the only one that really mattered was the one that couldn't be predicted—player salaries. Kurtz's advice was to pursue a strategy of developing young talent and stay away from high-priced free agents, especially in the beginning. "Real world is, in the first year or two, if you lose 110 games, which you're going to do, who cares? The fans are still going to come out." The average big league payroll then was running about $23 million. For Denver, just starting out, Kurtz thought $15 million was realistic.

For the bottom line, he predicted five years of tax losses totaling $20 million, though possibly some cash flow toward the end. But even that, Kurtz repeated, was predicated on the team's realizing substantially all the revenues from the new stadium; namely, tickets, parking, concessions and advertising. "Subject to negotiations with the stadium authority," Jacobs scribbled on his legal pad.

John McHale, Jr., head of the stadium district board, and Roger Kinney, a board member, had been asked by Kurtz to leave the room during Kurtz's presentation; it was McHale, after all, who would be representing the taxpayers in negotiations with the owner, whoever the owner turned out to be. But now the two district officials were invited back in, and McHale gave a brief rundown on plans for the new stadium. Site and design were far from settled, but what Hellmuth, Obata & Kassabaum (the Kansas City architectural firm responsible for the new Comiskey Park and Oriole Park at Camden Yards) was proposing already was enough to make anyone drool. Not a multipurpose concrete bowl but a lovely brick ballpark featuring steel trusses, open grillwork, asymmetrical dimensions and a big view west to the mountains. Capacity would be held down to about 40,000, in keeping with the new thinking in baseball that smaller is better, if for no other reason than it juices the demand for season tickets. Construction would begin within a year after the franchise was awarded, and was expected to take two years, pointing toward a move-in date of April 1995.

Finally, the governor himself stood up. All eyes turned to the front of the room. He took off his coat, rolled up his sleeves, and in his typically blunt manner said, "Look, we're going to try to put an ownership group together. This is an awkward process. I don't know most of you people, but I don't know any other way to get started. Tell me who you are, what you're doing here and how much money you want to put in." And with that, he turned to the first person sitting on his left— who happened to be Jerry McMorris, the owner of NW Transport Service, a Denver-based trucking company—and invited him to begin.

McMorris is a trim, middle-aged millionaire with a year-round tan, a full head of hair, a native Coloradan's flat nasal twang and a self-made man's devotion to the place where he made himself. Listening to Kurtz, he had not liked the business deal that was described, not at all. But that's not what he said now. Instead he told the governor he believed baseball would be good for Denver, good for the state of Colorado and good for business. ("There's only sixteen major metropolitan areas in the United States that have all three major league sports," McMorris would explain later, "and this was the last step to take Denver into what I would call the sweet sixteen.") And while he wasn't ready just yet to say exactly how much he was willing to kick in, he was definite about wanting to help.

"Colorado's been good to me," he said. "I'd like to give something back."

Okay, great, now who's next? Sitting next to McMorris was Mike Cassidy, another local real estate lawyer, who announced he was speaking on behalf of Doug DeCinces, the former All-Star third baseman for the Orioles and the Angels. "DeCinces will be here tomorrow with the money," Cassidy said, which sounded farfetched, but who really knew? Next up was Dave Elmore, whom most people in the room already knew as the owner of the class AAA Colorado Springs Sky Sox. Elmore owned three other minor league teams too. He wanted to contribute a ready-to-go minor league system in exchange for an equity position in the new team; interesting, possibly, except that the real need right now was for people with cash. Next, the blond kid with the white shoes said his name was Michael Graham, that he was in real estate (welcome to the club) and that he represented John Henry, a wildly successful commodities trader from Boca Raton, Florida. Graham, the former owner of the Fort Myers Sun Sox in the failed Senior Professional Baseball Association—a league for retired major leaguers—said straight out that coming up with $95 million would "not be a problem" for Henry. "Appoint us and we'll take care of this thing," he said. And on and on around the room.

At one point the door opened and in walked George Gillett, known in Denver at the time as "the man who owns Vail." There had been a lot of talk in the papers the last few days suggesting that Gillett might turn out to be Denver's white knight. Gillett proceeded to put those rumors to rest. He chose not to bring up the fact that cracks were beginning to appear in his own real estate and broadcasting empire, nor did he acknowledge (as some in the room already knew by then) that he, like Dikeou, was beginning to hear from his creditors. Instead he read a press statement which said, in part, "My involvement at this time would be inappropriate," and just as suddenly he had appeared, he was gone.

Mixed in with the hustlers and the fly-by-nights was a smattering of corporate heavyweights, some of whom were destined to join the partnership in the coming weeks and months:

Hensel Phelps, the construction company that had built the just completed Colorado Convention Center, hoping now for a piece of the action on the stadium; Coors Brewery; and the *Rocky Mountain News*. Jacobs, Ehrhart and Nicklous, by luck, were sitting just to the right of the governor, which meant they would speak last. Listening with growing excitement as the introductions continued, Jacobs concluded that while the corporate guys all seemed willing to play along, none was especially eager to take the lead. McMorris sounded serious, as did Cary Teraji, the young founder of a software company called Innovative Solutions, but other than those two Jacobs saw almost no one he regarded as a threat for control of the franchise. Granted, there were a lot of cagey lawyers making claims on behalf of "undisclosed principals." But by now Jacobs knew all the big players in town well enough to guess which lawyers represented which clients. "These people were talking off the top of their heads," Jacobs would say later. "My experience was telling me there were very few people of substance."

Halfway through the meeting, Jacobs kicked Ehrhart underneath the table. "Steve," he whispered in his ear, "there's nobody here. If we want to do this we can do it!"

THE MEETING lasted about an hour and a half. Nicklous, when his turn finally came, was circumspect; he talked about his experience with the Chicks (which was a plus, people respected that) and mentioned that he had recently signed a contract to buy the class AAA Edmonton Trappers. But like most of the others, he refused to put a dollar amount on the table. After it was all over, the governor gave out his home phone number and asked for written proposals from interested parties, to be delivered to Robinson over the weekend if possible. He concluded by calling a follow-up meeting for next Thursday, the twenty-third. "Anybody who's really serious about this," Romer said in closing, "you get back to me and we'll do something."

That weekend, Jacobs drew up a preliminary proposal, identifying Nicklous and Ehrhart as the general partners and

Nicklous as the moneyman. It was necessarily light on substance. Basically, Nicklous agreed to put up the $100,000 ap-
plication fee (of which $25,000 was nonrefundable), and to-
gether he and Ehrhart promised to seek other investors.
Jacobs hand-delivered the proposal to Robinson early Monday
evening at his home near the Denver Country Club.

Everyone reconvened at 7 A.M. Thursday at the Westin.
They met this time in room 1926. The Board Room, as it is
called, with its gray fabric walls, blond-wood conference table
and blue-shuttered windows which open on a panoramic view
of northwest Denver from Union Station to Mile High Stadium and the purple mountains beyond, was a more stately
setting than the week before. Not that it made any difference.
What followed, according to Jacobs, was more of "the same
bullshit." Except that now the sense of urgency ratcheted up
another notch. The deadline was seven days away. It was time
to act.

There were a few newcomers in the crowd: Barry Fey, the
concert promoter, who was interested in marketing the stadium; David French, a local developer, who wanted to syndicate the deal on behalf of whomever was chosen; and a bevy of
lawyers claiming to speak for, among others, former major
league pitcher Hank Aguirre (now a California builder), former A's owner Charlie Finley, ex-slugger Reggie Jackson and
the ubiquitous "unnamed Japanese investors."

Half an hour into the meeting, an exasperated Governor
Romer threw up his hands, called a recess, grabbed Jacobs
and Ehrhart (Nicklous was out of town), plus the members of
his search committee, and led them all into a cramped blue-
tiled service kitchen adjoining the conference room. "This
isn't going anywhere," the governor said to Jacobs and Ehrhart as soon as he closed the door. "We got a week to do this. I
liked your proposal"—what he didn't say was that it was the
only one submitted. "You guys are willing to put up the
money. I'm going back out there and announce that the
Nicklous-Ehrhart group has been selected by me to bring Major League Baseball to Denver, Colorado. I have no authority
to do this but I'm going to do it anyway because if I don't do it,
it's not going to get done." At which point the governor threw

open the door, strode back to the table, made his announcement, and left.

Instantly, the whole room was in an uproar. There were cries of "Unfair!" and "You have no authority to do this!" Some, including Michael Graham, gathered up their papers and walked out. Ehrhart and Jacobs moved to the head of the table. They announced that there would be a meeting the following morning at Holme, Roberts & Owen for all those who were serious about wanting to put money into the Nicklous-Ehrhart group, and that Mr. Nicklous would attend. Then, escorted by hotel personnel, they slipped past reporters and out the back door of the hotel.

JACOBS AND EHRHART had made it to square one. All they had so far was the governor's blessing to try to put together an ownership group, which carried some prestige, sure, but little else. There was still nothing to prevent Teraji—or Graham for that matter—from lining up other investors and submitting their own applications. But one thing Jacobs and Ehrhart could count on in the critical week coming up was access to money and power. Upon leaving the Westin, they walked the 12 blocks over to the City and County Building and were immediately ushered in for an audience with Mayor Pena.

Partly, Jacobs and Ehrhart were paying a simple courtesy call. Pena had made baseball a campaign issue when he first ran for mayor in 1983, and had stayed close to the issue ever since. He traveled with the Denver delegation to New York during the first round of presentations in '85, and would no doubt be involved if and when they ever reached the presentation stage again. His continued goodwill was essential to the whole undertaking. But beyond that, Jacobs and Ehrhart had come before the mayor today to begin the all-important work of lining up concessions. Specifically, they wanted to make sure they weren't going to be stuck paying a high rent to the city during the two years the team would have to play in Mile High Stadium.

"Just by looking at Kurtz's initial projections," Jacobs explains, "we knew that in a market Denver's size, unless we had substantially all the revenue from the stadium, we were going to have a very difficult time attracting investors and a lender. We always knew that was the key to putting the deal together. That's why right after the governor appointed us, the first two people we talked to were the city on Mile High and the stadium district on the new stadium lease. We flat told them that this was our objective. If they told us there was no way we were going to get there, we probably wouldn't have gone forward."

Jacobs and Ehrhart were direct. They told the mayor it "can't be a one-way lease," an interesting choice of words given that a one-way lease was exactly what they were looking for. Pena, what with all the political capital he had invested in baseball, was eager to please. After the meeting, he wrote a letter on city stationery to Ehrhart and Nicklous which eventually found its way into the packet of materials provided with the application to the National League. "I assure you that the City and County of Denver will cooperate with the franchise owners in an effort to make Mile High Stadium available on terms that are fair and reasonable," Pena wrote. (The mayor proved true to his word. The upshot, nine months later, was a two-year rent-free deal in which the city also agreed to give the team 92 percent of its cut from concessions.)

From there, Ehrhart and Jacobs walked over to Jacobs's office at 1700 Lincoln—known around town as the "cash register building" because of the distinctive shape of its crown—took the elevator up to Holme, Roberts & Owen on the 41st floor, and there began to structure the beginnings of a partnership.

Ehrhart, 43, was a key to the deal from the beginning. He had experience—running leagues, owning a team, negotiating leases. And he was a Colorado native, the great-great grandson of Jacob Ehrhart, a member of the territorial legislature. Ehrhart grew up in suburban Lakewood (his dad still lives there), played in the state high school football championship game at old Bears Stadium (before it was enlarged for football and renamed Mile High), went on to stardom at Colorado College, and later attended law school at Boulder on an NCAA scholar-athlete postgraduate scholarship. Although Ehrhart hadn't lived in Colorado since 1982, when he left to become legal counsel and later executive director of the USFL, he and Jacobs hoped that his deep roots in the community would help satisfy baseball's requirement for local ownership. Moreover, the guys like McMorris—locals with big money to invest—remembered Ehrhart and trusted him, if not unconditionally then at least more than they trusted an outsider like Nicklous.

As for money, whatever Ehrhart had to contribute, it wasn't going to make much of a dent in $75 million. That was where Nicklous fit in. A native New Yorker, passionate to this day about the Brooklyn Dodgers, Nicklous made a pile of money with Flynn-Hill, Inc., a company that builds and installs elevators. Nicklous sold out in 1988, the same year he bought the Chicks. Since then, he had tried all kinds of businesses—TV and film production, military housing for the Navy, waste-treatment technology—but lately had focused on sports, as an owner of minor league teams, a marketer and a promoter.

Nicklous flew to Denver the next day to take part in the first meeting with his potential co-investors. The challenge was to line up enough cash commitments in order to be able to assure the National League, with a straight face, that the Nicklous-Ehrhart group could raise at least $75 million. No one was expecting real money yet, just promises. Of course, the big thing everybody else wanted to know before they pledged was exactly how far Nicklous, as head of the group, was willing to go. But Nicklous still wouldn't say, other than to declare that money was "no problem." McMorris, for one, was disturbed by that. Immediately after the meeting broke up, he pulled Jacobs aside and told him, "Your man is dancing." Jacobs didn't really need to hear that from McMorris. He was already thinking the same thing himself.

Later that afternoon, at a big press conference attended by Governor Romer and covered live by all the local television stations, Nicklous and Ehrhart were introduced as the governor's personal choices to lead Denver in the coming campaign for Major League Baseball. But behind the broad smiles of those in the know—which did not yet include the governor—

was deep concern about Nicklous's ability to follow through on his promises. Already, Jacobs had conveyed his doubts to Ehrhart. And Ehrhart, playing it safe, had placed a call to Youngstown, Ohio, and the president and chief operating officer of Phar-Mor, Inc., Mickey Monus.

SATURDAY MORNING, the day after the press conference in Denver, John Antonucci awoke at his mountain home in Vail and headed for the local drugstore to pick up a Denver newspaper. There on page one of the *Rocky Mountain News* was a picture of Steve Ehrhart. Something to do with baseball, the caption said. Antonucci was shocked.

Antonucci was on vacation. Year-round he lived in Canfield, Ohio, a suburb of Youngstown. As a young man fresh out of Ohio State he had taken over from his father the management of the family's beer and wine distributorship, Superior Beverage. Only 35 years old, already an extraordinarily wealthy man, he bore a certain outward resemblance to Ehrhart—the same chunky build, the same light brown hair, carefully parted on the side and combed low over the forehead. But that is as far as the comparison goes. Where Ehrhart is circumspect, reserved, always fretting about one thing or another, Antonucci is brash, impulsive ("an animal when it comes to business," according to one who has faced him), an open book. Two years later, when Antonucci's closest friend and business partner was accused of masterminding a $350 million fraud, the best evidence another friend could cite to prove Antonucci's innocence had nothing to do with virtue; it was that Antonucci can't keep a secret. "I just don't think John's the kind of guy that could hold that within him for two or three years," the friend says. "It's not his personality."

John Antonucci's closest friend and business partner was none other than Mickey Monus, 42, the founder of Phar-Mor, at the time the fastest-growing retail chain in America. The Phar-Mor concept, as reported in an admiring company profile in *The Wall Street Journal,* originated with a visit one day by Monus to a discount drugstore in Cleveland. The prices were low, the profit margin was undoubtedly slim, but the place was packed, and that's what impressed Monus. In 1982, backed by, among others, shopping mall mogul Edward DeBartolo, Monus launched a chain of deep-discount pharmacies, selling an eclectic mix of cosmetics, sportswear, office supplies and drugs, always at well below list price. By 1990, Phar-Mor was opening its 200th store nationwide (on the way to 300 by 1992) and reporting annual sales in excess of $2 billion (on the way to $3 billion). "Our market," Monus told the *Journal,* "is the whole country and maybe parts of the world."

Antonucci and Monus—soon to be dubbed the Drugstore Cowboys by the Denver media—had known each other for years. Their fortunes were closely intermingled. Together they had invested in at least half a dozen companies. Antonucci owned a 2 percent piece of Phar-Mor (worth eight figures at the time and growing fast). Monus owned big chunks of two Ohio distributorships that were part of Antonucci's Superior Beverage group. Monus and Antonucci were joint owners of the corporate jet leased by Phar-Mor. They were partners in a real estate development company, Monus and Antonucci Enterprises, and co-owners of the 5,800-square-foot Vail home where Antonucci was staying that weekend. Both were active in charity and civic circles in Youngstown. Monus, a confirmed casual dresser with longish, gray-specked hair, which he combed straight back behind his ears, was a member of the board of trustees of Youngstown State University, and soon to become chairman.

Above all, the Drugstore Cowboys shared a passion for sports, crisscrossing the country to attend Super Bowls, World Series games and the Final Four, lining up Phar-Mor as a sponsor of two LPGA golf tournaments and, in 1988, cofounding the World Basketball League for players six feet five and under. Under the WBL's unique financial structure, as general partners in the league, Monus and Antonucci were majority shareholders in each of the league's ten franchises, as well as outright owners of the Youngstown Pride. Monus was also co-owner of Sure Shot Teleproductions and Transmissions, Inc., a satellite uplink service. The big dream shared by Ehrhart, Monus and Antonucci was one day to build a modern sports and communications empire to rival that of Ted Turner, who owns the Braves, the Hawks and TBS.

Baseball fit nicely into the equation; Antonucci was not displeased to see Ehrhart's picture in the paper. On the other hand, the last Antonucci had heard, Ehrhart was still working for him and Monus as commissioner of the WBL. He wondered what the hell was going on.

Antonucci found a phone and called Monus. "Hey," he said, "is Steve moonlighting or is he on a mission?"

"No, no, no," said Monus. "I haven't had a chance to talk to you in the last twenty-four hours. He's out there on a mission. There's an opportunity for us to get involved with the baseball process."

MEANWHILE, with only days remaining before the deadline, someone at the National League office in New York had looked at the calendar, realized that August 31 was the Friday before the long Labor Day weekend, and decided to give everybody until Tuesday, September 4, to turn in their applications. That meant that Jacobs and Ehrhart had not just seven days to pull everything together, but 11, which was good. Of those 11 days, however, five were weekends or holidays, which was too bad.

The league's formal application consisted of 39 questions, divided into five sections—location, ownership, stadium, government and market. Some of them were easy. For example, question 9: "Do any members of the proposed ownership have any ownership or management interest in any casino gambling or other gambling operations? If so, describe." Answer: "No." Elsewhere, in the stadium section (which Denver had to fill out twice, once for Mile High and once for the new ballpark), the National League wanted to know, among other things, about field dimensions, parking, lighting, whether or not the stadium was equipped with luxury suites (how many?) and a video board, whether it was owned outright or leased, and if it was leased, on what terms. On the key issue in Denver, the league asked, "What is the landlord's position regarding the retention by the club of parking, concession, signage, pay television and luxury box revenue?"

The truth is, no one knew the answer to that yet. The law directed the stadium district board to "pursue opportunities for privatizing" the stadium, and stated a "target amount of at least fifty percent." But the law also said, "Such amount constitutes a target which the district shall attempt to achieve but is not a mandatory requirement," a clause for which Steve Kurtz, the accountant, lobbied strongly while the law was being written. ("I told the people in the legislature, 'What you're proposing's not going to work, so give the stadium district enough latitude in the legislation to do whatever kind of deal they need to do.'") By the time of the stadium election, the 50-50 goal had already been abandoned, and in its place was the 70-30 plan drawn up by Lee White, the investment banker. White's plan missed the target, but not by much, and on that basis the stadium was approved.

What few voters realized was that White's plan was never meant to be binding. White was working on spec for the stadium district. The only way his firm, George K. Baum, would ever get paid was if the vote passed, a team was awarded, and the stadium got built. "My job," he later recalled, "was to put together a plan of finance that we could sell to the voters."

Now, armed with Kurtz's projections, Jacobs and Ehrhart were preparing to toss aside White's plan and reach for the stars. Their response to question 24 (d) was cautiously optimistic. "The stadium district," they wrote, "has acknowledged in preliminary discussions that revenues from these sources will be shared with the franchise. Final allocation of these revenues will be determined during lease negotiations."

By far the most difficult questions to answer were the ones relating to the composition of the ownership group. No such group existed, not yet anyway. In the week leading up to the deadline, Ehrhart and Jacobs went to work wooing potential investors, trying to translate good intentions into firm commitments and somehow come up with pledges for at least $75 million. McMorris was a "rock" from day one, says Ehrhart; he committed $7.5 million immediately, and six months later, when the agreement was finalized, he was up to $10 million. The *Rocky Mountain News* was the same way; it pledged $5 million and stuck with it. But after that, Ehrhart and Jacobs had to twist some arms.

A lot of people were plain spooked by the awful magnitude of the franchise fee. Thirty years before, it had cost the New York Mets and the Houston Colt 45s about $1.8 million apiece to join the National League. In 1969, the Montreal Expos and San Diego Padres had paid $10 million each. And in 1977, the last time baseball expanded, the Seattle Mariners and Toronto Blue Jays had come up with $6.25 million and $7 million, respectively. No one ever had any idea where those numbers came from; they were justified entirely by the fact that they turned out to be what the market would bear (albeit a market with a pent-up artificial demand). Former American League president Lee MacPhail, testifying in 1976 before the House Select Committee on Professional Sports, explained the Mariners and Blue Jays numbers as follows: "I think we could have gotten anything we wanted to ask Toronto for . . . [W]e had a legal problem in Seattle [which sued after the Pilots moved to Milwaukee and became the Brewers]. We had been there before. We had difficulties there. We were most anxious to settle the Seattle differences . . . [T]he Seattle price was based on exactly what the price of the previous Seattle expansion had been."

But $95 million? Right up until the announcement on August 1, the word around town was $75 million maximum, although Pirates owner Douglas Danforth, chairman of the expansion committee, would later admit that $75 million was the *minimum* price considered. According to Danforth, the owners used logic in arriving at the final figure. "We put a value on the players that we were all going to give up," he begins. "As you know, each major league team only produces about two major league players a year from their five or six minor league teams, so you have an incredible investment in each player you give up. That was one factor. And another, of course, we knew we were going to divide the [national television and licensing revenues] by 28 instead of 26, which in round numbers took a million dollars a year off of each club's income. And the third factor—and we did all this mathematically—the third factor was we knew from past history that the new teams do not draw nearly as well [on the road] as the established teams, so we were going to see a sacrifice in attendance fees for probably five years. You put all of this together and that's how we arrived at it."

But when Bill Giles of the Phillies, who also served on the committee, was asked about the $95 million, he laughed out loud. "Well," he finally said, "it was kind of picked out of the air, I guess." Steve Matt, an accountant with Arthur Andersen in Dallas who specializes in appraising sports franchises, finds it amusing that the number came in just under $100 million, like the sale item priced to go at $9.95.

Whatever the justification, the fee sent shock waves through the tight community of franchise seekers, and nowhere did it hit with greater impact than in Denver, where money was always a problem. "Good gracious alive," were the first words out of the mouth of Odell Barry, a member of the Colorado Baseball Commission when a reporter called with the news. "Oh my God," said John McHale when he heard. Potential buyers everywhere were moved to reconsider.

"That was what was scaring people off," says Ehrhart. "For a while we thought all the big cable television people in Denver would be interested, but they never put a penny in. There were a lot of big talkers; a lot of people showed up at meetings and said they were interested. We were beating the streets trying to find investors."

One way or another, everyone knew that Coors—the third-largest brewery in the United States—was going to have to be part of the deal. "We'd been told this by any number of people inside baseball," says John Frew. "Not only did we need their money but it was home state, well known, conservative Republican, all the things that the owners all identify with. Peter Coors, Bill Coors, these are their guys."

Coors had been mentioned early on as a possible partner with Dikeou. But after Dikeou bailed out, so did Coors, saying it still meant to bid for the right to put its name on the new stadium but wanted nothing to do with being an owner. The change of heart on the part of Colorado's best-known corporation was noted with concern at the National League office, and lately, after coming under intense pressure in Denver not to let the city down, Coors had begun signaling a willingness to reconsider, but only up to a point. "Guys like Peter Coors said, 'Look, we're in the brewing business, we don't want to be in the sports business, we don't know anything about sports. But you guys do, so we'll be a limited partner and you run the thing,'" says Ehrhart. "That's how John, Mickey and I ended up being the three managing general partners."

McMorris said basically the same thing to Ehrhart—that he had neither the time nor the inclination to run a baseball team, but nevertheless wanted to be involved. "There were several of us," says McMorris, "that if any one of us had wanted to be the managing partner, all we had to do was say, 'Fine, I'll take the oar and go do it.' But we got very comfortable with John and Mickey. And both Peter Coors and myself had a business relationship with them, so they weren't strangers to us." Besides, as long as the Drugstore Cowboys were so eager to take the lead, McMorris and the others were more than happy to let them. They were heroes already just for agreeing to help out. But if the deal fell through—and in those early days that still seemed likely—the Drugstore Cowboys, not McMorris and Coors, would be the ones to take the rap.

What emerged at the end of 11 frantic days and nights was a two-tiered limited partnership. On top were the general partners: Antonucci, Monus and Ehrhart (who together kicked in $15 million), plus Nicklous ($7.5 million, a soft commitment at best) and Dave Elmore (also $7.5 million, even softer; Elmore was still keen on swapping his minor league teams for an equity position). Those five, all of whom claimed expertise in sports management, agreed to take an active role in running the team. Underneath them were the limited partners, who together pledged the bulk of the capital: $37 million guaranteed, up to a maximum of $63.5 million.

The largest of the limiteds was Denver financier Oren Benton (owner of NUEXCO, the biggest uranium trader in the world), whom Ehrhart pursued on a tip from a law school buddy; Ehrhart got through to Benton in London late one night and came away with a promise for $10 million. The other two big hitters were McMorris of NW Transport and Charles Monfort, a member of the family which owns a giant meat-packing and processing plant in Greeley, Colorado; Monfort, after talking to McMorris, agreed to match his friend's initial $7.5 million guarantee. Coors, still wary of taking anything other than a token equity position, would commit only $1 million by the application deadline, but left open the possibility of going higher at a later date. All of the limiteds —corporations and individuals—were locals. That was important, given the fact that baseball had made local ownership a requirement, and not one of the generals, Ehrhart included, could claim residence within a thousand miles of Denver.

The final heading on the list of owners was "Other Investors," which was nothing more than a careful way of conceding that the partnership, as it stood right now, had come up short of the $75 million capital requirement. Under "Other Investors," Jacobs wrote "Names to be provided," and, without knowing what those other names were (or even if they could be found), he put them down for a cool $25 million.

Jacobs worked straight through the holiday weekend, sleeping as little as two hours a night, and finally came up with a package that in his words was "skimpy but doable." Too late even for Federal Express, he and Ehrhart flew to New York on Tuesday morning and handed over the completed application in person to National League vice president Phyllis Collins. Jacobs remembers seeing a stack of other applications piled high on her desk.

Mission accomplished, Ehrhart returned to Memphis. Jacobs checked into a hotel and slept through until Wednesday afternoon. That night, he caught a flight to Denver, and on Thursday morning, September 6, he arrived back at the office. Waiting for him on his desk was a fax from Collins, inviting the Drugstore Cowboys to New York for a formal presentation before the National League expansion committee on September 18.

Twelve days from today.

Oh shit, Jacobs thought, here we go again.

TIME NOW to call in the PR flacks (Nicklous sent a man out from New York), fill any gaps in the application, put together a promotional book (something they could leave behind with the members of the committee), and line up political support. Jacobs assumed that Governor Romer, along with Mayor Pena and Senator Wirth, would take part in the presentation on behalf of the partnership, the three of them forming a kind of political chorus line to sing the praises of Denver. Romer was willing, except that he'd already been asked by Cary Teraji. Teraji was the only one from the original group at the Westin who had refused to comply with the governor's request that all step aside in favor of Ehrhart and Nicklous. Instead he went ahead and formed his own group—with help from Doug DeCinces, Hank Aguirre and Hall of Famer Ernie Banks—and filed a separate application. Romer, however, was determined that Denver present a united front to the National League. He strongly urged Jacobs to work something out with Teraji and fast, before the eighteenth. Teraji drove a hard bargain, agreeing to abandon his own bid only after he was offered the chance to invest as a general partner. (The Drugstore Cowboys weren't worried; with only $1 million to invest, Teraji had no power anyway.) The upshot was that Denver, unlike Miami, St. Petersburg, Phoenix and Washington, went to New York united under a single ownership group.

Teraji's withdrawal left a total of 17 groups from 10 cities competing for two openings. The heavy favorite was St. Petersburg, on that everyone agreed. But how you handicapped the rest of the pack depended on which selection criterion you thought was the most important. Geography? Then you had to like Denver's chances, and possibly Phoenix's. Market size? Washington, no question. Enthusiasm and support? Denver again, but also Buffalo and even Nashville, all of which had set minor league attendance records of one kind or another over the years. Charlotte, Sacramento, Orlando? No chance, given the competition. Miami? Maybe, but not if St. Petersburg was already in. The only other contender was Malcolm Glazer, the Florida businessman who proposed to play an equal number of home games in whichever four out of five cities—Buffalo, Denver, Miami, St. Petersburg and Washington—failed to win a franchise of its own. Four cities, four fat local television contracts (all of them for 143 "away" games), four times the endorsements for the players and four sets of satisfied politicians who wouldn't have any reason to bother baseball anymore about expanding; maybe it wasn't so farfetched after all. "This is an idea for the 1990s," Glazer's 23-year-old son Joel told the *Denver Post* in November. "It's the future of baseball." Distant future, perhaps. Most people, if they had had to choose two cities in the fall of 1990, probably would have said St. Petersburg for sure, followed by Washington, Buffalo or Denver, in that order.

All 17 groups traveled separately to New York during September for step number two in the expansion process, the presentation. Because expansion was a league affair, and outside the realm of the commissioner's authority, the expansion committee was made up of National League president Bill White, plus three National League owners: chairman Doug Danforth of the Pirates, Fred Wilpon of the Mets and John McMullen of the Astros. Each applicant would have 45 minutes in front of the committee. Once the committee had had a chance to hear from everyone, it would trim the list of candidates down to one ownership group from each city. Only then would the finalists be announced. So everybody's goal in September was to make the short list. Only those who survived the first cut would be eligible to move on to step three, the visitation.

The Denver delegation flew to New York on the seventeenth and camped in at the Waldorf. There was panic that night during the final rehearsal when someone tripped over a wire and the television screen suddenly went blank. For 20 long minutes, it seemed as if the whole computer-directed show they'd cooked up back in Denver was history. That eventually got fixed, but then someone called from Washington with the bad news that Tim Wirth would not be able to join them in New York after all, something about a treaty vote on the Senate floor. But no big deal; Wirth put a three-minute spiel on videotape that night and had John Frew fly up with it in the morning on the shuttle. Frew ended up playing a small but significant role that day. Arriving at Willkie, Farr & Gallagher, the National League law firm, shortly before one o'clock, he saw immediately that the members of the Denver delegation were nervous as gerbils, and made a quick tactical decision to remove the coffeepot from the waiting room.

Shortly after one o'clock on the eighteenth, Ehrhart, Antonucci and Jacobs ushered Mayor Pena and Governor Romer into the same windowless conference room vacated before lunch that same day by Wayne Huizenga and his South Florida party. Seated at the table, in addition to the three owners on the committee, were Phyllis Collins from the National League, filling in for the absent Bill White, and two lawyers: Tom Ostertag from the commissioner's office, and Lou Hoynes from Willkie, Farr. Since no more than five presenters were allowed in the room at one time, Monus and McMorris waited outside. The plan was to let the politicians warm up the crowd, then bring in the moneymen to talk business.

No sooner had the mayor entered the room than Danforth greeted him in fluent Spanish. Pena was startled but recovered nicely—it turns out Danforth had spent years living in Mexico and South America as an executive with Westinghouse—and the two chatted away amiably while everyone else got situated. It was an icebreaker from heaven, and may have been part of the reason why later, when Pena and Romer stood up to leave, Danforth said, "Oh, why don't you stay and bring your other people in." If nothing else, Danforth's gesture had a calming effect on the bugged-out Denver delegation.

The presentation went the limit, and was followed by 15 minutes of questions and answers. The only tense moment came when McMullen asked Monus about Sure Shot, a sensitive topic. Monus tried to explain that Sure Shot was in the uplink business, providing only the hardware to handle satellite transmissions, but McMullen's eyebrows hit the roof.

"You're not in the superstation business, are you?"

"No—" Monus said, starting to elaborate.

"One thing we don't need is another Ted Turner!"

The birth of cable superstations in the 1980s had brought vast new profits not only to Ted Turner, whose TBS carried the Braves coast to coast, but also to the Tribune Company, whose Cubs went out over WGN. But partly at the expense of owners like McMullen, who felt cheated two ways: at the gate, on the theory that televised baseball eats into attendance; and in their local television markets, which before cable came along were protected monopolies. McMullen was right to worry; knowingly or not, he'd put his finger on the ultimate aim of the Drugstore Cowboys.

Lou Hoynes, the longtime lawyer for the National League, tried to calm McMullen down by pointing out that Sure Shot was a long way from becoming TBS. But McMullen was hot. "Lou, you never understood that anyway!" he shot back.

For the most part, though, the questions were all lobs, which was surprising to the members of the Denver delegation, given what was at stake.

"Frankly," says Jacobs. "I had the impression they were just going through the motions, that this was something that was part of the process, that they had to do. But that's okay. I just wanted them to remember us."

IT HAD BEEN a furious four weeks from the day of that first "bizarre" meeting with the governor in August until the presentation before the expansion committee in September. Now, back in Denver, Jacobs took a little breather. Like everybody else, he had heard the rumors that Huizenga had put on a stunning performance in New York, although the news did not affect him as much as it did the folks in St. Petersburg. Jacobs had figured all along that one city in Florida was bound to get a team. Unless now the National League was preparing to make a two-fisted grab for both major cities in the lucrative Florida market—a possibility he considered but did not take seriously—it really made no difference to him who won down there, as long as Denver won too.

On the surface, Jacobs knew, Denver was a logical choice, for all kinds of reasons: its long history of support for the minor league Bears, and later the Zephyrs; the fact that it had all but been promised a franchise by baseball following the collapse of the Continental League (of the eight proposed Continental League cities, only Denver and Buffalo were still waiting for a major league team); and above all its location, close enough to the West Coast teams to provide them with a convenient opponent but not too close—in fact, 550 miles from the nearest big league city.

Throughout the first half of the twentieth century, St. Louis was the western frontier of the baseball universe, which explains why so many people in Denver today are Cardinals fans (the Cardinals could still be heard on local radio as late as 1992). The arrival of the Philadelphia A's in Kansas City in 1955 was baseball's first foray beyond the Mississippi. It previewed the settlement of the West Coast three years later, when the Dodgers and Giants abandoned New York for California. But baseball leapfrogged the Great Plains and the Rocky Mountains, presenting the National League with an opportunity 30 years later to open up a vast new market hungry for baseball. "The Time Zone Without a Team" was the apt slogan Denver boosters came up with to drive home this point.

"The two things that they had going for them, in my mind anyway," says Phillies owner Bill Giles, who joined the expansion committee during the fall of 1990, "was the fact that it was new territory, it was bringing baseball to a part of the country that did not have it. And the fact that Denver had been trying so hard for so long to get major league baseball."

The Denver people would have been thrilled to know that Giles felt that way. On the other hand, there was no getting around the fact that Denver is not a large market by major league standards. With only 1.6 million people living within a 20-mile radius, Denver was a distant third behind contenders Washington, with 2.9 million, and South Florida, which claims 2.7 million. If Denver was chosen, it would immediately become only the 18th-largest metropolitan area served by base-ball. Denver could dress up its presentation with a lot of market babble about television viewing habits of "relatively affluent young families with children," which the region claimed to have a lot of. ("Although higher-educated consumers typically watch fewer hours of TV, they do watch sports.") And Denver could point out that the city's median income, $30,450, was relatively high. And it could, and did, claim as its own a geographical territory that stretched from western Kansas to eastern Nevada, and from Canada all the way to Mexico. But then all a visitor had to do was take the elevator to the top floor of any downtown skyscraper and look out the window to see that once you left the city proper, there weren't a whole lot of people out there, just tall mountains and wide, empty plains. Count all the people within a 70-mile radius of Denver —which is about as far as anybody would want to drive to see a ball game—and still you come up with only 2.6 million, a distant last among the six eventual expansion finalists.

Market size was not the only issue; if it were, baseball would have chosen Washington and probably Miami the day it decided to expand, and saved themselves and everybody else a lot of anguish. But there's no doubt that it was a big issue, probably first on the list as far as most owners were concerned, because it was a factor in everything from attendance to the value of local television and radio contracts to how much the team could reasonably expect to take in from sponsorship deals, and therefore the principal money-related item on the checklist. Steve Matt from Arthur Andersen, who advised three expansion hopefuls during the application process, contends that the $95 million asking price "severely limited the number of markets that could support a team," and as such "was the most important of the selection criteria. . . . It's kind of like if you say, 'I'm only going to hire people who have 3.9 GPA.' It limits the number of people you have to consider."

One way Denver had of overcoming its small-market disadvantage was by penetrating as much of that market as possible; in other words, by selling lots of season tickets. In the larger markets, attendance was almost a given. Huizenga, for example, apparently never gave much thought to selling season tickets until a year after the franchise was awarded, at which point someone from the Marlins called someone from the Rockies to find out if they were interested in having a competition to see who could sell the most. The guy in Denver just laughed. By that point, the Rockies already had $6 million in the bank from ticket deposits. They began selling in February 1991, and by the end of the month had racked up more than 20,000 subscriptions. It's true that the 20,000 were not yet final sales, just promises to buy, backed by a $50 refundable deposit. Still, 20,000 was a big number (worth a million dollars in cash to the partnership), and it sent a strong message to the National League that little Denver was primed to support baseball in a big way.

But no matter how many season tickets Denver sold, that alone wasn't going to be enough to convince the other owners that baseball, with its bloated economics, could make money over the long haul in Denver. Inevitably there would come a post-honeymoon slump. Denver, like any expansion team, could expect a couple of big years right off the bat, as fans lined up to satisfy their curiosity and sponsors reacted to the initial enthusiasm. And beyond that, unlike other teams, Denver could look forward to a second honeymoon once the new ballpark opened. But eventually fans and advertisers would begin to lose interest, at least until the team started winning. If the experiences of past expansion teams were any guide, just to reach .500 could take a decade or more.

Part of the solution to Denver's problem lay in raising more capital than its competitors, thereby easing its debt burden. The National League required only $75 million, which would have meant borrowing at least another $45 million just to get started, never mind coping with revenue shortfalls in the future. Jacobs, like the accountant Kurtz, thought Denver could and should do better than that—his goal was $100 million—but in order to raise that kind of money in a small market, Denver had to promise investors an attractive return. And the key to that promise, from the very beginning, was the stadium lease. "If we had a lease like some of these other teams have," says Jacobs, "we couldn't have put this deal together and raised $100 million."

Mining profits from stadium leases was nothing new in baseball. Astute owners such as Jerry Reinsdorf in Chicago and Edward Bennett Williams in Baltimore, to name just two, had been perfecting the process for years. But then no one had ever dared ask for the kind of lease Jacobs was prepared to demand. That it would be the best lease in baseball, if he could get it, goes without saying. The only way left to improve upon it would be to somehow convince the landlord to pay the tenant.

THE MAN in the role of public servant who stood between Jacobs and his goal of obtaining the best lease in baseball was John J. McHale, Jr., chairman of the seven-member stadium district board. McHale is a baseball blue blood, the son of the longtime president of the Montreal Expos. It was only natural that he get involved early on in the work of the Denver Baseball Commission. Steve Katich, the chairman of the DBC, was thrilled to have someone with McHale's connections on board. "John McHale knows more about baseball and how things get done than everybody else in Denver put together," Katich says. Through his father, McHale was able to obtain for the DBC an exclusive invitation to the general managers meeting in Palm Springs just as expansion fever was beginning to heat up. It was an early coup, one which Katich always regarded as "very valuable."

A former linebacker at Notre Dame, McHale went to law school at Boston College and settled afterward in Boulder, Colorado. His specialty at the Denver firm of Miller & McCarren was labor law. In recent years he had teamed up with former Astros general manager Tal Smith to provide professional services on behalf of major league teams during salary arbitration. (Rather than haggle with their star players and risk poisoning relations, teams these days often hire consultants such as Tal Smith Enterprises to do their dirty work for them.) McHale got results, and soon acquired a reputation as

Tim Wirth (D-Colo.), chairman of the Senate Task Force on the Expansion of Major League Baseball, with task force members (left to right) Dennis DeConcini (D-Ariz.), John Breaux (D-La.), Walter Fauntroy (D-D.C.), Dan Quayle (R-Ind.) and Lawton Chiles (D-Fla.). For Chiles, gunning simultaneously for Orlando, St. Petersburg and Miami, no hat is better than three. (Senator Wirth's office)

U.S. Supreme Court Chief Justice Oliver Wendell Holmes, whose 1922 landmark opinion in *Federal Baseball* removed baseball from the clutches of the Sherman Antitrust Act. (AP/Wide World)

Peter Ueberroth—travel agent, grand pooh-bah of the 1984 Olympics, commissioner of baseball and lately master rebuilder of Los Angeles after the riots—stonewalled the Senate task force and skillfully exploited expansion fever throughout the late 1980s. (AP/Wide World)

A. Bartlett Giamatti, commissioner of baseball from April 1989 until his death five months later, was an advocate of expansion. It was during Giamatti's tenure that baseball finally made a commitment to add two teams by 1993. (AP/Wide World)

Denver mayor Federico Pena (center) presents National League expansion committee chairman Douglas Danforth with the keys to the city as Colorado governor Roy Romer looks on. (Steve Groer/*Rocky Mountain News*)

Fan Matt McAleer of Denver waves from near second base as helicopters carrying visiting members of the National League expansion committee fly over the future site of Coors Field. (John Epperson/Denver *Post*)

National League expansion committee tours Mile High Stadium on visitation day. Originally built for the Denver Bears minor league baseball team in 1948, and later expanded for football, Mile High seats more than 76,000. (Denver *Post*/John Sunderland)

National League expansion committee members, left to right: Fred Wilpon (Mets), Bill Giles (Phillies), Bill White (president of the National League) and Doug Danforth (Pirates). The Rockies later sold over 24,000 season tickets, second only to the Dodgers. (David Zalubowski/ AP/Wide World)

Steve Ehrhart (left), Peter Coors and John Antonucci at the March 15, 1991, announcement that Coors will invest $30 million in the Colorado Baseball Partnership. The deal includes $15 million for the right to name Denver's new downtown stadium Coors Field. (Jerry Cleveland/ Denver *Post*)

Bob Gebhard (left), general manager of the Rockies, and John McHale, vice president, baseball operations. McHale, who resigned as chairman of the stadium district board after negotiating the sweetheart lease at Coors Field, was subsequently hired by the Rockies. (Ken Papaleo/*Rocky Mountain News*)

The Rockies' scouting director, Pat Daugherty (right), with 1992 first-round draft pick John Burke of the University of Florida. Burke agreed to terms only minutes before he was selected and signed for $350,000. (John Leyba/Denver *Post*)

Rockies investors at the August 6, 1992, press conference following the sudden resignation of Mickey Monus. Front row, left to right: Bill Fletcher (*Rocky Mountain News*), Cary Teraji, Jack Antonucci, Rob Klugman (Coors), Oren Benton and Charles Monfort. (Dave Buresh/Denver *Post*)

Of the three men appointed by Governor Romer in August 1990 to put together a Denver ownership group, only lawyer Paul Jacobs—shown here in his office overlooking the capitol—survived to opening day. Mike Nicklous, originally the lead investor, failed Major League Baseball's background check; Steve Ehrhart was forced out as team president in the wake of the Phar-Mor scandal. (Ron Semrod/Denver *Post*)

Mickey Monus, a.k.a. the Drugstore Cowboy, built Phar-Mor discount pharmacy into the fastest-growing retailer in America, created the World Basketball League, and committed $10 million in the Colorado Rockies. Then Phar-Mor accused him of embezzling $350 million and called in the FBI. (Bob DeMay/Youngstown *Vindicator*)

Built on spec at a cost to the public of at least $122 million, the Florida Suncoast Dome has stood empty ever since, a symbol of civic boosterism gone haywire. (Silver Image/Miami *Herald*)

Joe Robbie Stadium, home of the NFL Dolphins since 1987, was designed for baseball as well as football. Wayne Huizenga bought half the stadium in 1990 and spent $11 million to make it ready for opening day. (Florida Marlins)

Wayne Huizenga is joined by his father, Harry, at the grand opening of One Blockbuster Plaza in Fort Lauderdale. As a teenager, Wayne at times defended his mother against his father's violent outbursts. Today, father and son are inseparable. (Downtown Photo/Fort Lauderdale/ Kelly Foster)

Assistant general manager Frank Wren instructs scouts in the use of laptop computers at the Marlins' first-ever organizational meeting, January 1992. The Blue Jays and the Marlins are the first major league organizations to issue a laptop computer to every scout. (Margo Malone/Florida Marlins)

Carl Barger (with microphone), president of the Marlins, and David Dombrowski, general manager, at the unveiling of the team's sleeveless uniform. Barger collapsed and died at age 62 while attending the 1992 winter meetings in Louisville. (David Cross/Florida Marlins)

Gary Hughes, the Marlins' scouting director, at an all-comers tryout camp in Delray Beach, Florida. Although 600 came, only one—Brian Whitman, a 20-year-old right-handed pitcher released by the Expos—signed. (Margo Malone/Florida Marlins)

Charles Johnson from the University of Miami was the first player drafted by the Marlins. But when Johnson asked for "Brien Taylor money"—a $1.55 million bonus equal to that of the Yankees' 1991 first-round pick—Wayne Huizenga walked away. Johnson later signed for $600,000. (University of Miami)

Wayne Huizenga, chairman of Blockbuster Entertainment, Inc., and owner of the Florida Marlins, on July 5, 1991, the day the Marlins' franchise was awarded. Huizenga's willingness to foot the whole bill himself, and pay cash, was a deciding factor in Miami's favor. (Miami *Herald*)

an uncompromising negotiator. That reputation, plus his fa-
miliarity with the ins and outs of the baseball business, made
McHale seem to many an obvious choice to represent the district in lease negotiations.

On the other hand, those same family and professional ties
meant that McHale was apt to see things from baseball's point
of view. If one of the qualities that make a tough negotiator is
the willingness to walk away from a deal that stinks, then
maybe McHale was not the ideal choice after all. As much as
anyone, and more than most, McHale wanted to see major
league baseball choose Denver. So much so that from the start
he seemed unsure about what his job entailed. Was it to drive
the best possible bargain for the district and the taxpayers? Or
was it to do whatever it takes to bring baseball to Denver?

"I think one of the principles we had to guide us was that we
had to get the fairest deal we could get for the taxpayer," says
McHale, who is handsome, curly-haired and charming, a tea
drinker and a bow tie wearer (the tea and the tie are "affecta-
tions," but he says so himself, which saves him from ridicule).
"But we had been given a mandate by the taxpayers in this
district to get baseball, and it was not going to be consistent
with our responsibility to the public to have to go back and tell
them that we couldn't give on this issue or that, therefore we
can't have a baseball team."

It was an extraordinarily delicate assignment, one requiring
a balanced perspective, which McHale never had. Jacobs, on
the other hand, had but one goal, and therefore no need to
wrestle with cross-purposes. He knew exactly what he wanted
in a lease—more than that, what he *had to have*—and was free
to pursue it unwaveringly.

Beyond that, at least in Jacobs's case, there was never any
doubt about which master he served. Jacobs worked for the
partners; his interests were the same as theirs. As for McHale,
his loyalty was suspect from the start. He worked for the district; by law he reported to the taxpayers. But what the taxpayers wanted and what McHale wanted were not necessarily
the same thing, and Jacobs picked up on it right away.

"Oh, it was no secret to everyone who knew John that he

wanted a career in baseball," says Jacobs. "You could tell. He loves the game, his family's been in the game all his life. That's his passion."

ON DECEMBER 17, Paul Jacobs took a happy phone call from Phyllis Collins in the National League office. Stand by the fax machine, she told him. Good news was on the way.

"We were on the short list," says Jacobs. "We were excited about that. Once we made that, I figured we had a pretty good shot, because we had started from so far back. I said, 'Okay, now we've got some time. Now we can build this thing.' "

The original list of 18 hopefuls had been cut by two-thirds, down to one potential buyer in each of six cities: Buffalo (the Rich family); Miami (Wayne Huizenga); St. Petersburg (a group led by Joel Schur, owner of the class A St. Petersburg Cardinals, and backed by supermarket magnates Sidney and Allen Kohl, brothers of Herbert Kohl, the junior senator from Wisconsin); Orlando (Richard DeVos, president of Amway); Washington (John Akridge 3rd, a real estate developer); and Denver.

Buffalo, once a favorite to win a franchise on enthusiasm alone, was technically a finalist but effectively out of the running. Earlier in December, Robert Rich, Jr., owner of the class AAA Buffalo Bisons (and heir to a food products fortune built on a cream substitute made from soybeans), had written a letter to the *Buffalo News* questioning whether big league baseball could survive in a small market such as Buffalo and restating his unwillingness to invest in a franchise "at any cost." Rich's move prompted city officials, only hours before the short list was made public, to announce they were reconsidering plans to spend $2.5 million to expand the city-owned stadium. So in Buffalo, at least, the race was over before it started. Six months later when the winners were named, the *Buffalo News* was the only daily newspaper with a direct interest in expansion not to carry the news on page one.

That left three Florida cities—Orlando was the big surprise, its chances greatly enhanced by the last-minute recruitment of DeVos, whose wealth dwarfed even that of Huizenga—plus

Washington. The elimination of Sacramento and especially Phoenix was a big boost for Denver, assuming that the National League preferred to place one new team in each regional division. But again, geography was at best a secondary consideration, everybody knew that. The real issues, now as before, were money and markets. That point was driven home by the selection of Huizenga, whose big bucks—and above all, his willingness to spend them; DeVos, for one, was already wavering—would drive the process from here on in.

Unfortunately for Denver, Jacobs's goal of lining up $100 million in equity was still just that, a goal. Elmore, supposedly in for $7.5 million, had long since dropped out of the picture, unable to convince the others that his minor league franchises were as good as cash. As for Nicklous, the early doubts about his commitment turned out to be justified. Jacobs, Monus and Antonucci met with Nicklous in Florida the first week in February, during the Phar-Mor golf tournament. Nicklous was not well, physically (he said he was having heart trouble) or financially. He asked then that he be allowed to reduce his interest from $7.5 million to about $2 million. And not long after that, Jacobs was told by National League president Bill White that the league's own routine investigation into Nicklous's finances had raised some red flags. So there went Nicklous, taking with him his last $2 million and leaving the partnership at least $15 million light on a package that even at full strength, in Jacobs's words, had been no better than "skimpy but doable."

EARLY ONE MORNING in January, not long after Denver was named to the short list of expansion finalists, Jacobs, Ehrhart and the Drugstore Cowboys all piled into one car and headed west from Denver on U.S. 6, past the point where the flat edge of the Great Plains begins to buckle up against the steep wall of the Rockies, to where the road twists through gulches and turns around hills and enters finally the old mining town of Golden, the home of Coors Brewery. Jerry McMorris, the designated representative of the limited partners, met them there. They were five men on a mission, come

to beg, cajole, and if need be, twist arms. Still well short of
their goal of raising $100 million in equity, they had come to
ask Peter Coors for more money.

"In this state," says John Frew, "when these kinds of issues
arise, everybody looks to Coors to try to solve the problem."
The Coors family had been listening to pitches from the likes
of John Dikeou and the governor's search committee for
years. Time and again they had made it abundantly clear that
their business was beer, that they didn't know anything about
baseball, and that they had no interest in fronting and operating a baseball team. Or, as Rob Klugman, the company's baseball point man, explains: "While to some extent baseball is not
as foreign to selling beer as perhaps opera might be, it's clearly
not part of our mission statement for our company."

It's not surprising that Coors has seen fit to remain all these
years in tiny Golden, ensconced in a natural rock fortress,
rather than establish a corporate presence in Denver. Coors is
a secretive company, privately held, deeply suspicious of out-
siders, intolerant in the extreme of anything perceived by the
Coors family to be meddling in its internal affairs. A bitter
strike by plant workers in 1977 led to a national boycott by the
AFL-CIO which lasted for ten years. The boycott confirmed in
many people's minds an image of the Coors family as right-
wing extremists, which William Coors, grandson of founder
Adolf Coors, did nothing to dispel. The current CEO told the
*Rocky Mountain News* in 1984 that blacks "lack the intellectual
capacity to succeed," a remark that resonates with baseball
fans who remember the almost identical statement made a
short while later by former Dodgers GM Al Campanis.

But lately Coors was making an effort to soften its corporate
image, and promoting baseball was part of that effort. "We felt
it would be good for the region," says Klugman, explaining
his company's decision in August 1990 to commit $1 million to
the partnership. "This was an area that really went into somewhat of a nosedive in the early eighties with the collapse of the
energy business. I think we perceived the addition of major
league baseball as another important step in the resurgence of
this area. And to the extent that we live here, and the vast

majority of our work force is here, we would like major league baseball to be here."

And of course Peter Coors understands, as does Klugman, that from a marketing point of view, baseball and beer make a good match. Otherwise, two months before, he would not have offered the stadium district $15 million in what turned out to be the winning bid for naming rights to the new ballpark. As late as 1976, Coors beer was available in only 11 western states. In 1991, when Coors went on sale for the first time in New Jersey, it completed the rapid transformation to a truly national brand. The hope was that Coors Field, when it opened in 1995, would do for Coors Brewery what Busch Stadium in St. Louis does for Anheuser-Busch.

But it was one thing for Coors to make what amounted to an advertising buy with the ballpark and quite another to substantially raise its equity position in the partnership. As Klugman explains "Diverting relatively scarce dollar resources to noncritical businesses may not be in our best interest." The purpose of today's visit by the principal members of the partnership was to try to convince them otherwise.

In the past, Klugman had always been the one to represent the company in matters relating to baseball. Today, the partners met privately with Peter Coors himself. It helped that Coors, the nephew of William Coors and the president of Coors Brewery, was a fan; he considers Rick Sutcliffe a close friend, and even flew to Baltimore to watch him pitch in the first game ever played at Oriole Park at Camden Yards. Because he reads the sports page, Coors had already seen that morning's column by Woody Paige in the *Denver Post,* in which Paige called on Coors to step up to the plate and commit to baseball. The first thing Coors wanted to know was who put Paige up to it. The partners had seen the column, of course, and were thrilled that it ran today of all days, but they'd had nothing to do with it, and told Coors as much.

After that, Coors mainly listened: to McMorris, an old and trusted friend with whom Coors had been doing business for years (McMorris stressed the special role played by the two of them, plus Oren Benton and Charles Monfort, four prominent Colorado families "that live in this area and have a lot to be thankful for in this area"); to Monus, who did not have to remind Coors that Phar-Mor was a leading national outlet for sales of Coors beer; and to Antonucci, whose company, Superior Beverage, was a past winner of the Coors Distinguished Wholesaler Award.

The presentation was part carrot, part stick. Partly an attempt to seduce Coors with the idea that his company was in a unique position to make the "critical difference" in the success or failure of the whole undertaking; and partly a show of force, one aspect of which turned on the unspoken assumption that if Coors said no, the partners were prepared to go to Anheuser-Busch. "They couldn't *not* be a part of it," says Jacobs. "Because if we had gone up the road to Budweiser in Fort Collins, they would have done it. Or Miller would have done it, because of John Antonucci's connections with Superior Beverage and with Phar-Mor. Once we convinced them that [baseball in Denver] was going to happen, we concluded that they couldn't say no, they had to be a player."

Coors listened. He would make no commitment, but promised to get back to them.

ON A SUNNY WEDNESDAY in mid-February, Bill White flew out to Denver from New York with Bob Kheel, the new National League lawyer, for a secret powwow with Ehrhart, Antonucci and Jacobs. They met for lunch in the turn-of-the-century Brown Palace Hotel, upstairs in the Brown Palace Club—a dreary, men's-club room with brown carpets and lead-framed stained-glass windows—and afterward they all went up to Jacobs's office on the 43rd floor at 1700 Lincoln, a block away. It was a gorgeous, crystal-clear day, and as White stood looking out the window at snowcapped Pikes Peak rising above the jagged line of rock that fell away to the south, he mentioned for the first time that his daughter had gone to college at Colorado State; to Jacobs, making mental notes, that was one for the plus category.

Since White had missed Denver's fall presentation in New York, his visit was partly a long-overdue chance to get acquainted. But more than that, now that Denver was on the short list, there were a few things White wanted to go over with the partners. In structuring their deal, he told them now for the first time, they should keep in mind that while the $95 million would not be due until shortly before play began in 1993, the owners would be looking for "serious security" as early as the spring of 1992, in the form of irrevocable letters of credit. White also made a point of stressing the importance of baseball's local-ownership requirement, and strongly urged that someone high up in the partnership—either Monus or Antonucci—consider moving to Denver. He talked television territorial rights, and touched on the cost of getting up and running if and when the franchise was awarded. He wanted them to know that he thought their current payroll projection —$10–$13 million in the first few years—was probably unrealistic.

Above all, White went out of his way to be reassuring, and in so doing tacitly acknowledged the rumors of intrigue and influence peddling that were swirling around the expansion process. By now, everybody knew about Wayne Huizenga's ties to the expansion committee through his close friend Carl Barger, who as president of the Pirates was an employee of expansion committee chairman Doug Danforth. And it was certainly no secret that the Kohl brothers, picked to represent St. Petersburg, had a brother who was a U.S. senator; what was less widely known was that Jerry Reinsdorf (feeling guilty?) was lobbying hard for St. Pete, together with one of his close friends, the influential owner Bud Selig of the Brewers. Former commissioner Bowie Kuhn was said to be staunchly in D.C.'s corner. What White wanted the Denver partners to know was that while the final decision was not his to make— that would be up to the owners—he would do his best to keep control of the process. "Do what you have to do," he told them, "and don't worry about anybody else. I'll make sure the playing field is kept level."

And then White came to the heart of the issue. "This is a business deal," he said. "The franchises that are able to pay and to demonstrate financial stability are the ones that are going to get the award. One thing we don't want to do is put in a franchise that's in trouble two years down the road."

Soon the National League expansion committee would embark on the all-important last leg in the expansion derby, the series of on-site inspections—called "visitations," in expansion jargon, as if God himself were planning to drop by. They'd fly to Florida in late February, then visit Washington and Buffalo in March, and finish up in Denver on March 26. Looking ahead from the day of White's visit, Jacobs set himself four tasks to be accomplished in the next six weeks: one, to surpass 20,000 in season-ticket sales; two, to sign a lease with the city for Mile High Stadium; three, to sign a lease with the district for Coors Field; and four, to reach the magic $100 million mark in equity. The most important, of course, were the last two, intertwined as they were, and each of them absolutely critical, Jacobs believed, to addressing the last point White made before he returned to New York.

"Just get the money."

ON MARCH 14, Steve Ehrhart, as president of the Colorado Baseball Partnership, and John McHale, chairman of the Denver Metropolitan Major League Baseball Stadium District board, signed a seven-page memorandum of lease terms; not the lease itself, but a binding document. It was all the partners could have hoped for, and more.

To begin with, the district agreed to foot the entire cost of construction, estimated now at $156 million, including a $9 million scoreboard. Not 50 percent, which was the goal targeted in the legislation, and not 70 percent, as anticipated in the original plan of finance, but 100 percent. An out-and-out gift, in other words, preassembled and ready to use, from the taxpayers to the team.

One way the legislation had envisioned softening the blow to the taxpayers was to capture at least a portion of the revenues generated by the stadium. But under the terms of the memorandum, all such revenues were added to the partners' pile. Beer, hot dogs and other concessions? One hundred percent to the partners. Parking? One hundred percent to the partners. Novelties? One hundred percent to the partners. Luxury boxes? One hundred percent to the partners. Stadium advertising? One hundred percent to the partners. Rent? Zero, until the year 2000, after which the district would get 2.5 percent of the owners' net taxable income.

But "taxable" income can easily be made to look like nothing. Ball clubs have any number of ways of making profits disappear. One of the most popular is by depreciating for tax purposes the value of player contracts; attributing 50 percent of the purchase price of a franchise to player contracts is now standard in baseball. Another is with a generous "management fee," which in some cases amounts to taking profits before taxes. A key provision in the Denver partnership agreement called for Monus, Antonucci and Ehrhart, as managing partners, to skim off 5 percent of the team's *gross* annual receipts, payable in monthly installments.

It gets better. Another thing the legislation envisioned was that an outside manager would operate the stadium on behalf of the district. In the memorandum of lease terms, the district bestows that responsibility on the ball club. Which means that while the franchise owners must pay the cost of operating and maintaining Coors Field—about a $3 million annual expense —the stadium is theirs to do with as they please on the 284 days out of every year when they're not playing baseball. The revenue from tractor pulls, rock concerts, religious revivals, whatever they can book? One hundred percent to the partners.

And finally this. The naming rights to the stadium, once worth $15 million to the district? One hundred percent to the partners. And that $15 million, plus the additional money Coors felt comfortable putting up now that the team had such an attractive lease, was enough finally to raise the partners' combined equity above $100 million and set the stage for the triumphal visitation just two weeks away.

IN TIME, the media, politicians and outraged citizens would scrutinize the terms of this most generous lease and find much to criticize. But only after the franchise was won; and only after McHale, in a shocking move that raised a conflict-of-interest red flag, quit the stadium district board to pursue a job with the Rockies; and especially after McHale got the job, hired by John Antonucci as the new team's executive vice president for baseball operations. But not now. For the time being, at least, McHale was a hero.

"You have to have some people with balls that are willing to just put their heads down and bullet through," says the lawyer John Frew, whose firm represents the stadium district. "I think that's true of any major project, but on this one in particular, where you have some single person like John McHale who was in a position to make it happen or block it.

"They came to John and said, 'Here's the only way we can do it. Will you do it?' That was a big risk for John. Because our hopes, our expectations, were that we would have a certain healthy percentage of private capital in this deal, and that we would generate income from a variety of sources. We had no idea how much a stadium was going to cost, where it was going to go, how much it would cost to buy the land, all those things. We just had some rough guesstimates of where we were going. It was a big risk."

THE PRIVATE JET carrying the eight-member delegation from the National League touched down at the old terminal on the far side of Stapleton Airport at 10:30 A.M. on Tuesday, March 26, half an hour late. It was a postcard day, bright and cool but with a spring smell in the air, a smell of baseball.

As Doug Danforth got off the plane, smiling broadly all the way, he was greeted warmly on the tarmac by Governor Romer and Mayor Pena. Danforth wore a topcoat and a heavy winter hat and towered over both politicians, making them appear obsequious. He looked the perfect picture of the prosperous old-time capitalist, "right out of the John D. Rockefeller–Cyrus McCormick mode," is what occurred to Don Hinchey of the Denver Chamber of Commerce, who was among those waiting at the airport.

Romer barely had time for a quick hello. He had to leave right away for Colorado Springs, where he was scheduled to preside over the opening of a major new MCI facility. But Pena was free, and had set aside the full day for baseball. After presenting Danforth with the ceremonial keys to the city (carved out of a baseball bat), the mayor led him aboard a nearby waiting helicopter—one of four on loan that day from local corporations—and together with Monus and National League spokeswoman Katy Feeney, they lifted off on the first leg of the grand tour of Denver. Jacobs, Ehrhart and the Drugstore Cowboys followed in separate helicopters along with the rest of the honored guests.

They flew first over East High School, in front of which two hundred students (playing authorized hooky that day) had gathered themselves in the outline of a giant baseball. The students waved as the helicopters hovered briefly overhead. From there, they circled downtown Denver, passing over the old railyards at 20th and Blake, where the new Coors Field would be built. Far below on the empty lot, children who should have been in school and men who should have been working (Frew among them) had laid out chalk lines and were playing a game of true sandlot baseball; they too waved as the helicopters passed. And from there to Mile High Stadium, where the helicopters touched down on the lip of the outfield grass, and everyone piled out to have a look at the ballpark.

One idea the planners of the big day had considered was to try to pack Mile High Stadium with screaming fans, but in the end it was thought to be too risky; Mile High had 70,000 seats, what if they couldn't fill all of them? Instead, as the roar of the helicopters subsided, the dignitaries were greeted by the gentle murmur of crowd noise, pumped at low volume through the public-address system; not wild cheering, as one might expect at a football game, but that soft noise, peculiar to ballparks, that wells up on the radio during pauses in the play-by-play. Up on the auxiliary scoreboards, a game was in progress, Denver vs. LA (Denver was winning). And over on the main scoreboard in center field, a moving countdown to the first pitch of the 1993 season (741 days, one hour, 40 minutes at touchdown). Inside the home locker room, uniforms (the green and blue of the Zephyrs) hung in the stalls, and a post-game dinner spread was laid out for the imaginary players. Everything as it would be on the day big league baseball arrived in Denver.

Leaving Mile High as church bells pealed "Take Me Out to the Ball Game," they rode a specially outfitted bus to the governor's mansion. There, first lady Bea Romer and Governor Mike Sullivan of Wyoming hosted a luncheon attended by local dignitaries. And from there it was but a short ride to the corner of Broadway and 17th, where the bus let them off at the entrance to the 13-story atrium in the heart of the city's financial district.

Inside, more than 3,000 fans, all of them wearing baseball hats, all of them chanting "BASEBALL! BASEBALL! BASEBALL!," were waiting to greet the visitors from the National League. Denver was not supposed to do this. Each city had been given specific instructions from the league to keep the visitation low-key and not turn it into a spectacle. But from the moment Danforth stepped onto the red carpet laid out for him on the atrium floor, it was clear that the gamble was going to pay off.

The chant was deafening. Jacobs had hold of Phyllis Collins's arm and, close as they were, he couldn't hear a word of what she was saying. Together they followed Danforth to a small stage erected in the center of the atrium, where the committee members were presented with a giant ticket on which was printed "21,000+," symbolizing all the season tickets that had been sold. Then Norm Jones, the longtime radio announcer for the Denver Zephyrs, led the crowd in "Take Me Out to the Ball Game," and that did it, Collins was crying, Feeney was crying, even Danforth and Bill Giles were dabbing at their eyes.

Afterward, when they had left the stage, and crossed over to 1700 Broadway, and taken the elevator up to the Holme, Roberts & Owen boardroom on the 41st floor, and Jacobs and Antonucci and Wilpon had ducked into the bathroom, Wilpon turned to Antonucci and poked him in the chest and said, "We told you not to do that."

"It was just a few people to welcome you," Jacobs cut in, momentarily nonplussed. "We didn't really do anything."

But Wilpon wasn't mad. "That's the smartest thing anybody has done yet," he said. And with that, they all made their way to the boardroom, everybody smiling, everybody in a good mood.

THE WALL OF WINDOWS in the HRO boardroom faces northwest, up the front range to Longs Peak, which at 14,256 feet rises two miles above the Mile High City. The guests were placed strategically around the massive oval conference table (made of exotic makore with mahogany edging) so that they could enjoy the view. No sooner had everyone sat down than Governor Romer burst into the room, just back from the MCI opening in Colorado Springs. He circled the room, welcoming them all once again and handing each of them a Colorado lapel pin. But he didn't stay long, and neither did Pena. For what the partners and their guests had to discuss today had nothing to do with politicians, or fans for that matter, or even baseball. It was time now to get down to business.

Ehrhart, as president and chief operating officer of the partnership, led off. "Up until now, we have had to rely on words and pictures to convey our message to you," he began. "Now we have had an opportunity to give you a glimpse of Exhibit A itself: the dynamic and exciting city of Denver."

Ehrhart traced the history of Denver's unrequited longing for baseball, the near-misses involving the A's and the Giants, the long years of hope ending in disappointment. He touched on the market ("No other region can deliver to the National League 8.4 million fans in a market never before reached by Major League Baseball"; he was stretching it) and the climate ("day after day and night after night of perfect baseball weather"; ditto). He talked about Coors Field ("outdoor, natural grass, baseball-only"), stopping to point out that at a time when "the public's willingness to pay taxes is probably as low as it has been since the Boston Tea Party," local voters approved funds for a new stadium "even though the city already has a multipurpose stadium available for baseball." He mentioned the solid political support of Mayor Pena and Governor Romer, and came finally to the highlight of his portion of the presentation, the lease at Coors Field.

"The terms are outstanding for us," Ehrhart said, and launched immediately into a detailed discussion of those terms: "All costs of constructing the stadium will be paid by the district . . . the partnership will be the operator of the stadium . . . the partnership will keep all revenues generated by the stadium . . . the term of the lease will be 17 years with a five-year renewal at the partnership's option . . . the team pays no rent for use of the stadium."

The lease made a big impression on the owners, exactly as it was intended to do. During the question-and-answer session that followed, Bill Giles was moved to ask Jacobs, "Will you come to Philadelphia and negotiate my lease? This is the best lease I've ever read." Later Bill White, after he'd had a chance to fully digest its terms, would label Denver's lease "the prototype of what we ask our teams to look at. We will look at that lease in negotiating [future arrangements]."

In closing, Ehrhart told the committee, "We believe that these lease terms will provide a very strong foundation on which to build a profitable franchise. The control of operations and the cash flow from the stadium ensured by these terms were absolute priorities for us, and we were able to secure these benefits with the cooperation of the stadium district." And then he turned the meeting over to Antonucci, the chairman, whose job it was to go over the details of the partnership arrangement.

There were two points Antonucci wanted to hit on, both of which addressed concerns raised the month before by Bill White. One, the fact that Ehrhart and Antonucci had decided to move to Denver once the franchise was awarded, which together with the limited partners already in place would put 85 percent of the team in the hands of local owners; and two, the good news that the partnership had more than met its goal of raising $100 million in equity.

There had been some changes in the arrangement since the original application was filed in September. Gone were Elmore and Nicklous, leaving Antonucci, Monus and Ehrhart (who together raised their stake to $20 million) firmly in control. Nathan Monus, Mickey's dad, had kicked in $2.5 million, as had Jack Antonucci, John's dad. With Cary Teraji in for $1 million, that brought the total stake of the general partners to $26 million, the balance to come from the limiteds. Oren Benton, the single largest investor in the deal, was in for $20 million. Charles Monfort and Jerry McMorris were in for $10 million each. And Coors, as a result of the furious last-minute lobbying, was in for a total of $30 million.

Of the Coors money, Antonucci, explained, $15 million was payable in ten yearly installments of $1.5 million each and was the price they paid for the right to name the new ballpark Coors Field. Beyond that, Coors committed $5 million up front for advertising and stadium signs, and finally $10 million in equity, which was the coup.

"Coors and Colorado are synonymous," Antonucci told the owners now. "No company has done more for the state of Colorado. The Coors relationship will pay dividends to us far in excess of the $30 million committed by Coors."

"In sum," Antonucci concluded, "we have fourteen investors with an aggregate investment of $100 million. The limited partners are investing $74 million and the generals are investing $26 million." And with that, he opened the floor to questions. Plenty followed.

They asked for details on how the cash was going to come in under the terms of the partnership agreement, noting that the league would be looking for letters of credit totaling $25 million upon award of the franchise, with the balance in letters of credit due the following summer. Fred Wilpon of the Mets raised the issue of up-front expenses. Although the partnership had already taken steps to secure a sizable line of credit, Wilpon suggested they seek other means of low-interest financing to cover them during the initial period after the award.

(Acting on this advice, Jacobs later went to the stadium district board with a request for a $5 million no-interest loan. "Yeah, that request was made," says a source on the board. "I mean, they were scraping for dollars. There were some board members who just laughed in their face, said, 'You must be joking.' Max Wylie, who was the banker on the board, said he would consider an interest-bearing loan, but that's not what the owners had in mind, they wanted an interest-free loan. By that time they had come to the wall so many times and asked for so much, that was one of the first times, maybe *the* first time that the district said, 'Look, we've given you guys everything, we probably are gonna get skinned alive for what we've done, and if we give you anything else it's gotta be something that outside of this board would make business sense. What you're asking for simply doesn't, so you can't have it.' ")

It was during the visitation that the partners were told for the first time during the expansion process that national television money, which makes up the bulk of the distributions from baseball's central fund, might well decline after the current contract expired in 1993. "Nobody believes it's going up," Wilpon said. "You ought to figure it's going to be five to fifteen percent lower." More disturbing still was the frank admission by the owners that a work stoppage was possible, if not likely, in 1993, when both the players and the owners would have the right to reopen the Basic Agreement.

Far from feeling discouraged, the Colorado partners could barely contain their excitement. Jacobs was looking at his watch. Already the meeting was running 45 minutes late. The governor and the mayor were waiting downstairs, together with a roomful of reporters, and meanwhile the owners were still asking questions. Detailed questions. They were studying the Denver pro formas, telling them they probably had too much budgeted for spring training, too little for salaries, details that went way beyond the scope of the meeting as Jacobs had been led to understand it. "They're talking about things that are operational, once you have a team," Jacobs was saying to himself, "they're not talking about what you have to do to get a team." A feeling that things were going awfully well swept through the room.

After the meeting broke up, there was a brief press conference, and then all the members of the visiting party, escorted

by Jacobs and McMorris, climbed back on the bus for the return trip to the airport. Each was given a present of a genuine
Stetson cowboy hat, pre-sized, choice of black or white (most
chose black), plus a coffee-table book with lots of pretty pictures of Colorado. At the airport, there were hugs and hand-
shakes and kisses goodbye. Then everybody boarded the
plane and took off for New York. Everybody, that is, except
Bill Giles.

Giles wasn't going to New York, he wanted to go to Florida,
and since the Drugstore Cowboys were headed that way, and
they had the Phar-Mor jet, they had offered to give him a lift.
But Antonucci and Monus were late getting out of the press
conference, so Jacobs got on the plane with Giles to wait. Together they sat and talked for half an hour.

In the course of their conversation, Giles told Jacobs: "Before we came to Denver, it was probably St. Petersburg and
Miami. Some people like Miami better than St. Petersburg, but
before we came here, I would have told you that I thought you
were third." And now? Giles wouldn't say, other than to add
that the day had been "illuminating and instructive" and that
he was "real impressed." For Jacobs, who could still remember
eight months back, when Denver was dead in the water, even
that was enough to make him feel almost euphoric.

After Mickey and John showed up, Jacobs got off the plane.
He stood at the edge of the runway and watched it take off,
then he walked to his car. As he was putting his key in the
door, and thinking about what a fine day it had been, how
everything had gone so well, he felt something cold and wet
hit his nose. A snowflake.

It snowed all night. By morning, all of Denver was covered
with a two-and-a-half-inch blanket of white. Bad weather for
baseball. But by then it didn't matter. The visitors were long
gone.

# 4

## The Owner

*"This is the fundamental thing to remember in expansion. Cities are never awarded franchises. Owners are awarded franchises."*
—RICK DODGE, assistant city manager,
St. Petersburg, Florida

A SURPRISING NUMBER of people still think that Miami won the new National League franchise in Florida when the fact is, Miami was never even in the running. Wayne Huizenga won it. And Wayne is not a Miami guy.

Wayne lives with his second wife, Marti, in a big house in a part of Fort Lauderdale that is as far removed from the famous beachfront, with its high-rise glitz and its drunken teenagers, as it is from the infamous Federal Highway (fast food, strip joints, nerve-frying traffic). The grounds are spacious

and lush, a jungle garden of mangrove and cypress and bou-
gainvillea. Neon parrots inhabit the treetops. The house is
faced with natural stucco and adorned with Moorish arches
and an orange tile roof. It sits at the tip of a crooked finger of
land at the end of a lane so narrow and twisty that when Marti
eases her Rolls (not the '37 Rolls she presented to Wayne on
his 50th birthday, but the late-model, just-for-knocking-
around-town Rolls) through the automatic wrought-iron gates
and heads for the open road, a driver coming toward her has
no choice but to pull over and let her pass.

The property is bordered on two sides by canals dredged by
real estate developers and in back by the New River, which is a
circumstance rich with irony. A Seminole legend dating back
to the time of the lost Tequesta tribe tells how one night the
ground shook and the heavens roared and by morning a river
flowed over what was dry land only the day before; hence the
Tequesta name *Himmarshee*, or New Water. Centuries later, the
meandering bottom waters of the New River make up most of
what qualifies as old or charming about this fast-track Sunbelt
city whose first permanent dwelling was constructed less than
a hundred years ago.

But while no more new rivers have turned up lately in Fort
Lauderdale, new roads can appear at any moment, swarming
just-like-that with new citizens in new cars on their way to new
shopping centers, new office buildings and new homes clus-
tered around new (artificial) lakes, some of which filled up
with water, if not quite overnight, then close enough. Change
is a given in Fort Lauderdale. Growth is a religion. And
around here you won't find a more devout disciple or a more
shrewd exploiter of the South Florida gospel of fast change
and rapid growth, and its corollary—unlimited opportunity—
than the centimillionaire entrepreneur who came out of nowhere to win an expansion team for South Florida, Wayne
Huizenga.

THE FLORIDA MARLINS were born on Friday, July 5, 1991.
As sometimes happens with busy fathers, Wayne was among
the last to find out. He had planned on spending all of that

long Fourth of July weekend with his family at his remote vacation home near Linville Gorge in North Carolina. That is, until he spoke to the commissioner's office early in the morning and was advised that a vote was imminent. Rather than wait by the phone, Wayne decided to head for home. At 12:30 P.M. Eastern Daylight Time, the owners convened via conference call. Ten minutes later, it was all over. But where was Wayne? On his way down the mountain, headed for the airfield in tiny Hickory, North Carolina, where his $5 million, 28-passenger BAC 1-11 (one of three planes he owns, purchased secondhand from a Saudi prince) was waiting. Surrounded by rock walls, his car phone was useless. Not until he arrived in town almost an hour later was he able to get through to Fay Vincent in New York. "Congratulations," the commissioner told him, "it was unanimous."

Wayne threw a press bash late that afternoon down at Burt (Reynolds, a buddy of Wayne's) & Jack's restaurant in Port Everglades. Located on the southern edge of Fort Lauderdale, Port Everglades is a popular point of departure for cruise-ship passengers bound for the Caribbean. It also happens to be the only unbridged interruption in the coastal barrier island between here and the tip of Miami Beach, 25 miles south. And as such, it forms a natural chasm that helps protect residential Fort Lauderdale from the kind of scary urban characters who used to show up every Friday night on *Miami Vice* and who might otherwise be tempted to wander up the beach.

Ordinarily, Wayne does not like to do business or otherwise be seen in public out of uniform, which for him is a blue suit with a white shirt and a red tie. Tonight, this being a celebration (things having very quickly taken on a party atmosphere), he loosened up just a little, donning a wide red tie with baseballs all over it. (Marti told the *Miami Herald* she'd seen a picture of the tie in a magazine and called all over the country before she tracked one down at a store in Denver, of all places, and had it sent.) Anyway, flashbulbs were popping, cameras were rolling, and in the midst of all the hubbub and confusion someone handed Wayne a baseball hat. Wayne doesn't wear baseball hats, but he obligingly held this one up for the camera, which resulted in the six-by-ten-inch color photograph that ran on page one of the *Herald* the next day, under the headline "GREAT CATCH! The Marlins Are Florida's Team." The hat was orange with a nautical braid across the brim and on it was written in big blue block letters a message that pointedly contradicted the headline. "WAYNE'S TEAM," it said, and underneath that, smaller and in script, "Florida Marlins."

Wayne and his people had endeavored to keep the team name a secret, although it had long been assumed by those with an interest in the outcome that Miami would in no way be part of it. The *Herald,* hoping to exert its influence, had conducted a telephone poll in which respondents were asked to choose among Miami, South Florida and Florida for the geographic portion of the name. Of course Miami won, with 2,839 out of 3,482 calls received (only 37 picked Florida), but Wayne was unmoved. He said later that if St. Petersburg had won the other expansion franchise instead of Denver, he might have compromised and gone with South Florida. As it was, he happily embraced the whole state, to hell with the irrelevant civic types down in Miami, who were plainly miffed. As for the nickname, Wayne asked the fans for their advice, then chose to ignore that too. Club officials never did release the results of their name-the-team contest, but acknowledged that the favorite—and it wasn't even close—was Manatees. Miami Manatees? No way was Wayne going to name *his* new toy after a blubbery, slow-moving mammal native to Florida's warm coastal waters and currently threatened with extinction, not so much because of pollution or poachers as because it has a hard time staying out of the way of speedboat propellers.

But seriously, who was going to quibble over a silly thing like a name on a day like this? The point is, Wayne had won, Florida was in the big leagues, the long wait was over. Unless maybe you were from St. Petersburg, what more did you want? Florida, the biggest state by far without a baseball team to call its own; a carved-up peninsula with as many different fan loyalties as there are spring-training sites; a state long taken for granted by northern teams who teasingly drop by once a year, only to depart for distant cities in faraway states as soon as things begin to get interesting. Well, not anymore. Now Florida had the Marlins. Wayne really could have called it Wayne's Team if he had wanted to and most people still would have been thrilled.

Among those sharing the spotlight with Wayne that afternoon was Tim Robbie, co-trustee of the Robbie estate and representative of the family's half interest (the other half was Wayne's) in Joe Robbie Stadium. Long before Wayne entered the picture, it had been Joe Robbie's dream to bring a baseball team to South Florida. He had built the stadium that bears his name knowing that ten Dolphins games a year would barely pay the mortgage, that in the long term the success of the enterprise was dependent upon bringing in a baseball tenant. Joe tried to get it done on his own, but failed, at which point he turned to Wayne. Unfortunately, Joe died before the deal could be wrapped up, but then Tim took over and three months later, in March 1990, the Robbie family and Wayne were partners.

With Wayne at Burt & Jack's—as always in times of triumph—was Wayne's father, Harry, the 73-year-old patriarch of the Huizenga clan, who was born in the Netherlands and raised in Chicago. In a way it was Harry's decision to move the family to Fort Lauderdale in 1954 that set in motion the complicated chain of events culminating in this very exciting moment. Harry was practically beside himself, grinning wildly, pressing himself on total strangers, passing out a business card that identified him as the Marlins' second baseman. Jean was there too, Wayne's mom, who divorced Harry in 1954 but married him again in 1978. Jean confessed to a reporter from the *Herald* that at one point during the hectic months leading up she had worried so for her only son's health that she had told him, "Wayne, stop it, you're going to have a heart attack." Advice which Wayne, of course, ignored.

All the while, Wayne worked the crowd, lifting flutes of champagne, gladly repeating himself to reporters, posing for pictures for anyone who asked, frequently giving the old thumbs-up. The man was juiced. Within hours his mug would be plastered all over the newspapers and seen on every television news program. And by this time tomorrow, if you searched from Vero Beach to Key West, it would be next to impossible to find the proverbial man on the street who couldn't tell you that the Uncle Fester look-alike with the thin-lipped, skin-stretching grin, the squinty blue eyes, the bald pate and the faintly scarred complexion was Wayne. He might not know that his last name was Huizenga, and even if he did he might not be able to pronounce it (HIGH-zing-a), but he would know it was Wayne.

Which was strange, because a year and a half ago Wayne was about as anonymous as a guy with his kind of money could possibly be (he was not listed in Ft. Lauderdale's *Social Register* until 1987). Things began to change only when he bought half of Joe Robbie Stadium and 15 percent of the Dolphins, and soon thereafter announced plans to go after a baseball team. At the time not many took him seriously. Miami was hardly even in the running for an expansion franchise. It was understood that if Florida were to get a team—which it would, of course; there could be no question even then—the winner had to be St. Petersburg, which already had the Suncoast Dome, not to mention the sympathy and support (or so it was believed) of the many owners in both leagues who had been flirting with St. Pete for years.

But Wayne went ahead anyway, and after he blew away the local competition during the first round of presentations in New York back in September, people started to take notice. Then he was named to the expansion short list in December, and people in the know began to bet on him. Then the expansion committee visited Miami in February and satisfied itself that Joe Robbie Stadium was indeed okay for baseball, and after that suddenly everybody pretty much just *knew* that Wayne was going to get his team. It happened that fast. And still, people everywhere were asking themselves: How much do we really know about this guy?

Very little. That he is chairman of the board of Blockbuster Entertainment (the video rental store), a company he built from diddly into Fortune 500 in three years. That before that he was a co-founder of Waste Management, Inc., the largest waste-disposal conglomerate on the planet. That before that he picked up garbage in the predawn hours on the streets of Fort Lauderdale. That he is worth over half a billion dollars. That he is entirely self-made. And that while he takes pride in being the man Floridians must thank for the pleasures that major league baseball will bring, civic duty is hardly his main motive. Because for Wayne, more than anything else, baseball is a business. And Wayne has never taken an active role in any business that did not end up making him a lot of money.

WILBUR PORTER is 80 years old, often tired these days but not about to retire. Back in 1934 he hopped a freight train on its way through the South Georgia piney woods and landed in Fort Lauderdale. That same year he married Anna and eventually they had six children, four of whom are still alive. They moved into the Dixie Court housing project in Fort Lauderdale until Wilbur had saved enough money to buy a plot of land on the north fork of the New River (a few miles upstream from the mansion where Wayne lives today), in what was then unincorporated Broward County. He built his own house. When it burned down he built another on the same site. He has lived there ever since, and when Anna died in 1989, his daughter Ruth and her husband came to live with him. "I don't want for anything," Porter says, sitting at his kitchen table, a gold tooth shining through his smile. "I get along here and work, trying to live. Scared if I stop I won't be able to start back again."

Porter's backyard is full of stuff: a Chevrolet Vega; the hull of an old fishing boat; a rusty swing set; a doghouse with a mirror inside it (kind of a joke); three antique claw-foot bathtubs ("worth $1,700") full of muck and worms (the worms are for sale); a stand of palm-tree saplings (also for sale); and a garden bordered on one side with banana trees and planted with cabbage, rutabagas, turnips, sugarcane and mustard and collard greens. At various times over the years, Porter has also kept chickens, turkeys, goats, hogs and horses in his backyard. For a time he operated a riding school, Porter's Dude Ranch, which he advertised around town with the slogan "Exercise yourself the modest way!"

Porter has had lots of different jobs in his life. For 12 years after he came to Florida he worked in a dairy in nearby Davie. Later he tried landscaping, yard work and laying concrete. Somehow, he always managed to get by. But the one time in his long life when he really felt like he was getting ahead was during the time that he was in the garbage business.

Thirty years ago, Broward County's population was just beginning to explode. There was plenty of picking up to do in the vast unincorporated regions outside Hollywood, Fort Lauderdale and Pompano Beach. Porter got into it gradually at first, with a single flatbed truck. But as business improved he invested in more equipment, to the point where eventually he was running two 35-foot packers and a little snub-nosed 20-footer that used to tip back on its rear wheels whenever it was loaded past full. He brought his sons and in-laws into the business as drivers and helpers, even hired a white woman, whose job it was to go door to door through new communities like Plantation and Melrose Park signing up customers. "They thought it was her business," Porter says. "I didn't care what they thought. She could maybe go places I couldn't go at that time. So I got kinda large."

But early one morning Porter hit the streets only to find that the garbage along his route had already been picked up— an old trick in the garbage business, designed to intimidate. "Big shots," Porter says. They drove a fleet of brand-new dark-green packers. They were from New York, word was, and they all seemed to have Italian surnames. "It just kinda cut off my growth." Understanding what was coming, Porter began thinking about switching to another line of work.

It was about that same time that young Wayne Huizenga started coming by the Porter house afternoons, offering to buy some of Porter's customers. The year was 1962. Wayne was 25, a college dropout who had driven a bulldozer for a couple of years and done a stint in the Army before going to work for a friend of the family who was an independent hauler up in Pompano. Wayne was itching to get started on his own. "He wasn't working for that syndicate bunch," says Porter. "He was just trying to get his foot in the door. He knowed he had more chance than I would. I finally sold Wayne a truck (the 20-footer) and some commercial business and some houses, not too many. He done bought my stuff, and [the syndicate] didn't try to take his, 'cause, you know, he knowed how to fight it. He just stood his ground. He's a mighty man now."

Porter says Huizenga bought the truck and $500 worth of accounts. In time the lone truck became a large company, Southern Sanitation, and eventually a worldwide corporation, Waste Management, Inc., and Wayne became rich beyond Porter's imagination. Does Porter ever wonder what might have been? "Ooooh, yeah," he says, "I couldn'ta done nothing but made some money. But there's nothing to be done about it. What's done is done. It *was* like it *was*."

It was decades before Porter happened to run into Huizenga again, this time at a store in downtown Fort Lauderdale. Wayne remembered him and shook his hand. Though Porter thought about asking Huizenga for a contribution to the fund for renovations at his church, he never followed through. It awes Porter, sometimes, to think of what became of the skinny, determined kid he first laid eyes on in 1962. Porter has only to open his front door to be confronted with an amazing sight: dozens of clean, colorful Southern Sanitation packers parked in a lot across the street, all of them descendants of his old snub-nosed 20-footer, the one that couldn't always keep four wheels on the road. "He didn't fall back now a notch," says Porter, shaking his head. "He just held it on all the way, just kept climbing. Still climbing!"

BY FLORIDA STANDARDS, Wayne Huizenga might as well be a native. His parents, Harry and Jean, moved to Fort Lauderdale from Chicago in the spring of 1954, bringing Wayne, then 16, and Bonnie, 11. The Huizengas were part of the first big postwar wave of northern in-migration, arriving just as Florida was beginning to challenge California as a continental collection bin for mass murderers, social misfits and all manner of seekers after truth, happiness and riches. Consider that in 1950 the population of Florida was only 2.7 million, less than that of 19 other states, including Alabama. During the decade that followed, Florida's population swelled nearly 80 percent to 5 million. Since then, Florida's growth rate has averaged 38 percent per decade. With 12.8 million people as of the 1990 census, Florida is now the fourth-largest state in the country, after California, Texas and New York. Of the top ten states, Florida is the fastest-growing. Eight out of ten people who live in Florida were born someplace else. The fact that so many Florida newcomers these days are retirees, attracted by the tropical climate and the friendly tax code, is misleading. For the Huizengas and thousands like them were pioneers. They came to Florida not to kick back but to begin a new life. In Florida, anything was possible.

Wayne's dad, Harry, was the fourth son of Harm Huizenga, a Dutch immigrant who founded Chicago's first garbage-hauling company in 1894. Harm's first wife bore him three sons before she died, at which point he went back to the old country, remarried, fathered Harry, and returned to Chicago. All three of Harry's older brothers followed Harm into the family business. The luckiest among them lived to age 55. The other two never made it out of their 40s. Harry, making his own compelling case for nature over nurture, not only has outlived his half brothers by decades; he also never showed the slightest interest in garbage. Instead he became a carpenter, starting out making kitchen cabinets and eventually contracting to build houses. Florida, especially South Florida in the 1950s, was a natural place for a builder intent on making his fortune to wind up.

But that was not the only reason why, after 18 years of marriage, the Huizengas left a comfortable home and familiar surroundings in Evergreen Park, a Chicago suburb, for the Great Unknown more than 1,300 miles away. It wasn't even the most important. As Jean would later explain to the court-appointed special master: "We . . . agreed that maybe if we came to Florida we could make a fresh start. We came here with those intentions, but it didn't last very long."

AT 3:50 P.M. on Monday, July 26, 1954, Deputy Paul Radcliff of the Broward County Sheriff's Department knocked on the door at 1505 North Andrews Avenue in Fort Lauderdale and asked for Harry Huizenga. The purpose of the deputy's visit was to serve Harry with an 11-point bill of complaint, filed not 30 minutes earlier in County Court by Jean Huizenga, accusing him of "extreme cruelty" toward Jean and the children and seeking remedy in the form of divorce. Harry, apparently, was not at home. If he was, he chose to hide himself. In any case, court records show that Deputy Radcliff was able to leave the papers "with a member of the family then and there residing above the age of 15 years, to wit: Harry Wayne Huizenga, his son." It was not the first time that Wayne had been made to suffer for the actions of his father.

Part of the myth that would later emerge along with Wayne's own emergence as a public figure has to do with his austere religious upbringing; how as a teenager Wayne had to sneak out of the house just to see a movie or go dancing. The Huizengas were lifelong members of a strict Protestant denomination, the Dutch Christian Reformed Church, and joined a local congregation in Delray Beach after moving to Fort Lauderdale. So the myth is not untrue, as far as it goes. But to the extent that it suggests a structured, ordered family life, the myth is a lie. At best, home for Wayne was a place of unrelieved tension; at worst, of chaos spilling over into violence. Sometimes Jean locked herself in the bedroom, and sometimes Harry broke the locks. On New Year's Eve 1953, the last holiday the family would celebrate together in Evergreen Park before leaving for Florida, Harry allegedly terrorized Jean to the point where she had to call the police.

The Huizengas made their way to Fort Lauderdale in stages. Wayne moved down with his father in February, Jean and Bonnie followed in April. The house they moved into—a rented two-bedroom bungalow on a busy north-south thoroughfare six blocks west of Federal Highway—was both smaller and situated in a less desirable neighborhood than what they were accustomed to. Harry and Wayne shared one bedroom, Jean and Bonnie the other—ostensibly because the children were too old to sleep together.

Harry and Jean were not only trying to salvage what was left of their marriage; they were also intent on making a killing in Florida real estate, to which end they risked all the money they had. Unable to sell the house in Evergreen Park, Harry borrowed to the hilt in order to buy three empty lots in nearby Harbor Beach and begin building houses on them. He was banking on selling the houses once they were completed. But the plan backfired. Harry's new homes were destined to hit the market in the midst of one of Florida's periodic busts; even after three years, none had been sold. "Interest rates went through the roof," Wayne explained many years later, "nobody was buying, and the interest killed him. He lost everything he had built up. He was down to driving a five-year-old beat-up Chevrolet."

Things were not yet as bad as that during the first few months that the Huizengas were reunited in Florida. On the other hand, money was already tight; the living arrangement was such that it was impossible not to rub shoulders, much less nerves; and as far as Harry and Jean's relationship was concerned, there was no progress to report.

The divorce was ugly, as bad as it gets, played out in a flurry of combative legal maneuvers culminating in a brutally explicit hearing before a court-appointed special master. Wayne and his sister Bonnie appeared as witnesses on their mother's behalf. "I don't think we ever got one night's sleep around there," Wayne testified under questioning from Jean's attorney.

**Q.** Did he ever lose his temper?
**A.** Plenty of times.
**Q.** What would happen when he would lose his temper?
**A.** He would push us down on the floor, hit Mother, Bonnie and myself.

**Q.** When was the last time that you recall anything like that happening?

**A.** He hit her around in July. . . .

The incident to which Wayne was referring allegedly took place during the predawn hours of July 20, 1954, when Harry entered the bedroom where his wife and daughter were sleeping. "[W]hen I asked him not to wake the children and go back into his own room he hit me," Jean testified. "He walked around the other side of the bed and hit Bonnie and when Wayne came to the door to try and stop him from hitting me, he hit him, he hit Wayne too."

Bonnie, a seventh-grader at the time, confirmed her mother's version of events in response to questions from the special master:

**Q.** What happened when your brother entered the room?

**A.** He hit him with his fist across the face.

**Q.** Did it seem to hurt your brother?

**A.** Yes, the next morning he had a lump on his cheek.

Harry, for his part, strongly denied the accusations of his wife and children. He countered his wife's claims by accusing her of carrying on a long-standing extramarital affair and of disappearing for days at a time without explanation.

But the findings of the special master were conclusive and unequivocal: that "the Defendant . . . on a number of occasions became violent and dangerous to the physical and mental welfare of the Plaintiff"; that "therefore . . . the Defendant has been guilty of extreme cruelty to the Plaintiff." The divorce went through on October 21, 1954. Jean was awarded custody of Bonnie and Wayne, the right to occupy the house on North Andrews and $125 a week alimony.

Wayne stuck around for as long as it took to complete his senior year at Pine Crest School (as part of the agreement, his dad paid his private-school tuition). After Wayne graduated—with his family in ruins, no plan for the future and no good reason to stick around—he headed north.

For the better part of seven years, Wayne drifted. In Chicago, he went to work driving a bulldozer for one of the family outfits his father had spurned. Eventually he enrolled in Calvin College, a Christian Reformed college in Grand Rapids, Michigan, where he lasted until Christmas vacation his sophomore year before giving that up too. He joined the Army. Finally in 1960, despite continuing problems at home, Wayne returned to Florida.

By now Harry's finances were in ruins. He was forever falling behind on the alimony, and there were periodic confrontations. Jean accused Harry of breaking into her home and assaulting a guest. Harry, in a failed attempt to have custody of the children transferred to a relative in Chicago, accused Jean of "loose and lascivious conduct." In November 1960, Jean, who by now was working as a waitress, remarried, opening the book on a whole new family nightmare. Testifying at his mother's second divorce proceedings nine years later, Wayne would recall that "[m]any times she would call me at my home, and I would have to go over after he had beat her up." Asked what evidence he had that his mother was telling the truth, he replied, "Black-and-blue marks."

To have gone through what Wayne went through as an adolescent and a young adult is to be beaten down, defeated; or else to emerge as the one who winds up beating everybody else. To be overwhelmed by life and circumstances, a victim; or else, sometime before it's all over, finally to be the one in control. Wayne is an extraordinary example of the latter.

It took a while but at age 25 Wayne started to make his own way, slowly at first, with just the one truck and the customer list worth $500 a month that he had bought from Wilbur Porter. Wayne drove the truck *and* emptied the cans, which in itself was a sign of his resolve. "Back then," says John Currington, Porter's son-in-law, "to see a white guy picking up garbage was very rare." When he reached the point where he could afford to hire a helper, that meant he no longer had to drive the truck to the dump at the end of each day; instead he could go home and take a shower and put on a clean shirt and then go back out and sign up some new customers. Before long he had enough of those to justify buying a second truck, and for a while he rode solo again, Wayne in one truck and his helper in the other. Then he hired two more helpers. Then he bought a third truck. And a fourth. Wayne was really moving now. It was practically all he could do just to keep up with demand. During those years, the population of Broward County was growing by 50,000 every year. More people, more garbage, simple as that. Business exploded. By 1969, Wayne was no longer just Wayne and his helpers, he was Southern Sanitation, with 20 trucks running routes all up and down the east coast of southern Florida. By then Wayne was rich. Not nearly as rich as he was about to become, but getting there.

And what of Harry and Jean? In 1978, almost twenty-five years after the divorce, they remarried. Wayne and Bonnie attended the ceremony, performed by a Dutch Christian Reformed minister in Lighthouse Point, Florida. In their capacity as official witnesses, both signed the marriage certificate. In the years since then, Harry appears to have undergone a remarkable transformation. No longer a threat, today he qualifies as Wayne's mascot. Wherever Wayne goes, at least in times of triumph or celebration, Harry is sure to follow: to Burt & Jack's for the big expansion party; to the dedication of One Blockbuster Plaza in downtown Fort Lauderdale; to the first game ever played by a Marlins minor league team in Erie, Pennsylvania.

Wayne doesn't seem to mind. Until Harry was hospitalized last winter, Wayne even kept an office for his father at the Marlins suite in Fort Lauderdale. There, on any given day, while others labored, Harry mostly just poked around—sitting in on meetings, hanging out in the mailroom, pressing himself on visitors.

"Harry Huizenga," says the genial seventy-six-year-old, grinning and offering his hand. "Wayne's father!"

DURING THE YEARS that Wayne was in Florida building up the business of Southern Sanitation, Dean Buntrock was in

Chicago managing the family interest in a neighborhood outfit known as Ace Scavenger. The seed that became Ace had been planted the century before by Harm Huizenga (for years afterward the company was run exclusively by first-generation Dutch immigrants, known to everyone else in the business as "the wooden shoes"). Buntrock got involved when he married one of Harm's granddaughters (Wayne's cousin), and took control on behalf of the widows when the last of Harm's three older sons died.

The vision of a multi-city (and ultimately multi-national) garbage company, one with technical, engineering and financial capabilities on a scale never before imagined, belonged to Buntrock, not Huizenga. His inspiration was the ecology movement of the late 1960s and early '70s; more to the point, the new regulatory climate that was beginning to emerge as a result of it. New laws and new regulatory agencies meant vast new profits for a company prepared to meet the strict demands, and Buntrock set about building such a company.

"There was a keen awareness that public policy was about to emerge very quickly," explains Harold Gershowitz, a Waste Management vice president who came on board in 1972. "Back then [solid waste] was referred to as the third pollution, air and water being the first two. [Browning-Ferris, a competitor, and Waste Management] saw accurately that this was going to become an area of great attention, great expenditure— tremendous value-added about to be required in the way we manage waste materials. All of these opportunities were going to be localized, and if you were going to be a player you had to be there, you had to be in the market."

Waste Management was formed when Buntrock approached Wayne—whom he knew then only as a relative from Florida who happened to be in the same business—and convinced him to join forces with Ace Scavenger and a former competitor, Acme Disposal of Chicago, owned by Larry Beck. In June 1971, two months after Earth Day was celebrated for the first time, Buntrock, Huizenga and Beck took the company public at $16 a share. In 1972, the company issued three million new shares, and with that, Wayne hit the road, snapping up small- and medium-sized haulers coast to coast in exchange for stock in Waste Management; some 90 companies in nine months, according to company legend. It was a brutal, highly competitive (Browning-Ferris was doing the same thing), around-the-clock job—in other words, right up Wayne's alley. He gave it all he had, and by the end of the year, Waste Management was doing business in 48 markets in 20 states and Canada.

Today Waste Management is a $7.5 billion enterprise, twice as large as Browning-Ferris, its closest competitor. The company's market capitalization (the value of shares outstanding) —an indicator of size and strength, as well as the level of acceptance by investors—is in the $20 billion range, which is very big league, 20 percent bigger than General Motors, 50 percent bigger than Ford. A single share of Waste Management stock, bought at the initial public offering in 1971 and held, today would be worth around $3,000.

Over the years, Waste Management has expanded vertically as well as horizontally, adding an international division (three days after the end of the Gulf War, Waste Management had 100 employees on the ground in Kuwait City), divisions that specialize in disposing of chemical waste, radioactive waste and asbestos and even a division for cleaning up hazardous-waste dump sites; the same dumps, in some cases, that were originally contaminated by other divisions of Waste Management. While Waste Management bills itself as "the world's leading total environmental services organization" and claims that no one "is more committed to offering the services that protect the environment than Waste Management," environmentalists question those claims. Greenpeace, in a scathing 285-page report published in 1991, calls Waste Management "one of the world's biggest polluters," and points to a record $45 million in environmentally related fines and settlements the company paid between 1980 and 1990. Waste Management was a pioneer in the controversial practice of injecting pressurized toxic waste into deep underground caverns. The company operates two specially equipped incinerator ships, *Vulcanus I* and *II*, which are used to burn toxic wastes in international waters, beyond the reach of U.S. environmental regulations.

Greenpeace also cites what it calls "a history of . . . antitrust law violations . . . [and] attempts to gain illegitimate political influence," a conclusion reinforced in a recent study by the San Diego district attorney's office. Even before there was a Waste Management, Buntrock was sued by the state of Wisconsin in 1961 for his alleged role in a conspiracy to monopolize trash collection in Milwaukee County that may have involved threats of "physical harm to the owners of competing . . . firms . . . and their families and destruction or damage to their property and equipment." The charges were dropped in 1970 but fresh allegations of price fixing, bribery and mob connections have accumulated steadily over the years. For instance, in 1990 Waste Management paid a $19.5 million fine to settle its share of a national class-action suit charging Waste Management and Browning-Ferris with conspiracy to fix prices.

When Huizenga was asked by the *New York Times* about the influence of organized crime in the waste industry, he dismissed the question. "That reputation," he told reporter Richard Sandomir, "comes from your part of the country, up north." While no evidence exists to connect Huizenga to the mob, either during the early years at Southern Sanitation or later at Waste Management (which, by the way, is headquartered "up north" in Oak Brook, Illinois), Huizenga has had legal problems of his own. In 1976, he was cited by name in a case brought by the Securities and Exchange Commission, charging Waste Management with distributing $71,000 in "dubious outlays" from a secret "slush fund" to politicians in Florida and Ontario. Huizenga later signed a consent decree—legalese for "I didn't do anything wrong but I promise never to do it again."

Huizenga was coming up on 50 years old—the age by which two of his uncles were already dead—when he resigned as president and vice chairman of the board of Waste Management in 1984, sold the big house in Ginger Creek (one of tony Oak Brook's tonier subdivisions), and moved back to Fort

Lauderdale to be with his second wife, Marti. "I think he just opted for a saner existence," says Gershowitz. "He was commuting back and forth across the country every single week. I don't think he wanted to spend the rest of his life doing that."

Perhaps not, but neither was he ready to retire happily ever after. Wayne likes to describe himself as "a better builder than a manager." As long as he was building something at Waste Management, Wayne was happy; but after things settled into a predictable pattern (no matter that the company was still growing at a 20–25 percent annual clip), Wayne grew bored. Office-bound for the most part, he missed being *out there*, stirring things up, making things happen. There was that, and then there was the fact that no matter what, Waste Management was never going to be Wayne's company, it would always be Buntrock's. In the long run, that was an intolerable situation. What it came down to, basically, was that Wayne missed doing things and he missed being in control, so he quit. But it soon became clear that he never had any intention of slowing down.

"He loves the action," is the way Peer Pedersen, an old friend and a longtime member of the board of Waste Management, describes Huizenga. "He's an action guy. What else is there? 'Am I to sit back and sort of vegetate and live off my income and play bridge with my wife every night?' That wouldn't appeal to him at all."

BACK IN FORT LAUDERDALE, Wayne put together his own company. He called it Waco (short for Wayne's Company) Services, but when he realized people were pronouncing it "wacko," he changed the name to Huizenga Holdings. Huizenga Holdings was capitalized with Wayne's money and Wayne's ideas, and was set up by Wayne as a vehicle for investing in whatever businesses Wayne thought might be profitable, from insurance (Life General Security Insurance Company) to aviation (Suncoast Helicopters) to bottled water (Blue Ribbon) to auto parts cleaners (Sparko). Wayne had an eye for spotting winners, and Huizenga Holdings quickly became a huge success, accumulating over 100 companies in three years, and posting annual revenues approaching $100 million.

It was in early 1987 that John Melk, a fellow road warrior from the glory days at Waste Management (John and Wayne were the "dynamic duo" in charge of Waste Management's acquisition program), convinced Wayne to take a hard look at a little-known Texas video retailer, Blockbuster Video. Melk had been introduced to Blockbuster by Scott Beck, the son of Larry Beck, one of the co-founders of Waste Management. Earlier, the younger Beck had gone before a group of Waste Management executives and tried to interest them in Blockbuster, to little avail. In those days the video-rental business was still widely regarded as one step up from street vending and made most people think of pornography. "At the time I said, 'That's very interesting, but . . .'" Gershowitz remembers (later he accumulated six franchises of his own). But Melk was convinced from the start, and invested in a franchise, and as time went on he began to think that maybe this was a business Wayne would be interested in too. By April, David Cook, Blockbuster's founder, was out of the picture, and Wayne, together with Melk and Don Flynn, another Waste Management alumnus, controlled the company.

At the time Wayne bought in, there were only 19 Blockbuster Videos, all of them in Texas. Wayne took the basic concept—convenient location, huge selection, reasonable rates and a family atmosphere (nothing X-rated)—and sold it, opening company-owned outlets, selling franchises, and swallowing competitors coast to coast. By the end of 1991, there were 2,028 Blockbuster Videos around the world, in Japan, Chile, Venezuela, Puerto Rico, Spain, Australia, New Zealand and Guam. In January 1992, Blockbuster absorbed Cityvision, the largest chain in Great Britain with more than 800 outlets, which Wayne says will be the jumping-off point for expansion throughout Europe. Today, Blockbuster dominates the $13 billion video industry. According to PaineWebber analyst Craig Bibb, Blockbuster is "a McDonald's with no competition from Burger King or Wendy's or Roy Rogers."

Blockbuster's early growth was so steady and so spectacular

that when earnings for the first quarter of 1991 showed a less than 20-percent increase (compared with more than 100 percent the year before), something like panic set in, and the stock price plunged 50 percent. Earnings recovered the following quarter (Wayne blames the dip on the Gulf War), and in time so did Blockbuster's stock, but investors and franchise owners alike were left with nagging questions about the company's future. Thanks in part to Dan Dorfman, the widely read columnist for *USA Today*, the view has gradually taken hold on Wall Street that Blockbuster is about to hit the ceiling on growth; that soon, perhaps by the mid-1990s, cable systems will have the technology to serve up an unlimited menu of movies on pay-per-view, making the VCR, and with it the video-rental industry, obsolete.

"Wrong," says Wayne, his eyes flashing. "That is absolutely, positively not going to happen. Instead of having one choice, you might have five or ten or fifteen choices, but you still won't be able to watch the movie you want, when you want to watch it. Will there be more channels on television? Yes, there will be. Will some people stop coming to video stores and watch more pay-per-view? Sure, that'll happen. But the pie is big enough that you can share it. The industry's still growing at a billion dollars a year, and they still sell ten million VCRs a year. There's a whole bunch of people that are just now beginning to put the second and third VCR in their home—that means the teenagers can watch it in their bedroom, the little kids in another room and the parents in another room. I'm convinced that five years from now we'll have more customers in our stores than we do now. We're gonna be here big and strong and I'm not worried about it for a moment."

At the same time, Wayne is willing to concede that in the long run—"I'm talking about the year 2005, 2010, 2015"—technology will change the way we look at movies. But by then, he says, video rentals will be such a small percentage of Blockbuster's business that it won't matter anymore. "We'll be getting into other forms of retailing and entertainment," Wayne promises: video sales, as opposed to rentals (up more than 100 percent in the fourth quarter of '91); compact disc software (in partnership with Dutch giant Philips Electronics, which recently invested $66 million in Blockbuster); and music CDs and tapes (a worldwide chain of "megastores" jointly owned with Virgin Retail Group of London). "We want to use that same expertise that we've done building Blockbuster to go out and get another form going," Wayne says. "If that would be in the music business, for example, then we'd roll it out in music. We've got people that know how to put the shovel in the ground, get the building built, and get the store opened in the right location." There is even the option of one day entering the entertainment business from the other side, with programming. "I wouldn't be surprised in the year 2000 you turn on your television and you see the Blockbuster channel. That wouldn't surprise me at all."

With all that, Blockbuster remained a favorite of the short-sellers—speculators who sell borrowed shares on a bet that the price will go down—well into 1992. Among those strongly advising his clients to sell Blockbuster short was Jim Chanos of Kynikos Associates in New York. He said the stock was "outrageously overpriced," and cited concerns not just with developing technology but also with Blockbuster's "highly questionable" accounting practices, which he claimed provided a false picture of earnings.

To which Wayne responds, "Every day there's a new attack done on us by the shorts. I love it. Because when they start attacking us, you know they're nervous. Last year [1991] we got down to a low of seven, seven and a half, something like that, after the shorts jumped all over us. Fine, now we're fourteen. Next year we'll be higher, and the following year we'll be higher yet. It's action that's gonna stop the shorts. You keep doing the right things, keep increasing the earnings thirty, forty percent a quarter, and you kill 'em. Hit 'em right between the eyes, there's nothing they can do. It's just a matter of how much they want to lose."

WITH SUCCESS, Wayne acquired a reputation for shrewdness, toughness and smarts, for being a real businessman's businessman. It isn't so much that he is truly rich now (No.

151 on the Forbes 400, $560 million, according to the latest list), though rich is good. It is more his method that people have come to admire, precisely because it is so simple and straightforward.

He puts in long hours: seven to seven, as a matter of course, plus weekends. When he must fly, he prefers to fly at night because he finds it more efficient to sleep on a plane (it's his plane, after all, it has a bed) than to work on one. "People say, 'Boy, you must really be having fun with [Blockbuster],' " he says, genuinely puzzled. "I never thought about having fun. We work too hard to have fun."

He sticks to basics: The magic of renting rather than selling, for example. You buy something once—a dumpster, a video-cassette, a portable toilet (he once owned Port-O-Let)—and then you sell it over and over again.

He avoids debt: When Wayne and two partners bought into Blockbuster, they controlled almost 60 percent of the stock. Over the years, the partners generally have sold their shares while Wayne generally has bought, and yet today Wayne owns less than 10 percent of the company. "Okay," he says, "we've diluted ourselves. But we've built a big company. I just don't believe in a lot of leverage."

He follows through: "He sees sort of basic opportunities," says Pedersen, a member (with Carl Barger and Dean Buntrock) of Wayne's regular golf and bridge foursome, "and then he puts his ingenuity and entrepreneurial spirit and energy into it to bring it home."

And he has the capacity (absolutely required in Wayne's world) to kill without blinking: "Keep putting the pressure on the competitor," he preaches. "Hopefully someday he'll go out of business and we'll get all of his business, that's really what we're after."

Wayne's rather sudden decision to pursue a baseball franchise was interesting if for no other reason than because the popular notion of sports barons is that most of them are really buffoons, not businessmen. It's true that baseball is a departure for Wayne. Not only is baseball a cartel (Wayne may have to stifle some of his natural aggression); it's a mature industry (some would say geriatric), almost certainly overvalued, and headed for a crisis, if not in 1993, when the players and the owners both have the right to reopen the Basic Agreement, then in 1994, when both national television contracts—currently worth $14 million per team—expire, and the question becomes: How low can they go? Says Bill Giles of the Phillies, "I've been in the game forty-some years"—he remembers when owners made all their money from ticket sales, concessions, fence ads and scorecards, period—"and I've never seen a more important twenty-four months ahead of us than I do now. The value of everybody's franchise could go dramatically one way or the other."

Wayne is not blind to the risks. He'll tell you that if he lived in Buffalo, or even Denver, baseball wouldn't interest him. But sitting where he is in the geographical center of South Florida with its 4 million citizens (and 100,000 more coming every year), with the closest big league competition 665 miles away in Atlanta, and playing in a stadium he happens to own half of—with all that, Wayne thinks the numbers look pretty good.

"Just so we set the ground rules," he says, a trace of midwestern twang lingering in his vowels, "I don't care what people say or what people think. If I couldn't make a profit in baseball I wouldn't be in it. That's where we start right there. We're not in this business just for the love of the sport and wanting to do something for South Florida."

BASEBALL TEAMS have been described as "physical embodiments of tax accountants' minds." That was basically what Gerald Scully, author of *The Business of Major League Baseball,* had in mind when he outlined three excellent reasons why someone might want to buy one, even if it's likely to lose money. First, as a straight capital-appreciation play; you swallow the losses for two, three, five years—whatever it takes—then sell at a profit. Historically, that's been a sound strategy. But with all the uncertainty in baseball's future, franchise values are leveling off, even slipping. Wayne paid $95 million for the Marlins. When you add in the start-up costs ($15 million plus) and the money he won't be earning from national television in 1993 ($14 million), since both new teams were cut out of the pie, he'll end up having spent more for an expansion team than all but a handful of existing teams are worth in today's market.

A second approach is to use the losses generated by baseball to offset profits in other businesses you may own, and vice versa, in order to save money on taxes. In Wayne's case, his personal interest in the Marlins is only that of a limited partner; but Huizenga Holdings, the umbrella which he controls, is a general partner. "That was done for tax benefits," explains Rick Rochon, president of Huizenga Holdings. "We just happened to have some losses in Holdings that we would be able to utilize via the baseball." Wayne insists accounting tricks won't be necessary—that the Marlins will make money on operations—but if he ever wants to shuffle profits and losses, the mechanism is in place.

A third approach, which applies directly to Wayne, is to use baseball in combination with a related business to boost profits overall. That's what Ted Turner does with the Braves and TBS, what the Tribune Company does with the Cubs and WGN, and what Anheuser-Busch does with the Cardinals and beer. In Wayne's case, the possibilities are many. He looks forward to the day when the benefits of membership in Blockbuster Video might include discounts on Marlins tickets. And already, Blockbuster is the exclusive retailer for Major League Baseball videos. But more than anything else, when Wayne talks about the tangential benefits of owning a baseball team, he is talking about real estate—specifically, his half ownership of Joe Robbie Stadium, plus 65 acres of adjacent undeveloped land that he owns outright. Either investment alone—the team or the stadium—may have been hard to justify, but in tandem the potential is enormous.

Joe Robbie Stadium, which opened in 1987, sits in the middle of a grass-striped parking lot in northern Dade County, just below the Broward County line. What is unique about Joe Robbie Stadium, compared with almost all the other sports arenas in America, is that private investors, rather than taxpayers, put up the $115 million cost of construction. Granted, the land it sits on is leased to the stadium corporation by Dade County for a dollar a year. And beyond that, the county kicked in almost $30 million for improvements to access roads and utilities. Nonetheless, you'd have to go all the way back to Dodger Stadium in 1962 to find a comparable situation in which those who stood to profit most by the construction of a facility didn't have the gall to demand that someone else pay for it.

Joe Robbie built the stadium that bears his name ostensibly to house his football team, the Dolphins (before that they played at the Orange Bowl), although from the start he had a hidden agenda. Ron Frazier, the retired baseball coach of the University of Miami, remembers getting a surprise phone call early one Sunday morning years ago from Robbie, asking Frazier to meet him at the old Dolphins office on Biscayne Boulevard. He sounded excited. "I went in there," Frazier remembers, "and he had blueprints. He said, whispering, 'I want to show you a stadium.' We looked at it, and he said, 'D'you see this! Now look at the width!' He kept talking about the width. 'Look at this width!' He said, 'This is gonna be a baseball stadium! Here's where home plate will be! We'll play football, and it'll be a football stadium. But it's going to be a baseball stadium too!'"

Standing in the way of Robbie's dream were the mostly black middle-class homeowners who lived adjacent to the stadium site—a majority of them opposed to a stadium of any kind rising in their midst, much less one that would draw crowds year-round. So for obvious reasons, not much was said about baseball during the planning stages, at least in public. Besides, as far as the fans were concerned, baseball was an abstraction, football was real. And given the popularity of the Dolphins (Dolphin Expressway in central Miami was *not* named after Flipper), it made sense to rally support for the stadium around the team.

"Once people heard this was for the Dolphins," says H. T. Smith, the lawyer for the homeowners association, "and Joe Robbie said, 'If you don't let me build this stadium I'm taking my team and going somewhere else,' the support for this was as strong as the support for the death penalty in Florida. And I can't think of anything that Floridians are stronger for than the death penalty."

In the end, in order to begin construction, Robbie had to agree in writing to stage no more than 18 events per year at the stadium—eight regular-season football games, a couple of preseasons, the playoffs if necessary and maybe a rock concert or two during the summer. It was a promise made to be broken, as Tim Robbie now concedes. "From the very beginning," says the younger Robbie, "when we were marketing the suites and the club seats, we had the infield in place so that people who were selecting locations would know where they fit for baseball." Which explains why, of the 2,000-odd club seats that were never sold, almost all of them are in the east end zone (right field for baseball), rather than the west end zone (the third-base line).

Wayne leased a prime suite (#240A, midfield for football, first-base line for baseball) as soon as the stadium opened, and over time got friendly with Joe Robbie, whose own suite was right down the hall. In the fall of 1989, amid rumors of disarray in the Robbie family finances, Wayne approached Joe Robbie with an offer to buy the stadium. According to Tim Robbie, his father had no interest in selling out completely, but he was beginning to accept the fact that he needed help, and soon. It was costing him $4.3 million in annual payments just to service the stadium debt. At the same time, attendance—never a problem as long as the Dolphins were playing at the Orange Bowl in downtown Miami—was down sharply since the move. "He used to say, 'Well, I figured out how to put this place up, now I gotta find a way to keep it going,'" says Tim Robbie. "He was recognizing that he really couldn't make a go of it on his own, and that he needed to have a partner, and preferably a partner who would help bring baseball to the stadium."

Once Wayne brought up his own interest in baseball, the talks got serious. Joe Robbie died in January 1990, but negotiations proceeded with the estate, represented by Tim Robbie, and on June 29, 1990, the deal was closed. Wayne came away with 50 percent of the stadium plus 15 percent of the Dolphins, all for an initial cash outlay of only $17 million ($12 million for the team and $5 million for the stadium). Figuring in Wayne's share of the stadium debt ($45 million), plus commitments entered into for various joint ventures with the Robbies (land development, stadium improvements), the final price comes close to $75 million. Not a pittance but still a bargain.

"From Wayne's point of view, it only cost him five million dollars to get fifty percent of the stadium," says the accountant Steve Matt, who advised Huizenga on the purchase. "He was investing in the stadium because he saw it as an underutilized asset. He was banking on (A) getting the eighteen-event restriction lifted and (B) long-term, pursuing baseball. Wayne only wanted to buy part of the stadium but they made him invest in the team too, because that's where the Robbies needed the money." Huizenga has a four-year option to acquire an additional 10 percent of the Dolphins, one which Matt believes he is unlikely to exercise.

For their part, the Robbies got the help they needed to pay off the stadium debt (overnight, the family's annual interest obligation fell to $1.5 million), plus a commitment from Wayne to go all out in pursuit of a baseball tenant that would bring fans through the turnstiles on 81 days when the stadium would otherwise be empty. "Without baseball this stadium would never be much more than a break-even proposition," says Tim Robbie. "With baseball, it's a slam dunk, really."

The final agreement states in part: "Huizenga and the Robbie Estate agree that in respect to baseball it is their respective primary objective to induce a major league franchise to play its home games in Joe Robbie Stadium . . . and if necessary to participate in the acquisition of such a franchise either by expansion or by relocation of an existing franchise. In the latter instance, Huizenga and the Robbies agree to use their best efforts to support the decision of major league baseball to award a franchise to South Florida."

Six weeks later, on August 8, 1990, papers were filed in

Broward County on behalf of South Florida Big League Baseball, Inc., and Wayne went to work.

PRIOR TO THE SPRING of 1992, when Wayne finally gathered all his nonbaseball employees together in an 11-story glass tower in downtown Fort Lauderdale (bought for peanuts from the Resolution Trust Corporation, fixed up, and rechristened One Blockbuster Plaza), Wayne ran his worldwide video empire out of an elegant two-story building less than a mile from his home on palm-lined Las Olas Boulevard, the local Rodeo Drive. With its cool courtyard, its stucco exterior and its orange tile roof, the old headquarters felt more like a hacienda than a corporate office. Inside were big chairs, heavy tables and dark rugs, as in a study. On the walls were plaques ("1990 Florida Free Enterpriser of the Year," the Wharton School's "1990 Entrepreneur of the Year"), celebrity photographs (George Bush with granddaughter in a Blockbuster T-shirt—"My video adviser and I send best wishes") and framed personal letters, including a kind note from George's wife, Barbara, in which she thanks Wayne for the "oval wool rug," the one in the Oval Office.

Among the several small offices that opened directly off the lobby was one that belonged to Jim Blosser. A lawyer in private practice in Fort Lauderdale for 25 years, Blosser got to know his current boss during the 1988 presidential campaign (Blosser was Bush chairman for Broward County, Huizenga was a major contributor). Afterward, Huizenga persuaded Blosser to give up his partnership in the oldest law firm in town and come to work for him. Before he knew it, Blosser was spending almost all of his time on baseball.

"From day one it was Miami," says Blosser, unfolding a big map of Florida, flattening it out on his desktop and pointing. "Miami's way down here in Dade County. Miami's a million, almost two million people now. And Miami was going to be the place that the franchise was going to be located. Well, when you start thinking about making a baseball team happen, you don't think in terms of a million and a half or two million people. You think in terms of four million, five million, six million. Well, we got looking at the maps and we realized that Joe Robbie Stadium sits right there, and that the stadium—foresight of Joe Robbie and the other planners—is as close to downtown Fort Lauderdale as it is to downtown Miami. All of a sudden we said, 'Hell, this isn't a Miami team, this is a South Florida team.' So we undertook the job—by incorporating as South Florida Big League Baseball—to move the sales pitch from Miami to South Florida, which immediately more than doubled the appreciation of what this community was all about. No longer were we just Miami and the vision of *Miami Vice* and Cuban refugees and riots. We were in fact South Florida, a blended community of almost four and a half million people. And that was our first strategy, to sell South Florida as opposed to Miami."

The earliest expansion document in Blosser's file is a scrap of notebook paper on which is scribbled the names of four South Florida counties—Palm Beach, Broward, Dade and Monroe—and their populations. Together they total 4.1 million, or one-third of the entire state. Of that number, the vast majority live in a narrow, Chile-like strip of superconcentrated humanity stretching 85 miles along I-95 from West Palm Beach in the north to Miami in the south. East is the Atlantic Ocean, west are the Everglades. In some places the straight line from sea to swamp is no more than 15 miles long. "There is literally no green space," Blosser says excitedly, pointing at South Florida on the map. "Just one big metropolis. And Joe Robbie Stadium is right in the middle of all that."

When Huizenga and his advisers first sat down and began to make projections of revenues and expenses, they aimed low, for two reasons. First of all, that is Wayne's way. "If he could feel comfortable that baseball would work with conservative numbers, then in his mind he knew there was still some fairly significant upside from there," says Matt. "It made him more comfortable doing the deal." But it was also a tactical decision. Huizenga knew that he had to convince baseball that he was a capable businessman, a partner they could count on. "We didn't want to go into the presentation with real optimistic projections," says Matt, "and take the risk of the other owners looking at this and saying, 'There's so much blue sky in these numbers, it's ridiculous,' and lose credibility."

On the revenue side, Huizenga and his advisers made two key assumptions. One, that attendance would be strong—about two and a half million the first year (good for about $21 million), and settling down around two million ($19 million) once the novelty wore off. That was high—the major league average in 1992 was 2,148,933—but not outrageous, as shown by later developments. Months before opening day the Marlins already had sold some 16,000 season tickets, only two-thirds as many as the Rockies but enough to put them within reach of their initial projections.

The other assumption Huizenga made was more problematic—that revenues from the Major League Baseball central fund, currently running around $15 million per team, would continue to grow in the years to come. The big variable in central-fund revenues is television money. In the summer of 1990, those numbers still looked good. Baseball, basketball and football had all signed record-setting deals within the last 18 months, and the networks had not yet begun to complain about how much money they were losing. Today, though, CBS and ESPN are predicting combined losses approaching $500 million over the life of their baseball contracts, both of which expire prior to the 1994 season. Conventional wisdom has it that next time baseball will have to settle for less.

But Matt, for one, still sees room for growth. "If you go back through cycles," he says, "networks always whine, then when the next [contract] comes along it's for more money than the one before. It's true, they're coming off a higher base this time. And the market is fractionalized, so maybe this one really will go down. But we've got a couple years for the economy to recover, and things can be done to enhance the value of the television packages. An easy way is to expand the playoffs." Or with interleague play, which Huizenga strongly favors. "I think they need more of that interleague play, I really do," says Huizenga. "I know the purists and traditionalists don't like that but I think they've got to do whatever they can to keep it interesting for the fans."

As for local media—cable, free TV and English- and Spanish-language radio—Huizenga was conservative to a fault, forecasting only $8.5 million. In reality, the Marlins will take in $13.5 million their first season. If and when St. Petersburg gets a team and the Marlins lose their statewide monopoly, local media revenues would be affected. But not in such a way that the balance sheet would suffer, given how high the numbers already are. "Stations got caught up in the enthusiasm over expansion," says Matt. "The contracts they were able to sign with TV, radio and cable far exceeded projections."

After adding in concessions, stadium advertising, parking and the like, Huizenga and his advisers arrived at a total projected revenue of about $40 million in 1993. After the first year, when the expansion teams become eligible for a cut of the central fund, revenues were expected to rise sharply, reaching $60 million by 1996.

On the expense side, the key variable, of course, is player salaries. Theoretically, an expansion team could build an instant competitor by shopping the free-agent market and drafting high-priced stars left unprotected by the other teams. But the Marlins, like the Rockies, had no plans to do so. Huizenga's pro forma predicted a payroll of $10.1 million in 1993, increasing to $14.6 million by 1996 as the team begins to win and signs more expensive players.

Another big expense for most teams is rent. The Miami Dolphins currently have the worst lease in professional football, an arrangement agreed to by the Robbies largely to satisfy the stadium lenders. But the arrival of the Marlins as summer tenants greatly increases the stadium's cash flow, and has allowed both teams to negotiate what Matt calls "average" leases for their sports. The question is: Why would Huizenga want an "average" lease? After all, another reason why Joe Robbie was content to sign an unfavorable lease was that much of what he paid out as tenant came back to him as landlord, in the form of increased equity in the stadium. It's also not a bad way to save money on taxes, by making sure the Dolphins don't show too large a profit. Presumably, Huizenga would benefit from a similar arrangement.

But, strange as it seems, Huizenga doesn't want to do that because he may not want to play at Joe Robbie Stadium forever. As assets, the stadium and the team complement each other nicely. Assuming things work out, the upside potential is enormous. On the other hand, if things don't work out—if it turns out to be too hot during the summer to play baseball at Joe Robbie Stadium, or if it rains too much—then Huizenga has a problem. The weather in South Florida has always made the other owners nervous, so much so that Huizenga was forced to commit himself in writing to build a roof over Joe Robbie Stadium if need be. But he has another option. He could decide to move, perhaps to a new stadium farther north in Broward County. Which is why the Marlins signed only a five-year lease at Joe Robbie Stadium.

"From Wayne's point of view, yeah, it would obviously cost him something from the standpoint of his ownership in Robbie Stadium if he moved to a baseball-only facility," says Matt, "but theoretically he wouldn't do that unless the benefit to him outweighed the hit he would take on his investment in Robbie Stadium. He's perfectly positioned in that respect. As silly as this may sound, five million [his equity in the stadium] is not the end of the world to Wayne Huizenga. Even if he lost that five million dollars it's not going to make him lie awake at night."

Accounting, then, for player payroll, stadium rent, a top-flight scouting department (approximately $3.5 million, which is high) and the various other costs of operating a major league team, total projected expenses came to $35 million in 1993, on their way to $45 million by year four. Measured against revenues, that translates into a first-year profit of $5 million, on its way to $15 million by 1996. On that basis, Huizenga decided to go forward.

"Potentially," says Matt, "I think [Miami] is the best second-tier market in baseball," meaning everything outside New York, Chicago, Los Angeles and Toronto. "The market is big to begin with, it's growing like gangbusters, and right now there's no competition in the state of Florida for Major League

Baseball, though that may change over time. He should make money on operations in Miami. Absolutely."

BESIDES WAYNE, there were two other groups vying to represent the region: one led by New York financier Morton Davis and the other by Abel Holtz, a Cuban immigrant who founded Miami's Capital Bank, the largest minority-owned bank in the country. Davis's group was a late entrant, hastily organized and underfinanced; it was Holtz that Wayne had to worry about. A darling of the downtown establishment (2nd Avenue in Miami is Abel Holtz Boulevard), Holtz enjoyed the backing of powerful city councillor Victor DeYurre. The key to Holtz's bid was the city's promise, backed by DeYurre, to build a baseball-only stadium on the waterfront in downtown Miami, easily accessible to Miami's vast, baseball-crazy Cuban population.

Holtz, unlike Huizenga, is an avid baseball fan. His father was in the tannery business before the revolution; as a child, Holtz would sometimes accompany his father on business trips to New York, where he remembers seeing Mel Ott play at the Polo Grounds. He once tried to buy the Seattle Mariners from George Argyros (Argyros later sold to Jeff Smulyan), and early on he was talking to Joe Robbie about joining forces to go after an expansion team for Miami. After Robbie died, Holtz followed up with Huizenga—until the day Huizenga called from London to say that he had just closed on the stadium deal. With Huizenga committed to Joe Robbie Stadium, Holtz went his own way. "I was convinced and I am convinced," says Holtz, "that [Joe Robbie Stadium] is not going to work."

When Holtz thinks about playing baseball in a converted football stadium twelve miles north of Dade County's central core on always congested I-95, he sees nothing but problems. He thinks the sight lines for baseball are lousy, with so many seats strung out parallel to the foul lines instead of pointing in toward the pitcher's mound or home plate. He thinks the heat will be unbearable. "Joe Robbie Stadium was built for football in winter," he says. "You have no cross-ventilation whatsoever.

It's a complete concrete-enclosed situation." And above all he thinks the location is all wrong.

"Who are the most people in the community that are going to be attending baseball?" he asks, speaking from his spectacular all-white office on Brickell Avenue, overlooking Biscayne Bay. "In our opinion, it's going to be, one, the Latins. Ninety percent of them live south and west of Flagler Street, which is the opposite exactly of where the stadium is. Two, the retired people in Miami Beach. These people were raised in New York, in Boston, in Baltimore. They love baseball. But how are they going to get to Joe Robbie Stadium? There is no rapid transit, there is no easy way to park, there is no easy way to get there. And the third group is the black community. We figure that for the black community, it's going to be very expensive for them because of the driving distance from downtown.

"There is one good argument against my theory: that because [Joe Robbie Stadium] is closer to Broward and Palm Beach County, they will attract enough people from those counties to offset the people from Dade County who will not go. That's a good argument. But the market will tell."

Holtz and Huizenga weren't simply talking about two different markets; more like two different worlds. Miami, with its 1 million Hispanic residents and 400,000 blacks out of a total population of 2 million; and South Florida, with twice as many people and a demographic mix weighted more toward affluent white suburbanites—the "blended community," to which Blosser referred. By shifting his focus away from downtown Miami, Huizenga was acting in line with the dominant trend in baseball over the last 30 years. Just as jobs and middle-class families have fled decaying cities, so have new stadiums tended to be built on the outskirts, rather than in the center, to cater to suburban customers. The new generation of downtown ballparks may seem to buck the trend, but that's an illusion. As Peter Richmond observed in the *National Sports Daily*, previewing the new Comiskey Park, "Never have city and stadium been so detached from each other: The garages will attach to the park by elevated walkways, and thus fans who arrive by car will have the privilege of never actually setting foot on the South Side of Chicago."

"My feeling is that Joe Robbie Stadium sits in the middle of two million people to the south and two million people to the north but there's nothing around the stadium, no base," says Councillor DeYurre. "The key word is Miami, and this thing about regionalizing the concept doesn't really work."

To which Tim Robbie, speaking from his office at Joe Robbie Stadium, responds: "That's the old downtown Miami mentality. The people in the downtown power base don't really recognize the scope of South Florida. This is a lot bigger than they would like to see that it is. You can go from here to Palm Beach and it's wall-to-wall people and we're right in the middle of it. Downtown Miami doesn't run this community anymore."

THE TURNING POINT for Wayne, when he not only knocked out the local competition but also emerged as the national front-runner, was September 18, 1990, when he introduced himself to the National League expansion committee. All three groups from Miami were among those invited to New York that day to make their pitches. Rather than sit through what everyone assumed would be three identical recitations on the climate and demographics of Miami, the committee members asked first to hear a joint presentation covering all aspects of the market, after which they would consider the specifics of each competing bid. It was an innocent request, but one fraught with political implications, which Wayne was quick to exploit.

Holtz may have thought he had the inside track, what with Miami mayor Javier Suarez and Cheryl Hudson, president of the Miami Chamber of Commerce (who also happened to be Holtz's accountant), both scheduled to take part in the neutral presentation. But the task of scripting the presentation, and with it defining the market, was assigned to the Beacon Council, a regional economic-development organization chaired by the President's son, Jeb Bush.

"We said, 'No, it can't be a Miami presentation, it has to be a

South Florida presentation,' " says Blosser, the coordinator of Huizenga's effort. "If it were a Miami presentation, we couldn't be part of it. So we had some very serious discussions —negotiations—with the Beacon Council to cast off their perspective of just Miami and Dade County and take on the perspective of South Florida."

In the end, what was supposed to have been a nondenominational ode to Miami was really all about South Florida, precisely as Huizenga defined the market. Even Mayor Suarez wound up saying that he didn't care where the team played, as long as it was in Dade County. Holtz, when he found out about Suarez's betrayal, was stunned.

By the time Huizenga and the four members of his party— Blosser; Don Smiley, a Blockbuster executive; Glen Monn, the stadium manager at Joe Robbie Stadium; and Rick Deflon, an architect from Hellmuth, Obata & Kassabaum, which designed Joe Robbie Stadium—entered the windowless conference room at Willkie, Farr & Gallagher, the committee members were already primed to accept Wayne's bid.

Wayne and his entourage took their places around the U-shaped conference table. Of course they had a video to show the committee (shot on film for higher quality, then converted to video), and a stack of fancy leave-behind books (bound in imitation white leather and printed at a price that came to "more than my first house," according to Smiley), but all of that was icing, whereas Wayne was the cake.

Wayne didn't exactly walk in there cold. Most of the expansion hopefuls who would shake hands with chairman Danforth that day were meeting him for the first time; Wayne was renewing an acquaintanceship. Wayne knew Doug Danforth from having sat with him in the owner's box at Three Rivers Stadium in Pittsburgh. They met through Carl Barger, who worked for Danforth as president of the Pirates and also happened to be Wayne's closest friend in the world, a golf buddy and bridge partner from way back as well as a member of the board of Blockbuster Entertainment. That helped. It helped, too, that even those in the room who had never met Wayne before at least knew who he was, through Blockbuster's role as exclusive distributor of Major League Baseball videos.

By all accounts, Wayne was charming, forceful, a one-man show. He took care of both the intro and the closing argument, stepping aside long enough to let others tout the group's secondary assets—the South Florida market, Joe Robbie Stadium—then resuming his place at center stage for a brief discussion of South Florida's principal asset—himself.

Speaking to the committee members that day, Wayne talked about the fortunes he had made with Waste Management and Blockbuster, about his knack for spotting winners, and about his resources and his willingness to commit. To their eyes, he wasn't being boastful or showy, just giving them the straight dope. He said he would be happy to find a partner, or partners, if that's what baseball wanted, but at the same time he assured them that no such partner was needed, that even at $95 million he was prepared to do this deal alone. With cash, that was key; he promised to sell stock, rather than borrow, in order to meet his obligations. And toward the end of the allotted half hour, as he was handing over a copy of the presentation book to Danforth, he jokingly offered to write a check for the full amount then and there. Danforth chuckled, but he got the point. Summing up, Wayne said: "I've been lucky throughout my life by being in the right place at the right time, and I believe that this is the right place at the right time. I'll be a good person for you to do business with."

The owners were impressed as hell. Wayne came across as if he was already one of them, someone they knew, someone they liked, someone they could trust. Not only "knowledgeable" and "successful," as Danforth would later recall, but "a conservative guy and a nice guy." Or, as Bill Giles of the Phillies would describe him, after he replaced the Astros' McMullen on the expansion committee, "a solid man, not flamboyant, a steady-as-a-rock kind of guy."

And if, too, when they looked in his eyes (blue, cold, hard) they were reminded, as others have been, that a guy like

Wayne doesn't get as far as he has by *always* being a nice guy; that he appeared to be one among those people in the world who live by the creed that what matters most about money is that you have it, not what you had to do to get it; that, basically, he would be the kind of guy who knows how to play hardball—well, so much the better, welcome to the lodge, he was bound to fit right in.

"I think you can take everything this community did," Tom Ferguson, the former president of the Beacon Council, would conclude after all was said and done, "and everything that all the activists did, and you can boil it all down to one reason why we got Major League Baseball in Miami, and it's Wayne Huizenga. They like Wayne Huizenga. I don't know what it takes to get in their club of owners besides money but they look for certain qualities, and whatever those qualities are, he filled the bill."

By the end of the day, Wayne must have looked like a winner, even to those who were formally uncommitted up to that point. For among those accepting a free ride home on the Blockbuster jet were several members of the group that gave the neutral presentation, including Ron Frazier (whose job it had been to talk about the weather), Cheryl Hudson from the Miami Chamber of Commerce and Ferguson from the Beacon Council. "He offered," explains Ferguson, somewhat sheepishly, "and if you had the chance to fly back on his plane instead of commercial, you would. I think everyone felt that we had really put our best foot forward. When we came back from New York, we were all feeling pretty damn good."

Three months later, to no one's surprise, Wayne's group made the short list of six expansion finalists. That took care of the competition in Miami, leaving Wayne to worry about St. Petersburg and Orlando, the two other finalists from Florida. One of the three—but only one—was all but assured of winning a franchise.

THERE ARE SEVERAL WAYS to reach the St. Petersburg peninsula by car, some of them across the bay, some of them around it, each one a hassle in its own way. The most traveled

one, favored by tourists and commuters alike, is the Howard
Franklin Bridge, I-275, which crosses over from Tampa.
Tampa Bay looks lovely from the Howard Franklin—all blue
and sparkling and cool—but looks lie. The blue water is too
polluted for all but the most determined swimmers. And besides, it's full of sharks who follow the big ships up into the bay
from the Gulf of Mexico, eating the garbage that gets tossed
overboard.

Just across the bridge is a landmark billboard which for
many people is their first and most lasting impression of St.
Petersburg. "All Faiths Memorial Gardens" it says in bold
black print on a white background:

Cremation       $249
Direct Burial   $299
Shipping        $395

For years, St. Petersburg was a place where old people came
to die. Its most distinctive urban features were the rows and
rows of green benches, filled with rows and rows of retirees
whispering with the palm trees on the sidewalks of Central
Avenue. Most of the benches are gone now, and there's no
question that the city's demographics are changing—more
young people, more families. Still, it's hard to think of St. Petersburg as a real city, much less a home to Major League
Baseball. One joke making the rounds is that if St. Pete ever
does get a team, they ought to call it the Black Sox and San-
dals, in honor of the fashion-unconscious snowbirds who flock
here every winter.

Leaving the highway, heading toward downtown St. Petersburg on Central Avenue, one passes block after block of low-
rent businesses—the Wig Villa, the Emerald Cocktail, the
Young Women's Residence Thrift Store. So many plaster-and-
glass storefronts, each supporting a chunky marquee which
makes a patch of shade on the sidewalk. Suddenly, half a mile
from where Central dead-ends at Tampa Bay, a great gray
dome rises at the edge of an empty parking lot, its white-
ribbed top tipped over like an inverted satellite dish, pointing
northeast, away from the sun.

Inside, the brand-new Florida Suncoast Dome is being made ready, not for a ball game, but for a horse show. The 45,000 blue plastic seats are empty, bathed in the greenhouse light of the translucent dome. The concrete floor is covered with sawdust. A little behind and to the right of where the pitcher's mound ought to be, workers are assembling a horse jump propped up by two plastic killer whales.

By the time it's all paid for in 2016, the taxpayers of Pinellas County will have spent $234,164,931 on the Florida Suncoast Dome—assuming, that is, it remains empty. If a baseball team should ever decide to move in, somebody will have to come up with another $30 million to install the artificial playing surface and build dugouts, locker rooms and luxury boxes. Meanwhile, it costs $1.7 million a year just to keep the place open and available for rock concerts, basketball games, tennis matches, tractor pulls and, yes, horse shows.

The man who has made St. Petersburg's quest for baseball a personal crusade, who more than any other person is responsible for building the dome and probably feels most deeply the pain of repeated disappointments, is Rick Dodge, the assistant city manager. Dodge works out of a tall-ceilinged office in St. Petersburg's elegant stone city building, a few blocks east of the dome. On this late-spring afternoon the windows are open and the ceiling fan is turning. The walls are covered with paintings, the work of an artist friend who asked Dodge one night over drinks, "If you could have dinner with anybody who ever lived, who would that be?" Dodge, a man with eclectic tastes, could think of lots of people, and now all of them are hanging in his office: Thomas Edison, Joan Baez, Mark Twain, Louis Armstrong, Beethoven, Elvis ("that was a joke") and Dizzy Gillespie. On his desk is a bronze statuette of the Nike of Samothrace, a third-century-B.C. Greek sculpture popularly known as "Winged Victory," a reminder of what he's still waiting for.

Dodge is not your typical civil servant. An elegant dresser who favors monogrammed white shirts and a gold watch, he speaks with dignified, measured words, tinged with a trace of defiance to go with his jutting chin. When he is asked why St.

Petersburg aspires to be a big league city, his response is heart-felt and quick.

"Sport is one of the few things in life that transcends all strata of the community," he says. "It is one of the few things left in society that ties us together, regardless of race, economic standing or gender. You can go into New York's airport having an appointment downtown with an investment banker, and talk to the skycap, the cabdriver, the secretary and eventually the president of the investment bank about how the Mets are doing. I think that in cultures that are so fragmented nowadays, those kinds of bonding elements are particularly important. I think people have a great desire and need to have that. So that's the first point.

"Two, it is a driving factor for cities to compete for other pieces of the pie. If you are trying to relocate a General Motors plant or a major law firm or something else, the kinds of sporting events a town has are a very strong draw. Then focusing that down a little closer, what happens in terms of the economic spin-off itself? I have read probably fifty economic-impact evaluations and there's a variety of credibility given to all of them. But I think the most conservative view of the economic impact of a baseball franchise is about fifty million dollars annually, up to a high of about a hundred forty million annually. It's a nonpolluting industry with a big payroll and it provides a lot of jobs—directly within the confines of the franchise, secondary jobs at the stadium, and third-level jobs in support industries and restaurants and bars and transportation and cabdrivers and all that.

"Then we have down here on our waterfront about a hundred-million-dollar renovation of a hotel. They basically did that believing that we were going to score in baseball. Down the street, the Women's Tennis Association moved here from Miami in the belief that this is an emerging and vital area. We have a major developer doing a six-block development, with about thirty-five million dollars in it to date, again believing that the kind of people that baseball can bring are encouragement enough for them to step up to the risk.

"Granted, there are a whole lot of other issues in the community that are probably more important—health care, water quality, transportation, education. But you know, in our area, the only thing that brought this region together—Clearwater, Tampa and St. Pete—the first and only thing that did that was the pursuit of baseball. We're going to succeed or fail as a region, not as separate towns. And that realization has been made that much more poignantly clear to us by expansion."

"Say it ain't so!" was the headline in the *St. Petersburg Times* on June 11, 1991, the day after baseball formally announced it was passing over St. Petersburg in favor of Miami and Denver. For a while later that fall it looked as if the Seattle Mariners might be coming instead, but then Japanese corporate giant Nintendo came out of nowhere and put that rumor to rest. Next up were the Giants, and that was close. As had happened just four years before with the White Sox, a deal was signed and a lease was prepared. But then San Francisco rallied, a local buyer emerged, and the other owners voted to make the Giants stay put.

Dodge is no fool. He knows why the new Comiskey Park in Chicago is sometimes called the House That Dodge Built. And he understands the role his city has played in helping not just the White Sox but plenty of other teams, too, to play the field and gain leverage back home. "If you look at facts," Dodge says, "Ueberroth announced the criteria for expansion, and then suddenly they invited everybody to New York to make presentations, and then after that everybody in baseball who wanted to renegotiate their lease did so. It was pretty clear to any businessman that that was a show of strength to put pressure on local communities to reopen leases for negotiation, and that's what's happened. Oakland renegotiated, Minnesota renegotiated, Kansas City renegotiated. I mean, it was because a demand was demonstrated, and people were put on notice."

So does he feel used?

Dodge is silent for a long moment. "Unless you offered a truly viable competitive alternative," he says finally, "nobody would bother using it. You don't see anybody threatening to move to Buffalo. Is it better to be in the position of first in line and the most viable alternative? Or not even mentioned, and not even pursued, and not even in the game? The moves are almost sickeningly familiar about what you do to get what you want. It's become sort of a courting ritual that communities have suffered through. You only do it because you see it as having value. It's a game of leverage and those that are competing on the outside have none, except to offer their wares in the most attractive way. My only dream in life is to come back and for once in my life have leverage in a deal."

The ownership group chosen in December 1990 by the National League expansion committee to represent St. Petersburg was Sunshine State Baseball Associates. It was headed by Stephen Porter, a Washington lawyer, and Joel Schur, a businessman who moved to St. Petersburg in 1989 when he and Porter bought the St. Petersburg Cardinals of the class A Gulf Coast League. The group's principal investors were the Kohl brothers, Sidney and Allen, whose middle brother, Herbert, is a U.S. senator from Wisconsin. Herbert Kohl also owns the Milwaukee Bucks. A lot of people in St. Petersburg, Dodge included, were surprised when baseball picked the Sunshine group over other groups with stronger local ties. But baseball was impressed by the Kohls' commitment to put up $50 million for baseball. However, the Kohls reportedly backed away from their $50 million cash commitment, opting to finance the deal instead. Because of that—and *only* because of that, Dodge believes—St. Petersburg lost its franchise.

"The 'Wayne Huizenga' in the group walked from the deal and didn't tell us," Dodge says. "He jumped off the building and took us with him. The guy went from a fifty-million-dollar player to a five-million-dollar player, and with that went our franchise. It was particularly galling because it was a group *they* picked. Baseball picked the jockey for our horse, and then when the jockey failed, we lost."

Sidney Kohl denies he backed away from the deal, insisting to this day that the plan of finance which he submitted was approved by baseball. "That's not what I hear from everybody on the committee," says Dodge. "I talked to people on the committee whom I know well. I talked to his own partners. They told me the guy took a forty-five-million-dollar walk.

That breaks the fundamental code of what those guys look at. It wasn't just the money, it was the guy's commitment and word that got withdrawn. It violated one of the basic principles—'Are you one of the guys?'

"If you've got the stadium and the capacity to draw. If you've got the market, if you've got the corporate support, if you've got the fan base, if you've got all those ingredients, that's the ante to get in the game. But what separates it out then is not those ingredients. It's how they feel about the financial capacity and the character of the individuals that they're going to welcome in the family."

A year after the fact, Dodge describes the mood that descended on his community as a "malaise." "I think the feeling here had to be so much stronger than in Buffalo or Washington, it was just so . . . not to overdo it, but you ask your parents where they were when they heard Pearl Harbor was bombed. You ask people in this community where they were when they heard about baseball. We spent a lot of money and twelve years doing exactly what we were told to do. Exactly. And paying the dues. So I think it's also revamped people's thinking about what communities need to do to win." And then Dodge paraphrases Al Capone: "In this world you can get a long way with a smile, but you get farther with a smile and a gun."

As for the Marlins, Dodge has no plans to become a fan. "I think Miami has all the ingredients to deserve a baseball franchise," he concedes. "But they know that they're not going to be Florida's team. People outside the state of Florida think this is like Connecticut where you can see from one border to the other. But there are ethnic differences, cultural differences. We're worlds apart, and we're five hours apart. The Marlins will not be successful in marketing baseball as Florida's team for the west coast of Florida. There's strong feelings among the people here that the area was screwed."

("You know what?" says a Suncoast Dome employee who doesn't want his name to appear in print. "I'm praying that it rains every day in Miami. I'm not lying, man, I pray it rains every day they have games. I hope they have twenty percent rainouts. Hey, go ahead and play in Joe Robbie Stadium in the summer, go ahead. Just wait till those sudden storms roll up on you. And the heat! Not even at night do you want to sit out there.")

Meanwhile, the empty dome waits. A brooding, overwhelming presence in the middle of St. Petersburg, a daily reminder of the public debt, of the public's children's debt, and for Dodge personally, of failure. "There is nothing more humbling in the world than carrying around people's hopes and dreams in your pocket," he says. "That's not something that puffs you out. I don't mean to overplay my role, but when people look at you it's the kind of look they reserve only for surgeons in emergency rooms taking care of their children. 'Are we gonna get baseball?' It means so much to them. I'm not selfless, don't get me wrong. But you want this for the community. You want it because they've worked so hard and waited so long. You want it for them. As for me, when it happens, then I walk away. I'm released.

"I don't know if you've ever read any Camus, *The Myth of Sisyphus?* Sisyphus was a Greek who died and made a deal with the gods to go back and see his wife. And he got back to earth and kissed his wife, held his children, smelled the air, tasted water, touched the ground. And it was too sweet, he refused to come back. And the gods were pissed, they had to go back and get him. As his punishment, he was given this huge boulder on a mountain. And it took all of his effort to move this boulder up the mountain. And when he gets to the top of the mountain, there's no place for the boulder to rest, so it comes back down. So Sisyphus through eternity has to roll this boulder. Camus says at the end, 'Don't feel sad for Sisyphus,' for three reasons. One, it was his choice. Two, it's his rock. And three, in the time that he walks down the mountain, before he picks up his burden again, he is victorious over the gods.

"I'd like the sense of walking down that mountain, knowing that I don't have to pick up the rock again."

PAT WILLIAMS knows all about expansion, and not just because he helped bring the NBA's Orlando Magic to town three years ago. Williams has 14 children, and 10 of them are adopted.

"Fourteen kids!" says a visitor, the father of one daughter. "I can't conceive of that."

"I can't either," says Williams. "We got two Korean girls eight years ago, then twin Korean boys five years ago. Four Filipino brothers three and a half years ago, and two Romanian daughters kind of six months apart last year. And my wife's in Guatemala right now looking for more, which is scary. I'm not sure where it all ends."

Pat Williams, the general manager of the Magic, has had a busy day. A good chunk of it was spent in his office at the Orlando Civic Center. After work he drove at (or perhaps just above) the speed limit across this clean, green central Florida city—where even the buses have flowers painted all over them —to the local Christian Academy, where two of his boys, the catcher and the second baseman, are playing ball today. After an inning or two, Williams got back in his car and drove home, where two more kids were waiting—already in uniform—for their dad to give them a lift to a Little League game. Once those two were where they had to be, Williams headed back to the first game. In between he fielded calls on his car phone and tried to explain why he thinks Orlando, one of six finalists but a surprise to most people—almost a joke—ever really had a chance.

"Maybe we're all brainwashed here in Orlando," says Williams, who has the lean, almost gaunt look of a long-distance runner. "Let me put it this way. Orlando was on a roll and everything we had attempted was coming true. We had made the run at the Magic in the NBA and that had happened. The airport, the civic center, I mean, Orlando's on a roll. The power of Disney, I think, had given us all a great sense of self-confidence. The baseball effort we cranked up in '87. Everybody down this way was sure it was going to happen in St. Petersburg. Miami wasn't a factor. Orlando was not even considered. But we got into it. We argued that we had the strongest owner financially. We were in the fastest-growing area of America. We were going to build a modern-day Wrigley Field, the finest ballpark in the country. The future of Florida is here. Central location opens up the whole state. Number-one tourist spot in the world. On and on and on. All of those arguments, which we thought were very convincing, we believed. And I guess we thought that everybody else should believe them."

Originally it was William DuPont who was going to put up the money to buy a baseball team. DuPont started the Magic, and later bought Orlando's Southern League AA franchise, the SunRays. Had Orlando won a major league franchise, it would have been called the SunRays, too, and worn the yellow, black and red uniform the minor league SunRays wear today. But by August 1990, DuPont had pulled himself out of the picture, leaving Orlando in the same predicament faced by Denver—just days away from the application deadline, still looking for somebody who wasn't spooked by $95 million. "They set the price high and made the terms tough, I think halfway not caring if nobody could do it," says Williams. "They could not have set up tougher criteria to get in. We were hoping against hope that it wouldn't be that high. It was terrifying."

After DuPont pulled out, Williams had to scramble to find a replacement. A friend (Bobby Richardson, the former second baseman for the New York Yankees) suggested he speak to Rich DeVos, the billionaire co-founder of Amway. It took a while, but finally, on the Thursday before Labor Day, Williams found himself at Amway headquarters in Ada, Michigan, in a room with DeVos, trying to sell a salesman on buying a baseball team. DeVos let Williams talk for an hour, then asked him if he wouldn't mind waiting outside. Ten minutes later, DeVos called Williams back in. "Mail my name in," DeVos said. "I'll walk downstream with you and see what happens." It was a soft commitment—basically, DeVos agreed to put up the $100,000 application fee—but at least it kept Orlando in the game.

Williams, by nature an energetic promoter, worked hard to separate Orlando from the rest of the pack. He named his top baseball people, brothers Brian and Denny Doyle, and his manager, Bob Boone, long before he had a team for them to run. And he tried hard to put a positive spin on Orlando's obvious deficiencies. If Orlando is only the 23rd-largest television market in the United States, well, Williams wants you to know that it's up from fortysomething only a few years back. Population not exactly overwhelming? Go out a hundred-mile radius (which, by the way, takes in Tampa and St. Petersburg) and it's bigger than any other city in the Southeast, Atlanta included. "Our argument," says Williams, was: " 'Guys, have some vision, look to the future, the future of Florida is here. Ten years from now you'll look back and say it was the right choice.'

"Miami is very fearful of Orlando. You gotta understand the whole history of this state. For decades the state was Miami, that was all there was here. All the tourism, everything went there. Then twenty years ago Disney ended up here, and central Florida was completely transformed. This now is the destination spot, and it has impacted South Florida enormously. Suddenly there's a great tension, there's a rivalry over many issues. I think the business community has a great respect and fear of Orlando. The media pokes fun at us, still thinks we have no shoes on. My buddy [*Miami Herald* columnist] Dave Barry is constantly hammering at us, calls natives up here Orlandoids, describes all of us as low-foreheaded, nose-picking yahoos."

It was partly that perception that Orlando was never able to shake. On the day Williams got the bad news from National League president Bill White, Williams begged White for an explanation. " 'Can you tell me why?' " I asked him. " 'Just tell me why.' White talked for a while, but the one line that I do remember, he said, 'When we took our helicopter trip over Miami, we saw housetops. When we took our helicopter trip over Orlando, we saw a lot more treetops.' I wish I had had the presence of mind to say, 'Yeah, but, Bill, underneath the treetops were housetops.' "

DeVos, by far the wealthiest potential buyer considered by baseball—worth $2.5 billion according to the latest list in *Forbes* magazine, the 16th-wealthiest person in the United States—

was nevertheless reluctant to commit his family fortune to baseball. By March 1991, after the final round of visits by the expansion committee, at a time when a decision was imminent, DeVos was still wavering. "Huizenga had come out of the blocks early," says Williams, "very aggressively, 'I'll do the deal.' He dispelled all their fears. There was no negotiation, no quibbling over price. He came right out and was bullish, so that impressed them, obviously. The rest of us, all of us, the other five, were always nervous with price. We thought the deal could be improved, we thought the numbers would get better. Financially the deal never made sense to any of us. You run your revenues and run your expense items, you know, the deal doesn't work. If *we* couldn't make it work as a good business deal, how could anybody else? Well, Huizenga wiped all that out by committing to them early. He never quarreled or quibbled. He'd make the deal from day one."

Williams went back to DeVos in March and gave him another pitch. He told him he believed baseball was potentially a billion-dollar asset, that if it had risen in value ten times over in the last ten years, he didn't see any reason why it couldn't rise another ten times in the next ten years. And DeVos bought it, and finally did commit. But by then it was too late. "They did not have a solid feeling about us in that regard," says Williams. "They loved DeVos and liked what he could do, but it was never a case of him saying, 'I'll write the check.'

"Had Denver's ownership not been right and they couldn't get comfortable with it, I am convinced beyond a shadow of a doubt that they'd have gone to Miami and Orlando. What else could they have done? At that point they had two that would make the deal. It wasn't St. Petersburg or Buffalo or Washington, forget that."

Phillies owner Bill Giles, a member of the National League expansion committee, confirms Williams's belief that Orlando may well have been the committee's alternative choice. "There were three ownership groups that at least I felt definitely had the money," says Giles, "Orlando being the other one. Washington, Buffalo and St. Petersburg, as far as the ownership situation goes, all three of those were a bit weak." Still, says

Giles, Orlando was "not real serious because the market isn't there yet. I think Orlando will be a player if we ever expand again or somebody ever moves. Orlando's certainly a candidate."

"In my judgment Coors saved the bacon," says Williams. "I think it came right down to that issue. Coors came in and Denver's advantages then became too hard to overcome, because the one problem of ownership was resolved. In the final analysis, it was: Who can write the check? And who can keep writing them? That's even more important. If and when the losses start mounting up, who can keep this thing afloat? Basically, it was, you know: 'Write us your check, baby, on the date we say, and we don't want to hear from you anymore.' It's not like there was a hand-holding process. They were saying, 'We're beating you up real good, with the price, with the terms, no TV money, and we're not cutting you any breaks on the players you're going to get.' I mean, they really created a tough deal. And they don't want any whining or whimpering or remorse.

" 'Who can make the deal and keep writing the checks, and who do we never have to worry about?' That's my read."

ON JUNE 10, 1991—following nine months of mysterious deliberations dating back to September 1990, when applications were first filed—the four members of the National League expansion committee disclosed that they had chosen Denver and Miami to receive new National League franchises. The matter was now in the hands of the ownership committee. A ratifying vote by all 26 National and American League owners was expected soon, possibly at the owners meeting June 12–13 in Santa Monica, California.

That meeting, which took place at a hotel overlooking a beach populated by runners, roller skaters and homeless people, should have been a happy occasion, a time for the baseball lodge brothers to toast their two newest members, but it was not. Despite the genteel surroundings—the potted palms, the wicker furniture, the tuxedoed man tinkling "Take Me Out to the Ball Game" on the lobby piano—the mood was sour.

Once, when a newsman from Channel 8 in Tampa pointed his camera at NL president Bill White, White stuck his fist in the lens—"Look, I don't need my picture taken, okay?"—an in-your-face to the already battered fans of Tampa and St. Petersburg.

The immediate cause of much of the moping was the recent decision by Commissioner Fay Vincent to share some portion of the expansion fees with the American League. The National League said, "We're not sharing the money, it's never been shared before." The American League said, "Yeah, but nobody ever talked about money big enough to share before, and you need our consent to expand." In the end, it may have been the players union that forced the issue. Under the terms of the Basic Agreement, the league needs the union's approval for any plan to allocate players in an expansion draft. The union, according to one of its officials, wanted the players to come from both leagues rather than one.

"Essentially it meant more players that were close to the major leagues would move to the expansion teams rather than going down into the depths of the AA players," says the union official, "and we think it's in everybody's interest to have stronger teams faster. In the end we sent them over a plan, and told the commissioner's office and the league office this is the only player allocation plan we will approve. Either vote this one up or down or there won't be any expansion." That gave Vincent the excuse he needed, the theory goes, to divide the expansion moneys between the two leagues—$3 million to each AL team, $12.4 million to each NL team—a move which satisfied no one.

Denver and Miami overcame the second hurdle on the way to final approval on Wednesday morning, June 12. "The ownership committee, as almost all of you know, had the matter of the expansion cities on our agenda for today, in order to pass upon the qualifications of the ownership group in Denver and the ownership group in Miami," said the committee chairman, Cardinals owner Fred Kuhlman, shortly after lunch. "The ownership committee unanimously agreed to recommend to the National League owners and the American League owners the approval of the ownership groups in both Denver and Miami. That is basically the report of the ownership committee. The ownership committee's function is completed. The matter is now in the hands of the expansion committee and the leagues themselves. . . . The two leagues will meet this afternoon, and the recommendations of the expansion committee with regard to these two cities will be presented to the ownership in both leagues."

"Is this the last big hurdle?" a reporter asked.

"No, I don't think so. This was a hurdle. The last hurdle is the approval by the ownership in the respective leagues of the expansion committee's recommendation of the two sites. That still is the major question to be resolved. As far as I know, it's the only question left."

Later in the lobby, vice chairman Eddie Einhorn of the White Sox gave a hint of why that last hurdle might be difficult to overcome, at least here in Santa Monica. Einhorn, like many in the American League, was still mad at Vincent for the way he chose to allocate the expansion windfall. "We are prisoners of a system," he said, "where the only way right now of expressing displeasure is through the voting system."

The leagues met separately that afternoon. And at 6:30 that evening, Dr. Bobby Brown, president of the American League, stood at the podium in the pressroom. "Both the National and the American League discussed the recommendations of the expansion and ownership committees at their respective league meetings," Brown said. "While generally supportive of those recommendations, the American League has asked for more time to study a number of issues raised. The decision of the National League is to approve the recommendations of the committees."

"What are the objections?"

"I'll tell you what they're not. We didn't have any real problems with either the sites or the ownership groups. We had some internal issues that we needed to get straightened out and I'm not going to say anything more about those issues. I don't think we'll be ready to vote tomorrow."

"Are the differences mild, moderate or strong?"

"I would say mild. We just need a little bit more time."

"I don't think they're happy with the judgment I made," Vincent later conceded. "I don't want to sound defensive about this, but look, [Pirates owner] Doug Danforth and [Brewers owner] Bud Selig came to me and asked me to make the decision. I made a decision, I'm not going to apologize for it, I did what I thought was right. And the fact that people are unhappy about it cannot come as a surprise. That's too bad. They're unhappy. They will get over it. . . .

"I don't expect any problems, but until it's done, it's not done."

IN TIME, OF COURSE, it got done. And five weeks later, on July 17, at a four-star country-club resort called Turnberry Isle on Dumfounding Bay a few miles up A1A from Miami Beach, Wayne's team was christened. The setting was a ballroom as big as a basketball arena which had been decorated to look like a ballpark; the help wore baseball uniforms. Nearly 1,700 invited guests (including the governor and Jeb Bush, who delivered a telegram from his dad) clapped and cheered and chewed on free hot dogs and deep-fried Cuban tortillas. A full delegation of baseball officialdom down from New York for the day—led by Commissioner Vincent and National League president Bill White—presented Wayne with the charter declaring him a member of the most exclusive rich men's club in North America. Afterward, Wayne unveiled the new logo, a marlin jumping through a hoop. "The marlin is slick, powerful, alert, agile and proud," he explained. And Wayne's buddy Carl Barger, the new president of the Marlins, was heard to utter, perhaps more than once, "We are going to make this a competitive ball club in a hurry!"

It was a happy event—focused as it was on baseball and hope for the future—and as such contrasted sharply with the political war that was about to erupt two thirds of the way across the continent in Denver.

# 5

## Rounding Third

CARL BARGER sucked hard on his Salem, exhaled, and grinned. "I'm a little surprised at where they are compared to where we are," he said. Barger was referring, of course, to the Colorado Rockies. He was speaking in his new capacity as president of the Florida Marlins. Wayne Huizenga had offered Barger the job on July 8, 1991, three days after the franchise winners were announced. Barger quickly said yes, even though he already had a job that he liked—president of the Pirates. Not only that but the Pirates were in a pennant race, on their way to a second straight division championship. Barger, a Pittsburgh lawyer who in 1985 helped organize the public-private consortium that bought the Pirates and kept them from leaving Pittsburgh, had suffered through some pretty dismal seasons. Now that things were looking up, he hated to leave.

So for a while he tried to hold down both jobs. But that made for awkward situations. On July 16, for instance, Barger was in Pittsburgh trying to sign free agent-to-be Bobby Bonilla to a long-term contract, telling United Press International, "No one wants to keep Bobby Bonilla in Pittsburgh more than I do." The very next day he turned up at the Marlins' inaugural bash at Turnberry Isle, where this time he told UPI, "We are going to make this a competitive ball club in a hurry." Hmmmm. Under growing pressure to resolve what was plainly a conflict of interest, Barger resigned his position with the Pirates on August 2 and moved into what was then an otherwise empty office in Fort Lauderdale.

Images of Barger's past and future were contained in the picture frames on the walls. Here an unused 1990 Pirates World Series ticket (they lost to the Reds in the playoffs). There his close friend, Pirates manager Jim Leyland, locked in a pennant-winning embrace with catcher Mike Lavalliere ("Carl, this just about says it all," the inscription read. "You've done great because you love to compete. Forever in friendship, Jim"). And over there, Carl and Wayne posing with a Blockbuster Video floor display—a life-size blowup of Marilyn Monroe with her skirt lifted.

"For example, we have fourteen scouts signed already, and I don't think they have even close to that," Barger continued. Underneath his suit coat he wore a silk tie and a white shirt with his initials monogrammed on the left breast pocket. He spoke in a scratchy, smoke-scarred, somewhat arrogant voice. "I've been surprised at some of their hires. I think [GM Bob] Gebhard's a good hire. I have kind of put my emphasis on the baseball side. They appeared to put more of an emphasis on the [business] side. I wish them nothing but the best. I'm sure they'll catch up in a hurry."

Barger and the rest of the Marlins staff were camped out on the third floor of a low-rise glass office building in downtown Fort Lauderdale. Eventually they would move to Joe Robbie Stadium, halfway between Fort Lauderdale and Miami, but for now they shared office space with Huizenga Holdings. Although today was only November 1, and opening day was still almost a year and a half away, virtually all of the key front-office positions on the Marlins staff were already filled. General manager David Dombrowski, on the job now for six weeks, occupied the other corner office opposite Barger's. In between were some of the high-level baseball men Dombrowski had brought with him from Montreal: Frank Wren, Dombrowski's assistant, absorbed at the moment with the task of computerizing the scouting department; Gary Hughes, the scouting director ("There's people playing now, and we got scouts out there. Got a guy in Long Beach at a game tonight"); and Angel Vasquez, one of the few men in baseball employed full-time as director of Latin American operations, preoccupied just now with hiring scouts in the Dominican Republic and Puerto Rico. Cookie Rojas and Whitey Lockman, two veteran major league scouts, whose duties would keep them on the road for much of the coming summer, were already on the payroll. And later today, John Boles, another Expos alumnus, would join the Marlins as farm director.

In Colorado, by contrast, Gebhard was only now beginning to focus full-time on the Rockies. Although he had signed on just five days after Dombrowski, Gebhard, formerly an assistant under GM Andy MacPhail in Minnesota, elected to finish the season with the Twins, who wound up winning the World Series in seven games. So he was starting late—a disadvantage compounded by the fact that he had less money to spend than Dombrowski, and less freedom to spend it as he saw fit.

Gebhard's most significant hire to date was his scouting director, Pat Daugherty. Dombrowski and the rest of the Montreal Mafia in Miami all knew Daugherty, formerly the Expos' chief scout in Florida. They respected him immensely. ("He's like a second father," Wren says. "I named my first son after him.") But whatever his accomplishments, there was no denying that Daugherty's reputation had been earned primarily in the field—as a scout, a manager, and a junior-college coach. Now 56, he was being asked to take on administrative responsibilities. Furthermore, he was not even the Rockies' first choice. Gebhard had wanted Frank Wren, and had he got him would have made Daugherty his farm director, a job perhaps better suited to Daugherty's strengths as a teacher and friend to almost everyone he meets. But when Wren chose to go to Florida, Daugherty asked if he could have the scouting director's job. Gebhard was surprised ("He was even more surprised when Daugherty held out for more money," says a friend) but he went along. So far, Daugherty was way behind Hughes. Whereas Hughes already had a dozen experienced men on his payroll—not counting Rojas and Lockman, who worked directly for Dombrowski—Daugherty had only one, Tom Wheeler, whose signing would be announced in Denver later today.

On the other hand, as Barger himself had observed, the Rockies were ahead of the Marlins in ways that had little to do with putting a team on the field. To begin with, the franchise was jointly operated by a cumbersome committee led by the three managing partners: John Antonucci, whose title was chairman and chief executive officer; Steve Ehrhart (president and chief operating officer); and Mickey Monus. In addition, the lawyer Paul Jacobs was up near the top of the Rockies' organizational chart as executive vice president and general counsel. Under Jacobs was Michael Kent, the vice president for finance. And under Kent, perhaps surprisingly, was Dean Peeler, a PR man.

One reason the Rockies hired Peeler was that he was married to the sister of the wife of John Antonucci. The other reason, presumably, was that Peeler used to work for Exxon. His last assignment was Homer, Alaska, following the *Valdez* oil spill. That was a tough job for any PR man, but probably no tougher than the one he faced now in Denver.

On September 23, 1991, barely two months after John McHale resigned as chairman of the Denver Metropolitan Major League Baseball Stadium District board, McHale went to work for the Rockies. On one hand, hardly anyone was surprised by the move. McHale had been actively seeking the job ever since Denver won the franchise; it was the reason he gave for quitting the district in July. Still, having led the fight to persuade the taxpayers to pass the stadium initiative, and later having signed off on the mother of all sweetheart leases, when Mc-

Hale ended up on the Rockies' payroll as vice president in charge of baseball operations—well, people were shocked.

"Whether he did something wrong or not," says Neil Macey, McHale's most vocal critic, "it smells."

MACEY WAS A PARIAH in Denver, as much at odds with the local business and political establishment as his close friend and ally John Dikeou. It was Macey who came up with the idea for the stadium district in the first place, and later recruited Representative Kathi Williams to sponsor the stadium bill. After the bill passed, Dikeou was named chairman of the newly created Colorado Baseball Commission and Macey became executive director.

The CBC relied on private contributions. But as long as Macey was running the show, nobody wanted to contribute. Whether the issue in town was the convention center, the new airport or baseball, Macey had a history of gleefully staking out a contrary position. For example, it was Macey who supplied the lawyer and the money to sue the Greater Denver Corporation, an arm of the Denver Chamber of Commerce, for alleged violations of campaign laws in the Adams County airport election. In January 1990, a judge ordered the GDC to disclose its list of contributors, which happened to include the notoriously corrupt Silverado Savings Bank, as well as a number of prominent citizens who happened to own land on the site of the proposed airport.

"That pissed off the people over at the chamber," says Macey, trying to suppress a grin. "They went on a rampage to get me out of the CBC. My choice was either step down and have a chance of this thing passing or stand by my principles and watch it lose, so I resigned."

Macey was reappointed to the CBC by Governor Romer two days later, but only as a regular member, not the executive director. Soon after that, Dikeou announced he was no longer interested in buying a team. With Dikeou gone, Macey lost his connection. He had no ties to the new group of owners assembled by Paul Jacobs in August. For more than a year, he was hardly heard from at all. Then McHale went to work for the

Rockies, and Macey, outraged, looked up his old friend Kathi Williams.

Williams had recently lost her latest bid for reelection by some 300 votes, ending a six-year career in the state legislature. These days she sells commercial real estate in downtown Denver. Among the decorations on her office wall is a baseball poster, a small reminder of the role she played, together with Macey, in getting the stadium legislation passed and eventually bringing baseball to Denver. Williams is plainly protective of that role. "It was kind of our baby from the beginning," she reminds a visitor.

According to Paul Jacobs, Williams approached John Antonucci about working for the Rockies in the summer of 1991 and was rebuffed. Some critics have suggested that what lies at the core of her righteous anger is nothing more than sour grapes, a charge often leveled against Macey too. John Frew, the lawyer for the stadium district, says Macey looks at John McHale and "he sees himself: 'There but for the grace of God go I,' " on the theory that if Dikeou had bought the team, Macey would have gotten McHale's job. "That is just stupid," Williams says, dismissing any criticism of their motive. "Right is right and truth is truth."

"McHale had the reputation of being the contract negotiator of all contract negotiators," Williams begins. "He was supposed to be a tough SOB who had gotten concessions that no one was able to get before." Which is why she consented to his being named to the board in the first place. She knew he was from the enemy camp—coming from a baseball family—but she thought that his expertise would benefit the taxpayers. "Well, was I totally wrong. Absolutely totally wrong from the very beginning. It was bad judgment on my part. Because now I think that John had [a job with the Rockies] in mind from the very beginning. I should say that [Steve] Ehrhart, [John] Antonucci and [Mickey] Monus are no dummies. They are extremely shrewd. I think they knew how the game was played. Things happened [during the September 1990 presentation] back in New York that if I would have known about it, there would have been a red flag right then. They were partying and they were thinking how cute John was when he was drunk, and the relationship already was not one of a policy maker and a team owner. It was not the kind of relationship that you should have."

Then when McHale finally took the job with the Rockies, says Williams, "we thought something here just doesn't seem right. So we began to look at the memorandum of lease, and I think we were extremely shocked when we saw it—that it was not what we envisioned when we wrote the legislation. Basically we were told that our legislation was really a joke, it was a pipe dream, that we got baseball in spite of Neil and me, not because of Neil and me. We were told they had to give away all the revenues or Major League Baseball would not have awarded us a team, which was kind of interesting to Neil and me because we felt that we had some contacts in Major League Baseball also, and we didn't hear any of this. We were ranked anywhere from being in the top two to being in the top four at the very worst."

So Williams and Macey went back and talked to the other members of the stadium district board. "It was absolutely amazing to see how their philosophy had changed," she says. "They were just so pro-ownership. The guys from Ohio were pretty much the wonder boys, and had pulled off a miracle, and we should be extremely indebted to these gentlemen. My problem is this. I would really like to see baseball here, even though I've never seen a major league baseball game. I pushed the legislation very hard. As Neil probably told you, we lost the legislation on a couple of occasions and we brought it back to life. But I also feel—being a politician, or an ex-politician—that the promises politicians make are very, very important in terms of public trust and how you feel about yourself as an individual.

"There is a good ol' boys network, and the good ol' boys network is certain law firms here in town, the chamber and certain individuals. There's a certain spoils system that is no different from government that goes on here. I don't think it's my job to expose all that. My job is just to keep the things that I know about honest. I can't save the world, but I can at least do what I think is right. My total goal and objective is to improve what the taxpayer situation is, and if in fact [NL president] Bill White said tomorrow that the lease has to absolutely stay the same or the franchise will not come here or whatever, I would probably back off and say, 'Gee, I'm sorry.' "

The Rockies tried that. In September 1991, Antonucci made public a letter signed by White warning that major changes in the lease could lead the National League to reconsider. "Prior to the final formal vesting of the franchise," the letter stated, "the National League will require a detailed report with respect to implementation of the terms of the Memorandum." It caused a stir, until it was revealed that Paul Jacobs, the Rockies' attorney, drafted the letter and sent it to White for his signature.

THROUGHOUT THE FALL of 1991, while the Marlins were busy hiring scouts and otherwise thinking about baseball, the Rockies were preoccupied trying to defend themselves from a massive, multiple-front attack mounted by Macey and Williams. Wherever and whenever a city council met (not just in Denver but all over the six-county stadium district), or a political club (Democratic or Republican), or a legislative committee, Macey or Williams was sure to be on hand. Macey put together a 134-page source book, divided into 23 sections and conveniently contained in a loose-leaf binder, which he made available to members of the press. Besides all the relevant documents (the stadium legislation, the various plans of finance, the memorandum of lease terms), Macey's source book contained press clippings, a detailed financial breakdown of the Rockies partnership, tips for reporters (including questions to ask and documents to look for), even advice to the legislature on how it might legally void the memorandum.

By late November, Gale Norton, the Colorado attorney general, was set to begin a full-scale investigation into the terms of the lease and the circumstances surrounding its negotiation. Also, two bills backed by Macey and Williams were being readied for introduction in the state legislature. One sought to recapture a portion of the revenues handed over to the Rockies in the lease; the other to abolish the stadium district board and create a new one in its place.

"Once the announcement is made about these two bills," said Macey, "[Governor] Romer may then realize that, rather than just getting little letters from Kathi and Neil, he's in a real awkward political position, and he may call the Rockies and the stadium district board into his office and say, 'Guys, this isn't doing me any good and this isn't doing the Rockies any good. Soon you will be asking people to kick in their money for season tickets and you're asking them for a thousand bucks a ticket. If they have a negative feeling about the team, that may make the difference between sending in their check or not. So it's not helping you any to get all this negative press, and it's not helping me any. And since the stadium district board is about ready to be dissolved, why don't we rewrite the memorandum of lease and get these assholes off our backs.'

"That's probably a fifty percent scenario. The forty percent scenario is that the legislation will go through, the county commissioners will have the right to appoint new board members, and they'll start from scratch. And if the attorney general or somebody says, 'Well, we're not sure you can write a statute that conflicts with a preexisting contract,' the legislature will probably do it anyway. Romer may veto it, but politically it will be very unpopular for him to do that. Then you got ten percent—nothing really happens.

"Romer, if he's not careful—I mean, he's been riding on a tide ever since he was elected—but if he's not careful it could really nail him. He still has a chance to save himself, but soon that time will run out, and he's going to look like an absolute fool if he keeps defending McHale and defending the lease."

Both Denver newspapers—the *Post* and the *Rocky Mountain News*—went hard after the story all fall, trashing the lease and blasting the Drugstore Cowboys. Many of the same politicians who all summer had been clamoring for a seat on the Rockies bandwagon, leaped off in droves. Denver city councilman Dave Dowering, an early skeptic of the stadium bill, expressed what was now the prevailing point of view:

"In my mind, it's the classic case of the well-funded, big-bucks, heavy-political-operator type of businessperson coming in and totally tying the system up in knots and extracting every possible penny from the public while maximizing their profit. You're spending X amount for the stadium, and that supposedly is going to be funded by sales tax and other sources that are available to the board. The board gives those to the owners, so now it's going to be funded by sales tax. The team guarantees the managing partners a million bucks in salary, win or lose, profit or loss. So, in effect, if you put the accounting tricks to the side, you've got sales-tax dollars—money that should be used to reduce the public debt—directly flowing to the owners' pockets. That to me is a totally intolerable situation. We're in business, if you will, to provide service to our citizens. We are not in business to subsidize a major private toy."

John Frew found himself struggling to defend the stadium district—while half admiring Macey and Williams for their skill at driving the issue. "Neil and Kathi made a big deal out of what was promised and what was delivered," says Frew. "The voters were told, 'We need twenty years of the tax, it's going to cost a hundred forty million dollars, we think we can get rid of the tax in twelve years,' and they said, 'Okay.' Now, of that hundred forty million, the composition was seventy-thirty, a hundred million tax and forty million in privatization. Well, that was laid out when we thought that the team was going to cost sixty-five million. The team cost ninety-five million. That was revealed two weeks before the election. They vote for it anyway. I don't think anybody walked to the polls and said, 'Hmmmm, I like this thirty percent privatization business, I think I'll vote for it.' What the people said was: 'Go get a team.' And that's what we did. They voted for baseball.

"So what we have today, through aggressive borrowing and at very low interest rates, we'll get rid of the debt in twelve years, that's our projection. The stadium is still a hundred forty million. The difference is, now it's about ninety-two percent tax dollars and about eight percent private. The private interest will grow as we go through the completion of the lease. And if you include the operation and maintenance that they're going to have to pay every year, then it's even health-ier. With Neil and Kathi, there's a large part of them being good . . . well, I don't want to say good—them being slick politicians. They *know,* they absolutely understand that there are going to be changes in this lease, and so what they're going to do is bark now and take credit for it later.

"Look, the average Coloradan makes about twenty-three thousand dollars a year. Well, here come some guys from Youngstown, Ohio. The long-termers around here remember all this, where people came in in the early eighties, borrowed to the hilt, ran us all aground. You know, the poster child for the S&L industry, Silverado Savings, was from right here in Denver, Colorado, and they remember that. Took all the locals for a ride. Well, they see all this happening again. And it wouldn't be so bad, but two or three things happened. One, John Antonucci buys a two-million-dollar house, rubs it in everybody's face. Two, he tries to buy the [Denver] Nuggets, like he doesn't have enough things to do. And three, yeah, they cut a very lucrative deal. It kind of pollutes the atmosphere because people just see this incredible amount of money, and we try to say the lease is necessary in order to make this a good investment, and then people turn around and say, 'Well, wait a minute, if it was such a risky investment, why are these guys benefiting to such a degree that they not only get the five percent but they can afford to buy a house like this and the Nuggets and so on and so forth?' And you know something? We quit trying to defend them. I mean, we just said, 'Hell, I'm not gonna defend the guy. If he's gonna let us twist in the wind, then he's gonna have to figure out what it's like to live in Denver, Colorado.'"

JOHN ANTONUCCI leans back in his chair, hangs one arm over his head, tugs at his ear, and grins. "I don't think we're catching a lot of heat," he says. "I think the stadium authority is catching a lot of heat." He laughs. "The question I've asked myself, and I've asked our people over the course of the last three or four weeks when this negative press has come about, is how many season tickets have we lost, and the answer is, we've increased by twenty-four hundred since the World Series. So the average person wants baseball, this organization wants to play baseball, the consumer and the taxpayer out there essentially want baseball. I think it's just politics at its best at this point. We'll weather the storm. We can't be focused on that, though. We have to be focused on developing an organization, a first-class organization not only in the front office but on the baseball side of things. Let them go out and do their thing and we're going to get out there and touch and feel the politicians, and hopefully get this behind us."

Would he be willing to change the terms of the lease to make it more favorable to the taxpayers? "No. Without that lease, there would not be an ownership group, and there would not be baseball in Denver. It's that simple. I think it's just a matter of educating the politicians and for that matter the media about what really made this deal happen. It's not coincidental that Coors entered this partnership the day after the memorandum of lease was signed. Without that stadium lease and the way it's structured, it's financially devastating to this organization. I couldn't make any commitment to move forward and neither could our partners. Without those revenue streams there would not be a partnership. Without the partnership there wouldn't be baseball in Denver today.

"What are we talking about here? We're not talking about big dollars. It's a twelve-pack of Coke. And people aren't putting that in perspective. You have the political motivators out there who are using these fifty-million-dollar numbers. It's a twelve-pack of Coca-Cola per taxpayer in the district, it's not a big deal. Is that worth the price of having major league baseball in Denver? I think your average person would say yes, that's worth it."

Down the hall at 1700 Broadway, 21 stories above the atrium where the visiting members of the National League expansion committee were so warmly welcomed by the fans of Denver, sits John McHale, the cause of all the fuss. "I look back to August of 1990 when we were dead in the water," he says in a manner that is calm and detached, refusing to be drawn into the fight. "And we couldn't get it done. We were dying to have somebody come in, to have anybody come in from anywhere. Contacts were made and conversations were had and this group was put together, and I don't think that it's too much to say that they were really looked upon as heroes in this effort for some brief period of time. We negotiated and executed a memorandum of lease terms in March which was voted on in public session. It was released to the newspapers. Newspaper articles appeared describing its terms. And from that point through July, I guess, all we heard is what a great job the board had done, and weren't we lucky to have these fellows in from out of town, and so on and so forth.

"And then all of a sudden in September the whole calculus changed. I do not yet know why that is, except that you see it. We have to remind ourselves that forty-six percent of the people in this community voted against the tax, so there are at least four and a half out of every ten people you run into who didn't want to have to pay this tax and probably still don't want to pay it. That's a pretty sizable proportion. Other than that, I also probably believe that there are people who felt they played a bigger role in this process who have not been publicly recognized as having played that role by the media and others. Those are the elements that I've identified so far. How they fit together I don't know."

Meanwhile, elsewhere on the same floor, GM Bob Gebhard, assistant GM Randy Smith (the son of Tal Smith, with whom McHale worked on arbitration cases), scouting director Pat Daugherty and his assistant, Paul Egin, are trying hard not to think about leases and legislation, but about baseball. Daugherty is sitting in a tiny, half-height cubicle between Smith and Egin, his temporary office. Pinned to the fabric wall over his desk are pictures of his grandkids and a rental-car map of Greater Denver. Daugherty wears high-heeled boots—"I'm five foot seven and a half, and that half is important to me!"—and chews tobacco indoors, a real yahoo, it might seem, but everybody who knows him knows that's not the case. A former English teacher whose field reports are legendary for their vividly described scenes and raucous humor, Daugherty just happens to be one of those who are more comfortable having

others underestimate him. The big ring he wears is a me-
mento of his election to the Junior College Hall of Fame. "It's
a nice ring," he says. "I was happy to get that, means a lot to
me. Spelled my name wrong, but what the hell, I got a ring.
Spelled it D-o, which is, I think, the way it's supposed to be
spelled anyway, but somehow it got screwed up and spelled
D-a. No, I never mentioned it to them."

Daugherty spits a brown stream of tobacco juice at the trash
can under his desk. "When you're in the field, you're really
not privy to a lot of things. And I kind of enjoy that, because
when I was in the mainstream as [Expos minor league] field
coordinator, you know, there's so much shit, phone calls and
'Do this!' And I just kind of got up in an orange grove there in
Florida and loved it. You know, shit, I'm trying to grow flowers and go see ball games."

The phone rings. Daugherty picks up and does a live radio
interview. "Sure," he tells the interviewer, "we're going with a
smaller staff than the Marlins, but heck, I feel good about it.
John Antonucci has never told me I couldn't have anyone."
Off the air he says, "I don't want to go out and just start
finding twenty-four scouts—horseshit, old released scouts.
Christ, there's a hundred of those guys call me and they don't
go to games. Sons a bitches are sitting home watching TV and
drinking beer and playing golf. If I get enough of those guys
I'm gonna be fired. Shit, I'm not apologizing. It's not even a
skeletal staff. We're gonna stretch some guys out. But we've
got some part-time guys are gonna be in there. I feel good. I
feel like we got that thing covered."

All the Rockies' scouts are on one-year contracts. That used
to be standard for scouts, but lately more and more are signing two-year deals. When some of the young scouts Daugherty
hired asked for a two-year contract, Daugherty just said,
"Goddamn, you know, are you afraid? Are you afraid you're
not gonna keep your job? Holy Christ, if you're worried at
your age about a two- or three-year deal. God, show me some
balls."

Every fall, a scout's final duty of the season is to turn in what
is known as a follow list—a list of prospects who are high

school juniors and college underclassmen. Follow lists can be especially valuable to a scouting director who finds himself in a new job come spring. "I told Gary Hughes," says Daugherty, "I said, 'Hughes, how many nights did it take you to clean that goddamn office out?' He just laughed. That's an advantage he had that I didn't have. Before, they never wanted our follow lists before the first of the year, okay? So this year"—Daugherty lets loose a high-pitched chuckle—"all of a sudden I get a call on the voice mail. And I don't think Gary—I don't know, I'll never know what happened—but all of a sudden over the box I hear: 'This is to all scouts! Get your follow lists in. Have them postmarked tomorrow.' I'm thinking, you gotta be shitting me. Tomorrow? Why tomorrow?

"Well, I'm not blaming anybody, but somebody wanted all those lists in there in a hurry." Daugherty grins like an elf and spits in the can. "Am I making sense?"

MOST MAJOR LEAGUE CLUBS hold their annual organizational meetings in October, after the World Series. But since the Rockies and the Marlins are new, they're having theirs in January. And so to the Airport Ramada in Fort Lauderdale have come the five dozen new employees of the Florida Marlins. All the scouts, all the coaches and minor league managers, all the front-office people—even the trainers who will be working this summer with the Marlins' two farm clubs in Erie, Pennsylvania, and Kissimmee, Florida.

"We'll accomplish a lot in meetings here," says Dave Dombrowski after the welcoming cocktail party. His troops are settled in the banquet room for dinner. "But it's also a time to get to know one another and to have some fun. There are a lot of social activities that are planned. Gary Hughes always was good at the social activities." (Laughter.) "Frank Wren does all the work and Gary does all the social planning. But enjoy it. We're not starting our meetings until nine in the morning. You can stay up, you can talk, you can have a few beers, pick one another's brains. We're going to go out tomorrow night on a cruise, and we got a nice dinner planned Saturday night and Sunday a Super Bowl party. Have fun!"

.  .  .  .

FRIDAY, JANUARY 24. A little bleary-eyed, some of them, after a long night in Gary Hughes's suite, the baseball men reconvene in the ballroom for the opening session. Dombrowski stands behind the podium at the head table, dapper as usual. Next to him are Wren, Hughes, John Boles and Dan Lunetta. Facing him like students, each with a pad of paper and a pencil, are the scouts and coaches. They range in age from early twenties to late seventies, in experience from extensive to none. They share excitement at starting a new job, joy at working in the only industry in America undergoing expansion in the midst of this long recession, and, of course, love of baseball.

"Good morning and welcome, everybody, to the first Florida Marlins organizational meeting," Dombrowski says. "The success of the Florida Marlins organization in years to come rests in this room. You people—all of us—are the ones who are going to make it work. Our hard work, our dedication, the little bit extra that we do, will make the organization successful."

Wren—who made his reputation in baseball in part by being the man everybody else can count on to get things done—has a plan to break the ice. He wants to hear a few words from everybody in the room—who you are, where you came from, what brought you here—and he'll begin. "I spent fourteen years in Montreal," he says. "I signed out of junior college in St. Petersburg, had a brain tumor . . ."

*I was playing in West Palm Beach, class A ball. After a doubleheader one night, driving back to my apartment with my roommate, just like that I got sick as a dog. Thought it was food poisoning. We pulled off the interstate and I threw up all over the median. By the time we got home I was sick all night long. Never been so sick in my life. Throughout the night it just got worse and I really felt lousy and I went to the hospital the next night. They did a spinal tap and they found I had blood in the spinal fluid, I was hemorrhaging. So they did a lot of tests. Didn't find anything. At the time I went in the hospital I was leading the Florida State League in hitting, stolen bases and doubles. When I came out, I played the last month of the season at about twenty-five pounds under my playing weight and I went like one for seventy the last month of the season, just trying to get my eye back. Took the whole winter off. Tried to get healthy again and get my weight back up. Came back the next year and played AA. I was still about ten pounds lighter than I had been before. Everything started coming together like the last month of the season in 1980. I was the player of the month in the Expos' system. I hit like .365 with five home runs and 20-some RBIs, and everything started coming back. I was feeling like myself. Really had a great winter. Got stronger, and came back the next year on the AA roster. Fifth day of spring training I had another almost identical attack, only this time it came on a lot faster. Like nine o'clock one night in my room I'm sitting there, I start getting neck spasms, and by ten the neck spasms had gone up into my temples, and by eleven I was throwing up. At four in the morning I went to the hospital. They did a spinal tap. I'd had another hemorrhage. Blood in the spinal fluid again. And this time they did some more tests and they found the tumor. It took them three weeks to find it. About the size of your thumb, attached to the cranial nerve, back up under here [touching the nape of his neck], called the third ventricle. They split me from the top of my head all the way down my neck and went in the back. About eight or nine hours in surgery, took it out. I felt great after that. I just could not react at the plate. I could see the ball coming, I could see the break, I could see everything I could see before. I couldn't do anything about it. Once you come to the realization that you're not the same player, it's not fun anymore. When you're used to being a .300 hitter and all of a sudden now you're a .210 hitter, there's no fun left in it, I guarantee you that.*

". . . coached for four years. Had an opportunity to be a manager the next year, or else a minor league general manager. Took the job in Jamestown. So, after playing for four, coaching for four, was general manager for a year. Then at the end of that summer, Gary Hughes was hired as scouting director and they forced me down his throat. Was his assistant for three years, then took on additional duties in Latin America last couple of years. I have twin nine-month-old boys and I grew up in Kentucky, where my parents are from."

Next up, Gary Hughes: "My wife, Kathy, and I together have nine children, many of them are still in college, so please do a good job." Hughes was drafted out of San Jose Community College but didn't play professionally. "I was hampered by a lack of ability." And then, one by one, all around the room . . .

John Panagakis, a.k.a. the Greek, traveling secretary: "I was born and raised in San Francisco. No, I'm not that way."

Tim Schmidt, scout, southern California: On the heavy side. Also on the loud side. The life of the party last night up in Hughes's suite. "I'm not married, which is probably pretty obvious. I go by a couple of nicknames, Schmitty for one and Uncle Buck for another."

Jax Robertson, national cross-checker: Former scouting director for the Tigers. Signed Richard Dotson and Don Mattingly. "I was okay in college and a lousy pro player."

Dick Egan, western cross-checker: "I played for just about every minor league team that's ever been invented. Played briefly in the big leagues with the Tigers and the Angels and the Dodgers. If you've got a baseball encyclopedia you can look me up. I've got one win and two losses and two or three or four saves, something like that [two, actually]. Got into scouting with the [Major League Scouting] Bureau when it started, in charge of northern Nevada, where there's at least six schools, including high schools. Worked for five hundred dollars a year that year. Only thing I did there was set a record for expense accounts. One of the things that most of you have heard about me, I'm a prick. I don't talk to guys at games. I have an excuse, and I'll let you in on it—what we say in here stays in here—I don't talk to guys because I can't hear out of my right ear. So when people are on my right side they may or may not say something to me and then when I ignore them, they just think I'm really—uh, what I said I was. It's accidental most of the time, but sometimes it comes in handy. I got divorced after twenty-six years but I have a daughter in northern California, I have three grandchildren, I have a son—I don't know where the hell he is—and then I have two daughters by my wife's marriage, one of them a stewardess out of LAX, and she's already been instructed to stay the hell away from baseball people. She's a showstopper."

Whitey Lockman, major league scout: Signed out of high

school at age sixteen, came up with the Giants in '45, "and hit a dinger my first time up." Married in 1950 to Shirley, "my high school sweetheart." "I'm really excited. I picture the Marlins—it's a game fish, and we're going to be kind of swimming upstream in the game of baseball maybe for a while but not for long."

Rich Bordi, scout, Oregon, Washington, Idaho, Montana, Wyoming and northern California: Former big-league pitcher, been out of the game for two years. "I wanted to experience the real world. I was involved in ceramic tile as a tile setter. I wasn't bad at doing it, okay, but the bosses kept saying faster, faster. I said I can't do it that fast. So I said I got to get back in the game of baseball. It's me, it's in my blood, I wasn't put on this earth to be a tile setter. I was just doing it so I could see my family every day. They got tired of me and they said, 'Rich, get back in baseball.' "

Orrin Freeman, associate scouting director and national cross-checker: "I'm the father of Gary [Hughes's] goddaughter."

Greg Zunino, eastern cross-checker: "I didn't have the tools to play professional ball but Gary asked me anyway. . . . My son is Gary's other godson."

Jeff Wren, scout, Georgia. "I'm no relation. At least that's what Frank always told me growing up."

Scott Diez, scout, Oklahoma, Missouri, Kansas and Arkansas: Son of Al Diez, longtime scout for the Mets and the Royals. Drafted in the 38th round by the Pirates out of high school. Played seven years in the minors for five different organizations, quit in 1990, "not because I wanted to but nobody wanted me."

Bill Scherrer, scout, Pennsylvania, New York: Pitched for the Tigers in the 1984 World Series. Left baseball in 1988 and it "wasn't too fun. I was working in a food chain, as like an associate manager. Sort of demoralizing when somebody recognizes you, says, 'You're Bill Scherrer.' You sort of feel a little bit embarrassed. I found out after a month or two that I wasn't management material in the food business."

Jose Castro, hitting coach, Erie Sailors (Marlins farm club):
"I don't look Cuban but I was born there."

Cookie Rojas, major league scout: Signed at age 15. "Angel
Vasquez never thought I could make it." Played six years in
the minors, 16 years in majors, glad to be back home in
Miami.

Marty DeMerritt, pitching coach, Erie Sailors: Licensed
bounty hunter. "To be honest with all of you, I've had an
exciting life. I won't overwhelm you with intelligence, but I
will overwhelm you with enthusiasm. I not so much love the
game, I love pitching. The game's pitching, boys." Asked his
girlfriend if she could catch. "She said yes, so I married her."

Steve Minor, scout, Orange County, California: "I thank
Gary for everything. I'm a three-time loser. I worked for
Texas for a year, gone. I worked for Toronto for six years,
gone. I worked for Milwaukee one year, gone."

Angel Vasquez, director of Latin American operations:
Started in baseball as PR man for the Havana Sugar Kings.
Fled Cuba when he was a young man, lost everything, went to
Mexico City. Bought the Mexico City Reds, promoted bull-
fights and prizefights. At age 67, hopes finally to win a World
Series. "A lot of people think it takes a lot of years to do that,
but if I believed that I would not have taken the job."

Bill Serena, scout, northern California: "I worked eighteen
years for the Atlanta Braves scouting northern California, Oregon, Washington, Idaho and everything else including Canada, and then I got fired last year. I lost my dignity. I lost my
self-respect. This is my forty-sixth year. I couldn't compete
with this guy that had five years. He knew everything. He
never had no trust, he cared less. I'll tell you, Gary, David, you
guys gave me my self-respect back and I'm smiling. There are
a few others here that were in the same position that I was,
and when you lose your self-respect and you lose your dignity,
and somebody strips it from you, and then on top of it fires
you, after you've been with an organization, loyal and faithful,
it hurts a little bit."

Grady Mack, scout, south-central California: "I'm single. I

live about fifteen minutes from the LAX airport, and I'd like to meet Dick Egan's daughter."

Murray Cook, central cross-checker: Originally signed by the Pirates. Hired by George Steinbrenner as Yankees general manager—"I've never known why and never will." Moved on to Montreal, where he hired Dave Dombrowski.

Lou Fitzgerald, master scout: Played and managed in the minors for 22 years. Helped put together the original Houston Colt 45s. Married 47 years "and I don't know how I put up with her that long."

Jim Moran, scout, South Florida: Ran into John Boles last fall while still scouting for the Royals. "Boles says, 'Hey, you know Gary Hughes just got the job with the Florida Marlins.' 'Yes.' '*Hey, you know Gary Hughes just got the job with the Florida Marlins.*' 'So?' 'Here's the phone number, you asshole!' "

John Young, major league scout: "I think I'm an authority because I spent seven years with Dick Egan here. And Egan *is* a prick."

Finally: "My name is George Tebbetts," comes a geriatric voice from the back of the room. All are silent, straining to hear. "Before I say anything about myself, I want to tell all of you young fellows that in baseball, no matter where you go, no matter how long you stay, there will be only one group of people that you will associate with who sincerely love the game of baseball, and they will be scouts. Everybody else will be unhappy about something. You're not going to be paid enough to be unhappy about anything. [Laughter.] So I want you to be very proud of it. For the last twelve years I've been trying to get scouts into the Hall of Fame, and I think that before you're through scouting, that will come about. We will have scouts in the Hall of Fame. I signed at age seventeen and I'm a senior citizen. I started in nineteen hundred and thirty-four. I went to Detroit and played there with five Hall of Famers on that ball club, it was a great thrill for me to even be there. I was not a good ballplayer, I just lasted a long time. [More laughter.] For those of you who don't know, I was a catcher, sixteen and a half years at the major league level. I was a manager, a coach, an executive vice president, which means absolutely nothing [laughter], and the happiest days I ever spent were as a scout when I first started to scout. And I'm sincere about that. When I first started to scout, I was never so happy. I was single and I was drinking, and I had a hell of a time. [Laughter.] And you'll have the same opportunities as I had. The only thing I can say, and I guess I can say it because I hear it on the television all the time, is be sure to have a condom. [Widespread laughter, to the point of tears.]"

AFTER LUNCH, the group splits. Coaches and managers in one room with John Boles, the farm director. And scouts, all 40 of them, in another room with Gary Hughes. The scouting director of the Florida Marlins is a Captain Kangaroo look-alike—red face, jolly cheeks, bushy mustache, shaggy, once-blond hair—with a little bit of California thrown in—the glasses hanging on a cord around his neck, the turquoise pinky ring, the gold chain dangling on his wrist. The son of Howard Hughes (the paper salesman, not the billionaire), Hughes played college ball at San Jose State and eventually wound up coaching at Cal State Sonoma in the late 1960s, only to have the liberal student body vote out all funds for athletics.

Hughes started scouting with the Yankees as a bird dog, which is a part-time commission scout—no pay unless you recommend somebody that ends up signing (the first guy he recommended was Bob Knepper, who wound up pitching 15 years in the big leagues). He was hired full-time in 1978, and eventually became the Yankees' western cross-checker. When Murray Cook asked to talk to Hughes about the scouting director's job in Montreal, George Steinbrenner withheld permission for three weeks, or as long as it took him to sign all the Yankees' scouts he wanted to keep. In Montreal, Hughes enjoyed extraordinary success. He was mainly responsible, together with farm director John Boles, for the Expos twice being named Organization of the Year. As a rule, he prefers to draft high school kids rather than college, and likes pure athletes with size, speed and strength, even if their skills are undeveloped (see Delino DeShields, Marquis Grissom and Wilfredo Cordero of the Expos).

Hughes is worshiped by those who work for him (almost as much as he himself worships Jimmy Buffet). In addition to all those who made Hughes the godfather of their children, Julian Camilo, one of the Marlins' scouts in the Dominican Republic, named his son Gary; he is, in all likelihood, the only native-born Gary on the island.

"First off," Hughes says, once everybody settles down, "I couldn't be happier. Just looking at you guys. This whole thing, the whole Florida Marlins thing, to me is about one thing and that's opportunity. We've got an unbelievable opportunity here. . . .

"The first thing I wrote down is: 'Return all your calls and letters.' We're talking about doing the right thing, showing class in what we do. . . .

"We're not hiring anybody else, we're not putting on any part-time scouts, and we're not going to give your cousin a thousand dollars to cover his backyard. We're done. Bird dogs, however, are another story. We will not discourage you from having bird-dog scouts. You can have as many or as few as you want. I have a spot in my heart for them because that's where I started. I caution you, there are good bird dogs and there are bad bird dogs. A bird dog can end up being the most quoted guy in America because now he's a representative of the Florida Marlins, and all of a sudden he's got a theory on everything from world peace to how to cure the recession. Be careful who you have representing us. . . .

"The image we want is first class. We want you people to show us in a first-class light. One of the ways you can do that is in this hotel, leave a buck on your pillow every night for the housekeeper. You'd be surprised how those things come back. There's a person in this room, I'm not going to say the name, but there's a person in this room that almost didn't get in this room because of one thing. We were in a restaurant after a game one night, and there was this fan, just a little guy, stocky little funny guy that people kind of make fun of, but anyhow he asked this guy for a business card and the guy didn't give him a business card. He said, 'I'm out.' Well, fifteen or twenty minutes later, the owner of the restaurant—also a very nice fellow—comes up. And this guy who was with me hands this guy a business card. You should have seen the look on the little fan's face. Treat the little guy well. . . .

"There's a misconception here that we're throwing money around like crazy. It's not true. What we've done here with you people in this room is we've hired you for what we think is a fair wage and that's upset some people in this business and you probably read about it in the papers. We've got other organizations saying what the Marlins are doing is wrong, is bad, dangerous for the game. These are the same guys that are signing players to twenty-nine-million-dollar contracts, but it's dangerous to pay a scout what is a living wage. We're trying to treat you right but we're not throwing money away here. Wayne Huizenga didn't become the Horatio Alger story he is by throwing money away. Be alert to that. Be responsible with what you're doing with our money, with Wayne's money. And I'll just say this one thing—don't be an idiot. Don't jeopardize a good job and a good career over a ten-dollar expense item. Or a hundred-dollar item. We're fair with you. Be fair with us. And we ain't dumb. . . .

"Good things will happen if you do your job, which is what? To go to the ballpark. And once you go, stay. Hang around. Those of you who are new at the game, you're gonna see a lot of guys leaving early. Stay to the end of the game. If that's the hardest thing you have to do in life you got a pretty good life. . . .

"You're getting cars, most of you. Some of your blue cars are going to be white, but hey, again, if that's the worst thing that ever happened to you then you've had a good life. These cars are beautiful, they're marvelous cars, and even if you don't like the car, if anybody asks you, you love it. Everything we do here is the best. If something's not right, ask a question, don't complain."

Bill Singer, the former pitcher for the Dodgers and the Angels, now the Marlins' scout in Louisiana, Mississippi and Alabama, raises his hand. "Why Japanese cars?"

"Not my job to pick the cars," Hughes says. But then Frank

Wren cuts in, "They're all made in Georgetown, Kentucky."
Not union, but better than nothing.

"There are three things I look for in a successful employee,"
Hughes continues, "and the number one and the most important is loyalty. We expect you to be loyal. If you find that you
can't be, then you're in the wrong place. But number one,
loyalty. The second is hard work, you got to be hardworking.
We think you are. We know most of you are. Those we don't
know, you *will* be hard workers. You'll enjoy what you're doing but you will work hard. The last part, knowledge. You got
to have some idea what you're doing, but that's the third one.
You can know all there is to know about baseball, but if you
don't work at it and you're not loyal to us, it's not doing anybody any good. This is not original. Mel Didier said it to me
one time and he got it from Bear Bryant, who probably got it
from Moses. . . .

"Family, let's talk about family a little bit, in two contexts.
Number one, you guys are a family, you are the first Florida
Marlins family. This is not lip service, we really truly believe
this. Feel for the people in this room. We are all a family. The
other part of the family thing is your family itself. Most important. Birthdays, anniversaries, the kids in a play, first Little
League game. Stuff like that, you got to be there. There's going to be a lot of times when you'd love to be home and doing
stuff and you're going to be away, and that's why a lot of us got
up this morning and talked about our second marriages. This
game is tough on family life. Orrin Freeman [who is in the
room, and smiles], his wife was pregnant with their first child,
and he was in Chicago or someplace. They were talking together on the phone, which is how you get together with your
wife most of the time during the season, and she said, 'Orrin,
if you don't come home, you may not have a home when you
come back. I might have a nervous breakdown.' And his response was a good husbandly response. 'Can you wait till
Tuesday? I gotta see one more pitcher.' That's a tough sell,
trying to explain to your wife that the big dinner we're going
to have has got to be changed because it rained in Wausau.

That gets old, that gets real old after a while. Be alert to your loved ones' feelings, so they'll remain your loved ones. . . .

"Don't wrack your brains trying to figure out what I want. I'll figure out what you're doing. You scout the way you think. We had a guy with the Expos who spent an entire year trying to figure out what he thought I wanted, and that was his last year with the Expos. . . .

"The best source for knowing where to stay is other scouts, and it's good to stay there. It's great to be a loner and do your own thing, but a lot of times you go down to that office in the hotel and there's a bunch of scouts standing around and a lot of information gets passed around. That brings me to another one. You've been in scouting meetings all your lives and you've heard somebody just like me stand up here and say, 'We want you to get all the information you can from all the other scouts, but don't tell them anything.' It doesn't work that way. Eddie Bockman, one of our master scouts, has a rule —tell them anything they can read in the paper. We're all in this together. You're not going to say, 'There's a pitcher in Tonopah. You guys ought to go to Tonopah.' But if it's something they can read in the paper, fine. Don't be one of these guys that lets a guy go seven hundred miles out of his way and laugh as he goes. The information you give to us is ours, but we realize there are situations where one hand washes the other. . . .

"We are not in competition with the Colorado Rockies. We're in competition with the Minnesota Twins. We want to be the best. . . .

"Be real excited. When you were a high school kid and you were the big man on campus, then it wasn't cool to be excited. This is an exciting time. It's an exciting time in your professional career, it's an exciting time in your life, it's an exciting time in the history of South Florida, it's an exciting time in the history of baseball. Be excited. Be positive, be a positive scout. Don't be offended by a question. If one of us asks you a question, it's not an assault on your manhood or your dignity or anything else. I assume if somebody asks me a question they want to know an answer, that's all. . . .

"We don't grade by numbers. We don't put an OFP [overall future potential] on a player, we put a category. First category is definite. That's a player that you feel should be a first- or second-round player. Second is the chance category. Got three stages of the chance category. A high chance is a third- or fourth-round player. A chance player is a fifth-, sixth- or seventh-round player. A low chance is an eighth-, ninth- or tenth-round player. After that we have what we call a fringe prospect, and that's a guy you take in the eleventh- to the twentieth-round. The other category we have is an organizational player. An organizational player is a college senior only, and that's just somebody that you sign to do a job. Every one of these categories, there's big leaguers in there, fellas."

MASTER SCOUT LOU FITZGERALD signed out of high school, went to Americus, Georgia, got as high as AA in Dallas, started managing in '51, got into the Baltimore system, and then followed general manager Paul Richards to the expansion Colt 45s in '62. That was before they drafted players, when it was every scout for himself. The Colt 45s were especially aggressive under Richards and signed some big names—Rusty Staub, Joe Morgan, Jimmy Wynn, Jerry Grote, all of whom Fitzgerald coached in the low minors. He never managed Bill Singer, who was in the Dodgers' organization, but he managed against him, and when he ran into him today for the first time in nearly 30 years, he remembered a story.

"See, we won the pennant two years in a row in the Texas League," says Fitzgerald. "[Singer] pitched for Albuquerque. I want to tell you, he could really throw and we could hardly beat him. They had a manager named Clay Bryant. And Singer and one of my pitchers named Marvin Dutton was real good buddies. Well, we're in Albuquerque one night, and Jim Wynn—my outfielder—two strikes and no balls, Singer sticks a ball right there inside of his helmet. Oliveras, another guy, right-hand hitter, third baseman, his son now pitches for the Cardinals. Oliveras, okay? Two strikes and no balls, right back of his head. I said, 'What in the world's going on?' And Marv Dutton told me, 'Clay Bryant tells them when they get two strikes and no balls, they've got to knock 'em down.' Now, that's a shame with the young players we had, so I called Richards that night. I said, 'Paul, I got a problem, that Singer . . .' He said, 'Fitz, I tell you what you do. The next time he pitches, if you'll get a pitcher to break three or four ribs, I'll buy him a hundred-dollar suit of clothes.' So I get my pitchers together, and I had Darrell Brandon, he pitched in the big leagues, I had Joe Horner, he was a mean one, pitched for the Cardinals. So sure enough we're playing in San Antonio and Joe Horner's pitching. Score, I guess, is real close. They had a runner on second, Singer's up, and Joe Horner calls time out, says, 'Skipper can I get him?' I said, 'Well, looks like as good a time as any.' And he threw a ball back there, and I don't know how he dodged it, it just barely missed him and went all the way around that screen. So I called Richards, and he said, 'You know, Fitz, that looked like it stopped him, go buy him a fifty-dollar sport coat.' In 1963 that's a good coat. Two or three years later, Horner's pitching for the Cardinals, I'm in the hotel in Atlanta. He says, 'Come here, Fitz. I want you to look at this coat, that's the one you bought me!' "

BILL SERENA wears glasses with thick lenses shaped like TV screens. His ears slant away from his head like exclamation points, Ross Perot-like. He wears a brown-check sport coat. He plays the accordion. In 1947, playing for the Lubbock Hubbers in the old class C West Texas–New Mexico League, Serena hit 70 home runs—57 during the regular season and 13 in postseason. Another guy hit 72 a couple of years later, so Serena lost the record, but that guy never made it to the big leagues and Serena did, four years with the Cubs. "Baseball's been my whole life. I been married forty-two years and I been in the game forty-six, and my wife, she gets a little bit disgusted once in a while, but then that only lasts for about ten or fifteen minutes."

BILL SCHERRER: "Let's face it, the real world sucks. There's no reason to be there if you don't have to be. You get in the real world and go eight to five, and they pay people like bologna money, it's a no-win proposition."

Marty DeMerritt: "You shouldn't say that, 'cause that's going to go in his book, that's uneducated. Don't say sucks, just say the real world is inconsistent."

Scherrer: "I believe it, the real world sucks. People treat people like crap, and people bust their butts over a nickel and a dime."

GEORGE "BIRDIE" TEBBETTS has fine white hair, a pink complexion, blue eyes, a strong nose and big, thick hands appropriate to his former profession, catcher. Tebbetts is from Nashua, New Hampshire. He graduated from Providence College with a degree in philosophy. "When you can say I don't know," he says, "you're beginning to get smart." More than anything, he hates to hear a person say "you know." ("That's the goddamnedest thing. Really, the first suggestion I'm going to make is that we hire a guy to teach ballplayers how to speak.") Tebbetts owns a World Series record that "can never be broken and can only be tied and I'm very proud of it"—he went hitless in the 1940 World Series. He has been called Birdie since he was in the cradle, when his mother remarked on his small, round mouth—nothing to do with his high-pitched voice. He made it through the service without taking a drink, made it to 39 years old, then went overboard, then quit, and hasn't had a drink in 20 years. Late at night in Hughes's suite, he holds court. Jax Robertson, Uncle Buck and Hughes himself sit on the floor at his feet.

Tebbetts talks, they listen: "The only trouble with a roving instructor is he thinks he has to instruct. . . . It takes at least six years to learn how to scout. . . . The guys that cost you more money in this business are the guys that sign twenty guys cheaply. The guy that saves you money is the guy that signs one guy for a hundred fifty thousand. . . . If you want to see a guy's best fastball, take a look at the first pitch he throws after a home run." The reason Tebbetts doesn't like radar guns, he says, is that "there's too many goddamn good shitballers."

"There is no other group in sports that loves the sport like the scouts love baseball," Tebbetts says again. "It's a love affair. Otherwise, who the hell would take the job? You lose your wife, you lose your kids, you lose everything."

"THE ONLY STORIES that are perpetuated in baseball are perpetuated by the scouts, who continually keep telling stories, and the stories live on and on and on." Including stories a guy wouldn't want his wife to hear, like this one from a Marlins scout who shall remain nameless.

"I went down to Delano, where they had an Easter League, they had about a fifteen-to-twenty-team tournament down there. About ninety-five in the shade. Now, I'm coming back to Fresno, so I call this girl. She says, 'Why don't you come over tonight.' I stink. She didn't say shit because she worked in a delicatessen, she smelled like salami. Between the both of us we smelled pretty good. So I flip that kimono off and started to hit her nipples, and my goddamn teeth got loose. Sound like rattlesnakes, all over her fucking body. So I took the lowers and I threw them on the goddamn floor. Got through with what I had to do, I gave her a big kiss, I said, 'I'll see you in a couple of days.' I got down the road about forty-five miles. I forgot my teeth! Got to go back and get my fucking lowers. She says, 'What are you doing here?' I said, 'Left my wallet on the table.' She never batted an eyelash."

SATURDAY, JANUARY 25. The difference between scouts and coaches, according to Orrin Freeman, a scout who used to be a coach, is this: "We can always dream for the kids. The player development people have to deal in reality, and that's tedious." Scouts may bitch and moan about not seeing the results of their labor, never getting credit, the loneliness of the road, all that. But scouts start fresh every year, and the beauty of what they do is that they see talent, and catch it, and turn it over to the proper authorities. Then it's up to the poor coach to worry about what happens next. The coach is like the older brother, the one who worries, who always feels responsible.

The difference between the two personality types is evident

in Gary Hughes and John Boles as they pose for the first-ever group picture of the Florida Marlins baseball staff, Hughes holding back a laugh and Boles putting on a smile. Boles has a lot more on his mind. His father is a dentist and he inherited a dentist's well-scrubbed, clean-hands demeanor. He believes in "a systematic approach," and says, "I think that the most important thing is knowledgeable, hardworking people and a consistency of attitude and stability." And yet they're friends, the oddest couple.

"Angel Vasquez has a saying he taught me that I love," says Hughes. "He says, 'You're putting too much cream in my taco.' I really want to put cream in John's taco. I firmly believe that there's nobody better in this game than John Boles. There's no better person and we're lucky to have him."

"He's absolutely unafraid of his job," says Boles of Hughes. "You can say anything, he never gets offended. A guy can sign for two hundred thousand and I can say, 'Hey, Boomer, this guy, I don't see it,' and he'll laugh and say, 'It's only money.' I never thought it could be like this with a scouting director and a director of player development."

Like Hughes—and Dombrowski, and Pat Daugherty of the Rockies—Boles never played professional baseball. "I guess at first it used to bother me, people always asked me the question, 'Oh, you didn't play pro ball?' It was irritating because it was like I had to prove something." Boles went to the University of Louisville as baseball coach in 1980, expecting to lead the program to national prominence. But two years later a new athletic director came along and told him baseball was no longer a priority. "I said, 'Holy cow, thank you very much.' This is my second year at Louisville, I got a wife and two kids, left a great job in Chicago. I thought: Now what am I going to do?"

Then he got a call from Roland Hemond at the White Sox. Hemond had called before, but Boles had always said no, he wasn't interested in professional coaching, he thought his future lay in college. This time he said yes, and Hemond sent him to Florida to manage in the Gulf Coast League. Two years later he was promoted to Appleton, then Glens Falls, and then in 1985 to the White Sox AAA farm club in Buffalo. After a successful season in Buffalo, on the eve of the White Sox organizational meeting, Ken Harrelson took over as the club's new vice president in charge of baseball operations. Harrelson said he was going to "try to keep the casualties to a minimum," which reassured no one. That winter, while Boles was managing in Venezuela, he heard a rumor that Harrelson had someone else in mind for the job in Buffalo. So he called Dave Dombrowski, who was working for the White Sox at the time, and asked him what was going on. Dombrowski had exciting news. Tony La Russa, the White Sox manager, wanted Boles to be his new third-base coach.

"I said, 'Really?' I'm from the South Side of Chicago. All I ever wanted to be was with the White Sox. Eleven years old, you know, my father takes me down to Midway Airport to welcome the White Sox home from Cleveland when they clinch the pennant. Those guys walking by me, Luis Aparicio, Nellie Fox. That was my whole life. They used to go on road trips to California or something, I'd be up till two in the morning as a little kid, listening to the White Sox. So I'm all pumped up."

But there was a hitch, Dombrowski said. La Russa wanted Boles but Harrelson wanted Doug Rader. "I said, 'Oh, man, I know how this is going to turn out.' " Discouraged, Boles asked to be released from his contract with the White Sox. Shortly thereafter he was hired by the Kansas City Royals as director of player development, which turned out to be the beginning of a new, successful career in the front office. So the story has a happy ending. But to this day, Boles carries in his wallet a clipping from one of the Chicago papers, so small that he doesn't have to fold it. From time to time he will look at it, and remember the pain and disappointment he felt at almost, but not quite, making it to the big leagues.

"Footnote," the piece of newspaper says. "Manager Tony La Russa reportedly wanted White Sox class AAA manager John Boles to be his third-base coach. Harrelson refused, insisting on having a 'major league guy.' "

"We do not have a great situation with Erie," Boles tells the

Marlins' minor league managers and coaches who are sitting around the table. The picture-taking session is over. Across the hallway, the scouts are being taught how to work their new laptop computers. In here, Boles is preparing his staff for a season in which the Marlins will field just two minor league teams, and not until after the June free-agency draft: a Gulf Coast League team in Kissimmee, Florida, made up mostly of high school kids and Latin Americans; and a New York–Penn League team for college kids. Not until 1993, when the Marlins and Rockies major league teams begin play, will either organization field a class AAA team. And not until the year after that will they add class AA teams. As newcomers, both the Rockies and the Marlins had to settle for minor league franchises in less than ideal locations. "We come in new, we had to go to places where no one was, where nobody wanted to be. I'll give you the ins and outs and some of the communication that we've had, but that's it. During the year, let's not bitch about it. It's bad, but we can make it. It's a two-and-a-half-month thing. It's, uh, it's as bad as I've ever seen in baseball.

"Marty?" he says, looking straight at his pitching coach. "Right field. Two-fifty. Big, high monster, falling down. No locker rooms. The locker room is out in right field in a high school on a gymnasium floor that they've partitioned off. I mean, it's really rough."

"John," says Marty, still thinking about the short right-field porch, "when you evaluate me at the end of the year . . ."

"We don't worry about stats," says Boles. "It's two-fifty and they got great lights, figure that out. It's an embarrassment. The one good thing about Erie is that the travel's good and the fans are tremendous. It's an ethnic city, a blue-collar city, they're good people. And they love to come out. And the city's not bad. It's just the facility. I'm going to read you a letter from Frank Wren to David Dombrowski, concerning a trip we made on November 14 and 15:

> "We arrived to find two very ill-prepared men that were not real sure what to do or say. Skip Wiseman, new president of the

club, and Tom Lindon, who was former general manager, met us in a cluttered office at the park. It was very apparent that it was uncomfortable for them because neither of them knew who the spokesman was or what was acceptable to reveal about an obviously poor operation. . . . First stop was the playing field, which was being rebuilt by local landscape contractors with no baseball experience. . . . Outfield is covered in grass but is the roughest I have walked across in professional baseball. . . . The dimensions are very short in right field at about 270 and in the alley in right being 300 . . ."

Boles looks up. "Development of right fielders and center fielders will be prohibited," he says.

"To compensate for these differences they use a three-tiered fence. . . . The dugouts are built at a subterranean level with the headroom of the first few steps being around five feet. I have personally witnessed many players banging their heads both entering and exiting, in what could result in serious injuries. . . . The locker facilities are in the middle of the school outside the right-field fence and up three flights of stairs. . . ."

"Now it's been said," says Boles, "and now that's over. Because the big thing is, when we go up there, these players gotta think that we're the happiest staff in the world. 'So somebody else has got a better field, so what.' "

Then Boles starts going through the player development manual he has written, page by page. "These guys got to know exactly what the procedure is," he says of the young players they'll be getting after the draft. "What the plan is. There's a lot of startling, upsetting things going on in minor league baseball now, and I don't blame the players for going back and telling their high school or college coaches, 'Gee, you know, I was a little disappointed.' We don't want anybody disappointed in us. When it's over, we want them to go back and say, 'Oh, man, this is what I thought professional baseball was going to be.' We don't want to disappoint them because we weren't knowledgeable enough, we weren't detailed enough, we didn't work hard enough. We got to all be right there. If there's a weak staff member, the players pick it out in two days."

In Chapter 6 of the manual, this directive from the dentist's son: "In a concentrated organizational effort to promote and safeguard proper oral health, the use of smokeless tobacco by Florida Marlins minor league staff and playing personnel is hereby strictly prohibited."

Groans break out all around the room, from men who are chewing even as they listen. "We have a moral obligation to stop this before it starts," Boles says. "There isn't a guy in this room who doesn't wish he didn't do it. We have to do it, we just have to do it. We are eliminating smokeless tobacco from our organization from the outset."

THE RESULTS of the investigation into the terms of the lease conducted by the Colorado attorney general are released in early February, and they are encouraging for the Rockies. Is the lease binding? was the first question attorney general Gale Norton considered. Yes. Are any of the issues in the lease severable without voiding the whole agreement? No. Unlawful conflict of interest by board members? Perhaps, as it relates to Roger Kinney, who began consulting for the Rockies while he was still a member of the board. But not in the case of John McHale. Does the failure of the lease memorandum to address capital improvements violate the stadium act? No. Does the memorandum violate the act by letting the Rockies manage the stadium? No. Does the memorandum violate the Colorado constitution by permitting "an unlawful donation of public funds or an improper commingling of public and private funds"? No.

"It's reasonably encouraging," McHale says by phone. "She managed to take a few shots at the business judgment of the board, but she found the lease binding and enforceable."

"So you expect no major changes in the lease?"

"It doesn't look like there's going to be anything forced on us. Everybody has said that this is a preliminary document, there's a lot of things left to talk about. We seem to have trouble getting to talk about those because of the concerns raised about what's already been done. It isn't going to go away. I think the lease will continue to generate attention perhaps until we start playing baseball."

But in fact the issue dies. Neither of the two reform bills backed by Neil Macey and Kathi Williams gets past the legislature. And as the new season draws near, and attention turns to happenings on the field, what Macey thought three months ago was only a 10 percent possibility is what occurs—nothing really happens.

Elsewhere, Rockies scouts are in the field, conducting tryout camps, beginning to watch games wherever it's warm enough to play. McHale and Antonucci are looking for a spring-training site. Pat Daugherty is in Venezuela, temporarily detained by a military coup while trying to find scouts to cover Latin America. Bob Gebhard is getting ready to head for Florida. He'll be in West Palm Beach looking at the Expos, Braves, Yankees, Mets and Dodgers during spring training. Larry Bearnarth, Joe Niekro (hired as the pitching coach for the Rockies' class A farm team in Bend, Oregon) and Pat Dobson (a contract scout working part-time for the Rockies) will handle the rest of Florida. Eddie Robinson (another contract scout) and Randy Smith will cover Arizona. From now until the June draft, the Rockies office will be a lonely place.

But Rockies president Steve Ehrhart isn't going anywhere. He has plenty to keep him busy right here, giving speeches, "sowing seeds in the community" and coping with the business fundamentals—budget plans, banking arrangements, office furniture, all that. "This is a little bit different than a small business where you start with two or three employees and ten years later you've grown into a big company," he says. "We really have to materialize in a few months into a full-fledged organization, theoretically on a par with some National League teams that have been around for eighty or a hundred years."

The big news is that the Rockies have signed a $5 million radio deal with KOA, whose corporate parent, Jacor Broadcasting, is a limited partner in the Rockies. "It could be one of the finest radio contracts in the history of professional sports in the sense that it could be geographically one of the largest," says Ehrhart. "We'll reach from Canada clear down to the Mexican border. We might not be as big a market as LA or Chicago or New York, so we have to make up for that by stretching out, taking advantage of the fact that the folks in Montana and Wyoming, Utah and Nevada identify with Colorado more than they would with other major league teams."

"What made it really dicey," says Paul Jacobs, "was that KYGO, which is the other station, was going to pay us a rights fee and we were going to sell the time. The KOA deal was a rights fee where they sell the time, and they pay us. Because KOA was a partner, we didn't want to say no to KOA. We wanted KOA to say no to us, if they just couldn't match the other offer. So I went over to [KOA station manager] Lee Larsen and laid out two offers for him that morning, and said, 'You can do it either way, and this is what it takes to in effect beat the competition.' Either arrangement, we tried to make it apples and apples for them. He said he didn't think he could do either one. And I really believed that we weren't going to get it done. So we called KYGO, and they came down, and we were negotiating the last few points in their deal when Lee called me back and said, "I want to come over and see you.' Okay! And he came over with one of them signed. He signed the one that he said he could never sign, so that's what made it a little tense. We have a deal, and he's happy and we're happy."

LARRY BEARNARTH is camped in the sun behind home plate at the Blue Jays' spring-training park in Dunedin, Florida, wearing a white Rockies baseball hat and juggling a Jugs radar gun, a stat sheet, a stopwatch, a mechanical pencil, a cigarette and a clipboard. "Took me about ten days to master that," he says, meaning the gun and the watch—he was gunning runners to first base and timing pitches. "Mostly the other major league scouts here are looking to fill some gaps on their team. I am looking to fill every gap. I'm looking for a first-string catcher that might be a second-string catcher right now, or a prospect catcher who wouldn't be afraid to play in a hundred twenty games next year. I'm looking for a shortstop who can play every day. Two or three good pitchers to build around and a closer type to solidify the pitching staff. And a center fielder who can go get the ball." So far, he says, catching worries him the most. There are plenty of guys with one tool only, instead of two or three.

"Some guys have this high anxiety level," Bearnarth says, "where you're never gonna be able to count on them to do any real specific critical role—like being a starting catcher or a starting pitcher or a shortstop or a second baseman or a center fielder or a guy to get the last three outs in a game."

Across the peninsula in West Palm Beach, Bob Gebhard is focusing down on the Expos and the Braves. Geb won't talk during a game, not when he's working, but he's happy to share breakfast at the Days Inn in West Palm. Like everybody else, he has noticed the many veterans who are trying hard to hang on, those who are happy to accept an assignment to AAA this year in the hope that there will be a place for them next year on an expansion team. "I think players look at expansion as a new avenue," he says, "a way to stay in this game longer. Every player that's ever put on a uniform thinks they can play forever and they think they're probably better than they really are. And none of them ever understand why they're not tendered a contract, why they're released. It just doesn't make sense to them. And those that are released this year obviously are going to try to do anything they can to stay alive for the possibility of expansion. I think sometimes they forget there's only going to be fifty additional players in the major leagues."

Looking ahead to the June draft, Gebhard says, "Everything being equal, we'll probably draft a few more college players than high school players because we don't have a system full of prospects. As for the expansion draft in November: "There's not a quick fix," he says. "There's going to be names out there that if you just drafted the veteran players you could have a payroll of thirty million dollars easily, and also have fifteen players that are thirty-five years old on your club too. And unless you get awful lucky, you're not going to win the world championship that first year or two. But you also wake up when you should be competitive and those players that you wasted those drafts on, they're gone."

Down the coast, the Marlins are hosting a series of exhibition games at Joe Robbie Stadium. Last spring, before he even knew he was getting a franchise, Wayne Huizenga spent $5 million to rip out the north grandstand and replace it with a retractable system for baseball, part one of an $11 million renovation in preparation for opening day. But baseball is new to these environs and there are kinks in the system. Last week the Yankees nearly walked off the field because of the poor condition of the bullpen mound. And today, with the Blue Jays in town, instead of playing the Canadian national anthem, they play the Russian national anthem, which ought to be enough to keep Miami's fervently anti-Castro Cuban population preoccupied for a while. (It's also a fitting start to a season that will end six months from now with the Canadian flag being presented upside down before a World Series game in Atlanta.)

David Dombrowski is here, fresh from a scouting trip to Japan. Once the season starts, he'll be on the road nearly every day. "Ideally," he says, "I would like to be in a position where I see every major league club play at least five times, so I have a feel of what's going on and my own opinions. I think that's very important. But our most important people calling the shots are going to be the major league scouts."

Out in the bleachers, the fans seem to be enjoying the sunshine more than the baseball. Lucas Cuadrado, an air-conditioning repairman originally from Cuba, admits he's not really a fan, the only thing he'll watch is the All-Star game and the World Series ("I think it's un-American not to"). "I love the Dolphins," he says. "I just really can't see myself spending the money that's required to buy a season ticket. When is the baseball season? Does it start right at summer?"

Hal Kobrin, formerly from Lynn, Massachusetts, says he thinks the Marlins will be a success, but a small one. "Personal opinion? I think if they sell fifteen to twenty thousand season tickets they'll be very happy. I was talking to my father about getting season tickets and he said, 'It's not necessary. We'll be able to come get tickets to whatever game we want.' "

ON JUNE 1, the Colorado Rockies, having won the coin toss with the Marlins, use the 27th pick of the draft to select John Burke, a left-handed pitcher from nearby Cherry Creek by way of the University of Florida. Later that day, Burke is introduced to the press, a tall blond kid with a big smile, surrounded by his parents and his girlfriend. Burke was represented in contract negotiations by Scott Boras, by consensus the toughest negotiator in the business. Knowing that, the Rockies were determined not to draft Burke unless they had an assurance in advance that he would sign, and for a while it looked like they weren't going to get it. Even as other teams were choosing players, John McHale and Bob Gebhard continued negotiations with Boras on a separate telephone line in the draft room. Minutes before it was the Rockies' turn to choose, terms were reached. "The undefeated Colorado Rockies pick John Burke," Daugherty said. Burke got a $350,000 signing bonus, plus the standard $800 a month salary.

Down in Miami, the Marlins were not so lucky. They chose Charles Johnson, a catcher from the University of Miami. "The once-defeated-by-coin-flip Florida Marlins pick Charles Johnson," is the way Hughes made the call. Hughes knew all about Johnson, having picked him once before out of high school when Hughes was with the Expos. But Johnson refused to sign then, and right away it was clear he was going to be just as hard to sign now. Inspired by the record-breaking $1.55 million contract high schooler Brien Taylor obtained from the Yankees last year, Johnson—also represented by Boras—demanded $1.5 million to sign with the Marlins.

Hughes was philosophical. "If we sign him, great. If we don't, we'll feel bad, just like we did three years ago. He's a local guy and all that, but Wayne's not going to go crazy on him, and I have no plans to recommend that he should."

EARLY WEDNESDAY MORNING, July 29, Paul Jacobs picked up John Antonucci at his big stone house in southeast

Denver. Jacobs thought they were on their way to the airport for a planned trip to Youngstown, Ohio. But as soon as Antonucci got in the car, he told Jacobs, "We're not going to Youngstown. I've been up all night talking to Mickey. Mickey's coming to Denver."

All Jacobs knew about Mickey Monus was what he had read the day before in a press release from Phar-Mor—that there had been a "restructuring of executive responsibilities" at Phar-Mor, that Monus was no longer president and CEO of the company, and that he'd been kicked up to vice chairman. Jacobs correctly read that as a demotion, but he was totally unprepared for what he was about to learn back at the Rockies office.

Monus showed up around eight-thirty. He wore khaki pants and a blue polo shirt and he looked like he had been up all night. Inside Antonucci's office, in the presence of Jacobs and Steve Kurtz, the team's financial consultant, Monus said simply, "I have to get out of baseball. I'm no longer acceptable to baseball."

Jacobs did not know what Monus was talking about, but he knew immediately that he did not want to hear any more. "Mickey, I don't want you to talk to anybody in this room about anything you just said," Jacobs said. "I'll get a partner down here and help you get counsel somewhere."

That done, Jacobs took steps to temporarily transfer ownership of all those shares in the Rockies partnership held by Monus and his father over to himself and to Kurtz. "My feeling," Jacobs later explained, "was: 'I'm never going to see this guy again. His problem is so great that he could wrap this franchise up in lawsuits for years about who owns his stock if he goes bankrupt.' Who knows? I just knew the franchise was better off if we got control of his stock."

Two days later, Phar-Mor fired Mickey Monus, along with chief financial officer Patrick Finn, and turned both their names over to the FBI. The news stayed quiet over the weekend but on Tuesday, August 4, Phar-Mor went public with the firings and announced it was taking a $350 million write-off against earnings after uncovering what it said was an "intricate criminal activity to defraud the company and its investors," including alleged "criminal activity" on the part of Monus and Finn. The write-off left the company with a net worth of only $220 million. (That set off a chain reaction. Creditors demanded payment, suppliers cut off supply, stores closed and employees were laid off. By October, when Phar-Mor filed for protection from creditors in bankruptcy court, the company listed assets of $1.095 billion against liabilities of $1.085 billion. What was once America's fastest-growing retailer was left with a net worth of only $10 million.)

Jacobs and Antonucci had flown to New York on Sunday, and they spent the next two days reassuring the commissioner's office and the National League that the Rockies were in no danger of going under. Letters of credit had already been posted for the full $95 million franchise fee, so the league was protected. The challenge to Jacobs and Antonucci would be to replace the $20 million commitment abandoned by Monus and his father.

Which turned out not to be a problem. Jerry McMorris, Oren Benton and Charles Monfort, the three most prominent limited partners, stepped in and gladly made up the difference, assuming new roles as general partners in the ownership group. McMorris took over as chairman and chief executive officer of the partnership, bumping Antonucci, who stayed with the club (for now), but in a subordinate role. "John says he is clean and I accept that . . . ," McMorris said at an August 6 press conference, responding to questions about Antonucci's business ties to Monus. "If it doesn't hold up, we'll address it." Steve Ehrhart, formerly president and chief operating officer, was removed as general partner, stripped of his duties with the club and reassigned to look after the Rockies' interests during construction of Coors Field.

IN THE END, the downfall of the Drugstore Cowboys was welcomed by most Coloradans, for it left the team largely in the hands of local owners. Moreover, that the so-called Big Three—McMorris, Benton and Monfort—were perfectly willing to increase their stake now was eloquent testimony to what a good investment the Rockies had become. Proof that what once was thought of as a high-risk venture—one requiring a substantial public subsidy just to get off the ground—was turning out to be something else altogether. Thanks to the best lease in the business, a terrific set of radio and television contracts, and 24,000 advance orders for season tickets (second only to the Dodgers), the Rockies partners—as much as Wayne Huizenga—could see now that they, too, were going to make a lot of money.

"Initially, it was a charitable contribution for these guys," says Jacobs. "By the time the ownership situation changed, they'd figured out we had created a hell of a business. That's why they stepped up to the plate—eagerly, I might add."

# Epilogue: The Draft

ON A WARM, humid Sunday morning—November 8, 1992—inside the Marlin Room (next door to the Dolphin Room) on the second floor of Fort Lauderdale's Marina Marriott (which is not the Marriott that Wayne Huizenga partly owns; that's the Harbor Marriott), the baseball men of the Florida Marlins are making final preparations for the expansion draft, to be held nine days from now in New York City.

Some of them have hardly left this room since early October, two days after the season ended. Since then, they've been painstakingly ranking every player on every club in every major league organization, from the big leagues all the way down to the short-season rookie leagues. Not all of the players are eligible for the draft. Free agents, anyone with a no-trade contract, college draft picks with less than three years experience in pro ball, and most high-school draft picks with less than

four years are among those who will be off limits to the Rockies and the Marlins on draft day. On the other hand, there's
no telling how some of those players might figure in roster
moves in the coming weeks and months. And since professional coverage is one area where the Marlins figure they have
the Rockies beat, GM David Dombrowski means to exploit his
advantage.

The dominant feature of the room is a long rectangular
conference table covered with overlapping tablecloths—teal,
like the Marlin hats. All around the table are high-back uphol-
stered chairs that swivel and tilt, executive-style, and all of the
chairs are filled. Dress is informal: lots of short-sleeve shirts
with Polo logos on the left breast, pleated slacks (Dockers), an
occasional pair of shorts. ("No shorts in New York," Dombrowski will warn. "The most important thing is that you're
comfortable. But if you do feel comfortable in a coat and tie,
great.")

Bunched near the head of the table are the same five scouts
who met for the first time almost a year before in Dombrowski's suite at the Doral in Miami Beach: Cookie Rojas, John
Young, Ken Kravec, Scott Reid, and Whitey Lockman. From
the first day of spring training to the last day of the season, all
five were on the road. (Rojas, who lives in Miami, slept in his
own bed all of thirteen nights in a span of seven months; while
he was away, Hurricane Andrew blew the roof off his house.)
Rojas, Young, Kravec, and Reid covered one division each—
from the big leagues down to class AA—with help from assistant GM Frank Wren, who took care of Kansas City, and scout
Murray Cook who took care of Milwaukee and Montreal. To
Lockman was assigned the numbing task of compiling a com-
prehensive report on virtually every player who played in the
big leagues in 1992. He almost pulled it off, missing only the
Braves, not counting (as scouts do not) what he was able to
pick up from watching TV.

After the amateur draft in June, the regular pro scouts were
assisted by Dick Egan and Jax Robertson, who cross-checked
the minor league pitchers and hitters respectively. Both Egan
and Robertson are here, along with minor league pitching
coordinator Rick Williams (the club's most recent hire, just

over from Montreal but not yet announced because 14 former Expos work for the Marlins already and president Carl Barger doesn't want to have to do any more explaining about that until after the draft), scouts Greg Zunino and Jim Hendry (two more crossovers from the amateur staff who helped out toward the end of the summer with pro coverage), scouting director Gary Hughes ("Boomer," one of the few wearing shorts), John Boles and Dan Lunetta from player development, Caribbean expert Angel Vasquez, international scout Orrin Freeman ("O," who visited Holland, Australia, Brazil, and Japan this year, and was away from his wife and two-year-old daughter 260 days out of the last 365), new manager Rene Lachemann ("Lach," until recently Tony La Russa's third-base coach in Oakland, also wearing shorts), his brother Marcel (the pitching coach, formerly with the Angels), trainer Larry Starr (here to advise on injured players), traveling secretary John Panagakis ("Greek," responsible this week for meals, snacks, caffeine beverages, and maintaining Lach's personal supply of Red Man chew), and a couple of eager interns (one of them Jay Hemond, the son of Dombrowski's mentor, Roland Hemond). A total of twenty-five cooks in all, packed together in a cramped and stuffy kitchen for what Dombrowski promises will be "a week filled from early in the morning until basically all night long."

Last week, while everybody else took a few days off to get reacquainted with their families, Dombrowski (still a bachelor, fortunately), Wren, Lockman, and Rene Lachemann flew to Palm Springs, California, for the annual GMs meeting. The Marlins have known all along that there will be players left unprotected whom they wouldn't want on their club (mostly, aging stars who make too much money) but who nevertheless have value as trade bait. With that in mind, the Marlins canvassed the competition in Palm Springs. Boston wants a cleanup hitter and starting pitchers, Dombrowski is explaining now, but mostly they want to get rid of some high salaries, namely Jody Reed and Jack Clark. California is looking for a center fielder who swings from the left side and can run. The White Sox are looking for a left-handed–hitting first baseman who can drive in runs. Cleveland wants a number-two starter to complement Charles Nagy. Detroit wants starting pitchers and an outfield bat. Kansas City wants an outfield bat and a shortstop. . . . And so on, in alphabetical order, through all twenty-six teams. First the American League, then the National League. Everybody takes notes.

"If we're going to make a pick based on a trade," Dombrowski warns, "we need to make sure we really have a deal." In order to be sure, of course, both clubs need to know exactly who they're getting, and that's where the Marlins and the Rockies will enter a gray area in the days ahead. Tomorrow afternoon the fax machine on the table behind Wren's chair will begin delivering the long-awaited protected lists, forwarded one by one as they are received in the Marlins' main office in downtown Fort Lauderdale. Every Marlin employee in the room has had to promise in writing not to reveal the names on the lists to anyone outside this room under penalty of a $250,000 fine from the commissioner's office. So the challenge during trade negotiations will be to describe available players to other teams as precisely as possible without actually coming right out and saying who they are.

For now, at least, Dombrowski means to abide by the letter of the law, if not the spirit. Thus, he explains in answer to a question from a scout that yes, it's okay to talk to other clubs about a possible deal for, say, the Royals left fielder—the chunky one, good power, played college ball at Arkansas—but try not to say Kevin McReynolds. "If someone calls and asks about a specific player, tell them they need to speak with me," says Dombrowski. "That's a touchy situation. Don't anybody put yourself in a situation where you have to mention a player's name."

Dombrowski might have shown more respect for the rule's intent did he not feel so strongly, along with Marlin president Carl Barger, that the expansion clubs were being screwed by the baseball establishment in so many ways. Charging them $95 million just to get in, for example; then cutting them out of the lucrative national television contracts; then leaving them with the last two picks in the free-agent draft; and now the latest twist of the knife—it was rumored that at least two high-profile free agents, Kirby Puckett and Robin Yount, had already reached agreements to re-sign with the Twins and the Brewers respectively, but were persuaded to put off signing until after the draft so that their teams would not have to protect them. No wonder that when a Royals official approached Dombrowski in Palm Springs and asked him if he would ever consider drafting George Brett, Dombrowski smiled and said, "We might." Fat chance—at age thirty-nine, Brett is no longer the star he was—but why should Dombrowski do the Royals a favor, especially if it would only allow them to protect another prospect?

"They're sticking it to us," Dombrowski tells his troops before lunch. Then he gives them the rest of the afternoon off. There's really not a whole lot they can do until the lists come in. And tomorrow will be a long day.

"HELLO, BILL? Bill?"

Nothing but white noise is coming from the tiny speaker at the head of the conference table. "Third world," Egan mutters derisively.

"Bill?"

"Hello!" comes the response, suddenly clear. "Hello!" It is Bill Scherrer, calling from Venezuela. The Marlins have scouts all over Central America and the Caribbean, covering the winter leagues. The morning will be devoted to hearing their reports and making last-minute adjustments, if necessary, in the player rankings. But the one big name that jumps out is Andres Galarraga, a big league first baseman who was originally signed by the Expos and consequently is well known to Dombrowski and many others in the room. Scherrer is not impressed by Galarraga. He ranks him number fourteen overall.

"Fallen that far, eh?" says Dombrowski.

"He wants to pull all the time," says Scherrer. "He's a mediocre first baseman with power. He's not overweight at all, he's strong." (In a few days, Galarraga would sign a one-year contract with the Rockies for $600,000.)

Next to call is yet another new hire from the Expos, Jesus

Alou, covering the action back home this winter in the Dominican Republic. "I feel very happy to be part of the big fish!" Alou says before launching into his report. His assessments, unlike Scherrer's, are anecdotal and seemingly imprecise. And yet it is obvious that Dombrowski values his opinions. On a catcher in the A's organization: "I don't like him too much. Balls are always flying away from him." On a back up shortstop for an AL East team: "I like him as our shortstop. Not for a long time, but maybe for a few years." On Jose Martinez, a highly regarded pitcher in the Mets organization: "I watched him the whole game and he never threw what you call a fat pitch. This kid is a pitcher."

All morning and on into the early afternoon the calls keep coming—from Puerto Rico, Mexico, and finally the Arizona Instructional League. Scouts Tim Schmidt and Jeff Pentland are in Arizona, and as soon as Dombrowski has them on the line, he brings up the name of a switch-hitting outfield prospect in the Yankees organization, Carl Everett. Dombrowski has just learned that the Yankees have left Everett unprotected (the fax machine started humming shortly after lunch). He wants to know exactly what his scouts think of him.

"Great" comes the first voice through the speaker. "First of all, he's the best athlete here. He's got a lot of life in that stick. He's stronger from the right side of the plate. His biggest problem is pitch selection."

"Has this guy got *star* written all over him?" Dombrowski wants to know.

"There's a good possibility. Maybe a year away."

"How's his attitude?"

"Improving. Supposedly on the right track. He's really playing hard here."

The other prospect both scouts like very much is a right-handed pitcher with the Blue Jays. "He's the steal of the league," says the voice on the speaker.

"Who would you take, Carl Everett or [the pitcher]?" Dombrowski asks.

"That's not a fair question!"

"It's a very important question," says Dombrowski seriously.

"I would take Carl Everett," says one scout.

"I would take [the pitcher]," says the other.

IN THE BACK OF THE ROOM, next to the coffee urns and the fruit plates and the platters piled high with cranberry muffins and cheese danishes, are the telephones. When Dombrowski calls a ten-minute break, Boles grabs Lachemann and asks him if he wouldn't mind saying hello to a free-agent journeyman catcher the Marlins are hoping to sign before the draft. The catcher is playing hard to get. He had his best season ever last year in the AAA, and thinks he has a chance to play in the big leagues next season. He wants to wait and see what happens in the draft before making up his mind.

"I can't promise you anything," says Lachemann, "but we don't have a starting catcher. And we don't have a backup catcher either."

After Lachemann, it's Dombrowski's turn. Normally a player like this would not be getting so much attention from the manager and the general manager. But things are different in an expansion year, and the catcher knows it, which is the problem. "We're going after only a select few," Dombrowski says respectfully. "The Rockies have signed sixteen [minor league free agents], we've signed only two. We are extremely interested in you. We think you have a chance to make our big league club, or we wouldn't be sitting here talking to you."

Mostly, though, Dombrowski listens. After he hangs up, he turns to Boles. "I think he's going to sign with us," he says.

Maybe, but he's going to make them wait. "The guy thinks he's Johnny Bench," says a scout disgustedly.

AT 7:30, AFTER a room service dinner (pizza in boxes and thirty individual slices of key lime pie), and after pausing to watch ESPN's SportsCenter together on the conference room TV, it is time, finally, to examine the protected lists. Everyone in the room has his own copy of the confidential Florida Marlins Pro Player Composite Report. For the scouts who compiled it, the report is the fruit of a lifetime of accumulated wisdom, capped by an exhausting summer of dedicated observation. The report has twenty-six parts, one for each major league organization. Each part consists of a one-page list of the most attractive draft-eligible players in that organization, ranked purely by ability, without regard to salary, age, or position played. In the case of the major leaguers, the scout's judgment comes down to an appraisal of how well the player performed in 1992. But for the minor leaguers, the ranking is an educated guess as to what that player might become. The best players are those with the highest "ceiling," as scouts say. Those whose raw tools, once refined, will likely take them the furthest.

One by one Dombrowski reads the names of the protected players, fifteen in each organization, pausing just long enough between names in order to cross them off the list. "Wow!" comes a muttered exclamation from somewhere down the conference table. The Orioles have left four players unprotected that the Marlins like very much. Notable among them is Kip Yaughn, a twenty-three-year-old right-handed pitcher from Arizona State who has averaged almost a strikeout an inning in three pro seasons. Yaughn moves immediately to the top of the Marlins' revised list.

The shocker of the evening comes two clubs later at California, when Dombrowski says that relief pitcher Bryan Harvey, is available. Harvey, an All Star, saved 46 games for the Angels in 1991 and was equally brilliant last season until he went on the disabled list with a sore elbow in early June.

Kansas City protects George Brett (no surprise there), and perhaps because of that makes Omaha's power-hitting first baseman Jeff Conine available, along with two younger prospects, right-handed pitcher Andres Berumen and center fielder Kerwin Moore ("Ooooh!"). By the time Dombrowski finishes with the American League, and it is apparent that not only have the Twins left Al Newman unprotected but the Yankees have exposed Carl Everett, Charlie Hayes, and Danny Tartabull, Texas has left off Rob Nen, and Toronto has made available a trio of super prospects—Nigel Wilson, Aaron Small, and David Weathers—the mood in the Marlin Room is bordering on ecstatic.

And, it turns out, there are just as many happy surprises in the National League. The Braves, rich with talented young pitchers, have to draw the line somewhere, and they draw it at David Nied, who is coming off a breakthrough year in Richmond. The Cubs offer Shawon Dunston; the Expos, Ivan Calderon and Bret Barberie; the Mets, Eddie Murray; the Phillies, Mitch Williams; the Cardinals, Lee Smith. "This is better than key lime pie," says Egan, dropping his usual poker-face composure and giving in to the moment.

The only other task Dombrowski wants to accomplish tonight is to comb through the final list of unprotected players for trade possibilities and medical question marks (under the rules of the draft, the Marlins and the Rockies are entitled to full disclosure from other teams' trainers and doctors). The trainer Starr is joined by team physician Dan Kanell. Both take notes as Dombrowski flips through the lists of names, speaking only when necessary.

"Harvey is a big, big one," he says when he comes to California. "They're taking a heck of a gamble with him . . . Conine, we had a red flag about his wrist. . . . Tartabull—"

"Wouldn't Boston look at him," Egan interrupts, thinking trade.

"I would think so. . . . Cleveland is dying for a guy like Pete Smith. They said they'd give us a quality guy for Pete Smith. . . . Eddie Murray"—he purses his lips and shakes his head—"Al [Harazin, general manager of the Mets] even said publicly, 'Can you imagine if we lost Eddie Murray?' Publicly!"

"Maybe they sent the wrong list," says Cook, laughing.

"Mitch Williams, I'm surprised. Jeez . . . $2.4 million"— scanning his salary sheet—"that's not a lot for Lee Smith. I guess they figure if they lose Smith they can sign Worrell. . . ."

Time now to begin making preliminary offers to clubs that might want to make a deal before the draft. With so many GMs to contact, and so little time, Dombrowski divides the assignments among the senior members of his staff, based on who knows who. They'll start making calls from their rooms that night.

"PREPARE FOR AN EXCITING DAY!" Dombrowski says, closing the door and rubbing his hands together. After the meeting broke up last night, the interns stayed late to set up the magnetic boards. On the side board this morning, under yellow headings for each organization, are hundreds of colored tags with the names of the available players: white for position players, orange for right-handed pitchers, and pink for the rarest of all baseball commodities, left-handed pitchers. Beginning today they'll take one more look at each list and try to settle on a final ranking. Later in the week they'll transfer the tags one by one to the big board at the front of the room in overall order of preference, creating a master list for draft day.

But first, the Marlins have learned that third baseman Jack Howell, a former California Angel who's been playing in Japan, may be interested in coming back to the United States. Freeman watched him play the previous summer and thinks he may be worth a shot. "I've seen Jack Howell forever and know him like you guys all do," says O. "But the point is, he got better. He moved up on the plate. He's hitting more with power. I don't think he's a *great* third baseman, I never did. But . . ."

"Jack's biggest problem to me was always himself," offers Marcel Lachemann, who remembers him well. "In California he was being compared all the time to Wally Joyner. I thought Jack Howell was going to be a better player than Wally Joyner, but he pushed himself past the point where it was productive."

"If you can tell me that Jack Howell is going to hit .220, .230, I'd take him in a minute," says Rene Lachemann.

Dombrowski is convinced. He asks Boles to call Howell's agent and try to find out how much it would cost to sign him.

Okay, on to the lists. Dombrowski stands up, walks over to a small magnetic board propped on an easel at the front of the room, and pulls back a white sheet, revealing the names of the players in the first organization they'll consider, the Baltimore Orioles. Of the fourteen teams in the American League, only eight will lose as many as three players in the draft; the others will lose only two. Baltimore is one AL organization the Marlins believe has enough talent to warrant three picks, so they'll need to decide on the eleven players they like best (between rounds, each AL team can protect four more players). One name they discard right away is first baseman Glenn Davis, not because the Marlins don't like him but because he earned $3.4 million in 1992. "He's a guy we'd take only to trade," Dombrowski says.

Same with Greg Harris, Jody Reed, and Joe Hesketh on the Red Sox (a two-pick franchise), all of whom are judged too expensive by the Marlins. Money is definitely a factor. On the other hand, Dombrowski now has a 14-million-dollar payroll budget to work with—2 million more than the Rockies—and so he has enough money to spend on "a couple of quality guys." Bryan Harvey, for example, who's under contract through 1995 for 11.25 million. "I don't think there's any question that under normal circumstances, Harvey is the number-one guy in the draft," Dombrowski says. "This is the kind of guy you normally can't even trade for." But doctors removed bone chips from Harvey's elbow in August. The question is, can he come back?

Starr, the trainer, is optimistic. Bone chips don't worry him as much as a ligament problem would, he explains, especially for a relief pitcher, who needs to gear up only for short bursts. Marcel Lachemann, who coached Harvey in California, points out that "he's been cleaned out before, and he responded to that like it was nothing."

"Okay," says Dombrowski, "assuming he's healthy, is he a person we want to gamble on?"

"No doubt," says Lachemann, "you're talking about a first-class guy." Lachemann says Harvey tried to call him at home the night before. "I talked to his mother-in-law this morning. She said Brian was pretty upset when he found out he was unprotected. I think his reaction is going to be 'Get me the hell out of here.' I think California just wants someone to take them out from under the money. They think Joe Grahe can be their closer. The only chink in Brian's armor is that he does not hold runners on."

"How good is he without the forkball?" Lockman wants to know.

"Only average. But if he goes strike-one on a hitter, that guy's in deep shit."

"It's a gamble," says Dombrowski, "but it's an appealing one." In the end, Harvey stays at number one. Number two, after much debate, is Junior Felix, the Angels' leading run producer with 72 RBIs in 1992. Everyone agrees that Felix is an exciting young outfielder, potentially an All Star. But they question his makeup.

"He's not a bad kid," says Marcel Lachemann, "just very immature. The things that excite him are like throwing pillows on an airplane. He just lights up like a Christmas tree. I'm not saying that throwing pillows isn't fun, but that may account for the swings in production."

At the other end of the table, Cookie Rojas, another ex-Angel, nods his head in agreement. "You never know what he's going to do," he says. "You give him a sign to steal, if he don't want to steal, he won't."

"He has the mind of a ten- to twelve-year-old, tops," adds Angel Vasquez.

"Sounds like Pascual Perez," says Dombrowski, who reminds everybody that under the right circumstances, Perez was nevertheless outstanding. "What it comes down to," says Dombrowski, looking at his manager, "is do you want to put up with him?"

Lach is noncommittal. He remembers, though, that Doug Rader, the Marlins' new hitting instructor and first-base coach, happens to like Felix. Rader will be here tomorrow. Lach will talk to him then.

By the time they finish with the White Sox, it is time for lunch. Before they break, though, Dombrowski dials scout Birdie Tebbetts at his home in Anna Maria, Florida, and puts him on the speaker phone. Today is Tebbetts's eightieth birthday. "Hey, Birdie," Dombrowski says when Tebbetts picks up, "I got about thirty friends of yours here!" And with that the whole room launches into a rough rendition of "Happy Birthday."

"I don't know the ages of all you guys," says the firm voice on the speakerphone after the singing stops. "But can you imagine anybody being eighty years old?"

"THIS IS an interesting group" is the way Dombrowski introduces Cleveland. "Here we're talking about guys we like a lot as prospects."

If the Marlins have an overall strategy for the draft, it is always to take the best player available. For more than a year that's been Dombrowski's pat answer to every reporter who asked. Partly, it's just a line to keep the competition guessing. (The Rockies, by contrast, have talked openly for months about their plan to stockpile pitching, on the theory that down the road, finding hitters who want to play in Denver's mile-high stadium will be no problem. Knowing that, the Marlins can plan accordingly.) But there's truth in it too. Dombrowski knows there will be plenty of passable big leaguers looking for work the following spring, should he need to fill a hole; while prospects with high ceilings are always hard to come by.

Still, Dombrowski can't afford to ignore entirely the needs of next year's club. No one on the Marlins expects to win it all in '93, but no one wants to finish last either. Hence the strong interest in the closer Harvey, and in a guy like the Indians' Jack Armstrong. In 1990, his first full season in the big leagues, Armstrong got off to an 11-3 start and was the National League starting pitcher in the All-Star game. Then he fell apart, finishing the season 1-6. After he dropped to 7-13 in '91, the Reds traded him to Cleveland, who eventually put him in the bullpen. There, late in the season, pitching mainly in a set-up role, he showed tantalizing signs of regaining his touch.

Rumor has it the Indians think Armstrong can be a closer but kept him back last year for fear he would excel—and excite the Marlins and the Rockies. Cook, who was GM in Cincinnati in 1987 when the Reds made Armstrong their number-one draft choice, likes the idea. "I really don't see this guy as a starter anymore," he says. "Put him where he's had success and make him a closer." (Cook's only reservation is personal.

"He was a pain in the ass in Cincinnati. He thinks he's smarter than anyone else.")

Dombrowski seems ready to go with Armstrong as number one simply because he's "such a good arm," and not worry yet what his role will be. But the consensus of the scouts is that Darrell Whitmore—a fleet, power-hitting outfielder who played college football at West Virginia—has the higher ceiling.

"They'd die if they lost Whitmore," Dombrowski concedes.

"Let's kill 'em," says Hughes.

Whitmore number one, Armstrong number two.

AT 2:05 IN THE AFTERNOON, in the middle of a listless discussion about Detroit ("There's a good chance whoever we take here with our second pick, we'd take him right off our roster"), the phone rings for Dombrowski. It's Bill Murray, director of baseball operations in the commissioner's office, calling to complain about leaks with regard to the names on the protected lists. Dombrowski listens, a sober, concerned look on his face. "You can be assured we haven't told any of the papers," he says before he hangs up. Which is true, no doubt.

"CONINE, is there any question that he's number one?" Dombrowski wants to know, scanning the Kansas City list. The medical report on Conine's wrist has turned out to be encouraging.

"Not in my mind," says Wren. "This guy's going to hit twenty-five home runs in the big leagues."

"Can he play left field?" An important question, with so many designated-hitter types available who can't play anywhere else but first base.

"I think so," says Wren.

Rene Lachemann, who has watched Conine in his brief appearances with the Royals, disagrees. "It's going to take some work," he says.

But Boles, who was farm director in Kansas City when Conine was drafted, is high on him—"The KC minor league people will be shocked when they find out he was left off the protected lists"—and that settles it in Conine's favor. Number two is Berumen, who excelled at class A last season after he was converted to a reliever. "I would be ecstatic if we could take Berumen in the second round," says Dombrowski. Moore, the outfielder, is third.

All three are among the top twelve players in the Royals organization, according to Wren of the Marlins. Yet all were left unprotected, while shortstop David Howard, for example —only number twenty-three on the Marlin list—was held back. All of which just goes to show that evaluating players is an art, not a science. When Vasquez is asked one day during lunch about what goes into the process, he smiles, turns over his butter plate, and divides it in two with his finger. One half, he explains, is made up of the five standard performance categories, all of which can be measured with varying degrees of accuracy: running, throwing, fielding, hitting and hitting with power. And the other half? Vasquez sits back in his chair and touches first his head, then his heart, then his balls. Brains, will, and courage. And it is will, or desire—"*volunta*" is the word Vasquez uses—that Vasquez believes is often the determining factor. "In the type of civilization in which we live," says Vasquez, "sometimes willpower is more important than brains."

At the heart of the process is ambiguity, and yet ambiguity is a sentiment a scout must always beat down. He is paid to be sure, to know what God knows.

"I think he's one of those good-body guys who's never going to do it," one scout says of a Royals prospect.

"His stuff is better than his performance," says another scout of a different player. "He's the type of guy that managers don't love because you want him to be better."

And, "He's a four-A pitcher"; in other words, capable of excelling in AAA but lacking whatever it takes to succeed at the highest level. Ouch.

CHARLES JOHNSON—the Marlins' top choice in last June's amateur draft—finally signed a contract today. Dombrowski called a break around four and everybody went downstairs to watch the press conference. The University of Miami senior got $585,000 plus an invitation to spring training and a promise that no matter what, the Marlins would put him in a major league uniform in September and let him travel with the club, just to get a taste of life in the big leagues.

For most of the summer it had looked like this day would never come. Johnson originally wanted $1.55 million, which Huizenga refused to pay. Finally, at one minute before midnight on Friday, November 6—the deadline, after which Johnson would have reentered next year's draft—Johnson gave in, accepting almost a million dollars less than he thought he was worth in order not to lose the chance to play for his hometown team. Score one for Huizenga.

Back upstairs in the draft room the talk turns to another local hero, Orestes Destrade. Born in Cuba and raised in South Florida, the power-hitting first baseman struggled with the Yankees before signing with the Seibu Lions in Japan. There he became a star, winning home-run titles and MVP awards and inevitably inviting comparison to another veteran of Japanese baseball who later became the leading home-run hitter in the major leagues, Cecil Fielder. Word is out that Destrade wants to come home. He'd be perfect for the Marlins, who would love to have a Cuban star on the team. But he's expensive. "Does he have Fielder-type potential?" Dombrowski asks Freeman. No other scout has seen him play in years, but Freeman was in Japan the past summer.

"Knowing what I knew about Cecil at the time [he signed with the Tigers]," says Freeman, "I'd take this guy."

"You're as confident as you could be that he's a big league player?"

"Yes."

According to Dombrowski, the Lions are offering him $6 million for two years, which would be the highest salary ever paid in Japan. That's much more than the Marlins are willing to pay, but the signal they're getting is that Destrade, like Johnson, would be willing to accept less money for the chance to play in front of his hometown fans. Yesterday, by the way,

Jack Howell decided to go back to Japan for another season, so the Marlins have some money to play with. Maybe three million for two years, Dombrowski suggests.

"How many major league cleanup hitters make only a million and a half dollars?" Hughes asks. Not many.

"I would be very, very, very surprised," says Freeman, sticking his neck way out, "—and out of a job—if he hit less than .240 and less than twenty home runs."

"So you'd give it to him?" Dombrowski presses.

"Yes. I'll take the credit either way."

Dombrowski decides to open with an offer of a $1.5 million signing bonus, a $500,000 salary the first year, and one million the second year. "Jay," says Dombrowski to the intern, handing him a piece of paper. "Could you make a call to this number and ask Carl [Barger, still in Scottsdale] to call me."

Barger calls back around 7:30. He tells Dombrowski to go ahead, offer Destrade three million, but try to keep the signing bonus down—better to pile more money into the first year's salary than risk paying for a player they won't be able to use if there's a lockout the following season. Barger has just emerged from the meeting in which the National League owners voted not to allow Giants owner Bob Lurie to sell his team to a group of investors from St. Petersburg. That's good news for Huizenga, who was appalled at the prospect of having to share the Florida market with an established major league team. He worked hard behind the scenes to block the sale, infuriating fans in Tampa Bay, who organized a boycott of Blockbuster Video and burned their membership cards in protest. In the end, opposition by other owners was strong enough, so Huizenga was able to go on record as voting in favor of the move. (Which fooled no one. Not the despondent fans of Tampa Bay, who continue to hold Huizenga personally responsible for what is only the latest in a series of crushing disappointments. And not the Tampa Bay investors, who would soon file suit against Huizenga.)

The meeting drags on into the night, past the point where caffeine does any good. Throats are dry, eyes are red. (Lach, for one, has resorted to dipping his fingers in a glass of ice water and flicking himself in the face. So far he has been able to avoid mistaking his spit bottle for his bottle of Pepsi. But the meeting's not over yet. . . .)

As for an AL West pitcher, whose availability surprised Dombrowski, word has filtered through to the Marlin draft room that the problem may be alcohol. The trainer Starr has checked with his sources. "There's nothing wrong with him physically," Starr reports, "but they can't get him in shape because he likes his liquid refreshment."

"Grover Cleveland Alexander!" says Hughes, recalling the legendary pitcher who drank so much that by the time he retired in 1929 "he couldn't shake hands without taking three stabs at it," according to a biographical sketch in *Total Baseball*. Alexander is in the Hall of Fame but Dombrowski seems disinclined to gamble. He makes a note to check with major league baseball's employee assistance program, a supposedly confidential referral service for those who voluntarily seek help with substance-abuse problems.

On the Yankees, the consensus number-one is Everett, who the Marlins feel is "one of the top guys in the draft." Everett suffered a deep leg bruise during the past year but no one seems worried. "We think that injury was milked for all it was worth," says Wren, implying that the Yankees may be trying to discourage the expansion clubs from taking him.

On to Oakland. So many A's are free agents this year—and therefore ineligible for the draft—that GM Sandy Alderson has been able to protect almost everybody worth protecting in his organization. Not much is left. "I don't think there's one guy on this list we would really want to take," says Dombrowski. Earlier, when Alderson asked Dombrowski if he would agree not to draft a player from Oakland in the third round as compensation for hiring Lachemann and Rader, Dombrowski politely said yes.

"Weren't they a two-pick club anyway?" asks Hughes.

"Yeah, but we don't have to tell them that."

Next is Seattle—"and it ain't getting any better," says Dombrowski. Finally, after Texas ("an injury-filled organization"), Dombrowski calls an end to the day's proceedings. They'll start with Toronto in the morning, then begin the National League with Atlanta. Both clubs are overflowing with talent, and Dombrowski wants everybody to be fresh.

"I could have gone one more club tonight!" says Boomer.

"WHEN WE TALK about Toronto," Dombrowski says, pausing to apply the first swipe of lip balm of the day, "right off the bat we're talking about two of the top guys in the draft. We've got a chance to get one. We're not going to get the other. So I need you to bear down. This is as important as it gets."

Toronto has also left two established stars unprotected—Kelly Gruber and Jack Morris. GM Pat Gillick's hope, presumably, is that Colorado or Florida will take one of them and trade him, after which he can pull back his prospects. But the Marlins, at least, have already decided that no other prospect they could hope to get in a trade for Gruber or Morris would be worth more to them than the prospects Toronto has to offer.

Wren punches a button on the remote control and a shaky image of Nigel Wilson at the plate—lean build, long legs, sweeping left-handed cut—appears on the television screen. Marlin scouts spent the summer taping scores of top minor league prospects. "Hits with power," explains Kravec, who scouted Toronto. "Better on offense. Weak arm."

"Does he ever make contact, Ken?" asks Lockman. So far, all he's done is swing and miss. Then, crack. "Okay, there we go."

"He's a raw talent," says Wren, who filed a supplemental report. "I saw him a little bit better defensively than Ken."

"Can he play center field?" asks Lockman.

"I would say no, he's a left fielder."

Then a tall right-handed pitcher appears on the screen.

"Big frame," says Kravec. "Potential to fill out. Fastball-curve-change pitcher. Above average action and change. Needs innings to solidify his control. Command is his problem. When he has command, he is dominating."

"He's their prize jewel," says Dombrowski, watching closely, "and they're hoping nobody takes him. We talk about Toronto building up their prospects. Well, this is a guy they're trying to keep quiet, but his name keeps leaking out."

After a while Wren points the remote control at the screen and it goes blank again. Dombrowski turns to face his staff. "The choice," he says, "is between a guy who has a chance to lead the league in hitting, albeit with a weak arm. And a guy who's got a chance to be a dominating number-one or number-two starting pitcher."

Kravec, whose opinion in this case carries the most weight, has already made up his mind. "I never wavered," he says. "Nigel is my guy. He's got a chance to hit .320 and twenty-plus homers. Nigel is an offensive force. I never saw it as a tough decision. Nigel is my guy."

"Great," says Dombrowski, playing devil's advocate, "but I've got to throw in more information here. The reports on [the pitcher] are that he keeps getting better and better."

"I understand your problem," says Robertson, the former scouting director of the Tigers. "You've got a tough call. But Nigel is the most impressive offensive player I saw all summer in Double A or Triple A."

"He was head and shoulders the best player I saw all summer long," adds Wren.

"How bad a left fielder is he going to be?" Dombrowski asks the group.

"Average," says Kravec, which amounts to an endorsement. He means as good as the average major league outfielder.

"I think he can be better than Tim Raines," says Wren.

"The throwing problem may just all be in how he sets up," says Boles, the farm director. "That can be corrected."

"Philosophically, I feel more comfortable taking a position player because they don't get hurt as much," says Dombrowski. "We're talking about the first pick of the draft. Right now with what I'm hearing I'm leaning toward taking Nigel Wilson. Who wants to debate that?"

"I can't argue that there's a lot more of a gamble with a pitcher," says Marcel Lachemann, speaking as the pitching coach. "You're talking about one tool and that tool can break."

"My job is to watch pitchers," says Egan, "but I can't help but watch Wilson."

With that, Dombrowski asks for a show of hands. "Who likes Wilson first?" Every hand goes up except Cook's. ("I must have been scratching my face," is what he says later.)

Dombrowski ducks into the bathroom. "Time for a five-minute break?" Hughes wonders out loud.

"No!" comes the voice from the can.

TIME FOR TWO MORE CLUBS before lunch, Atlanta and the Cubs. The Braves have left four outstanding young pitchers unprotected—"They couldn't decide on their four top guys, so they're going to make us decide," says Reid, who covered the NL West. But Reid knows what he wants. "Nied. He's as good a minor league pitcher as you might want to see. He's ready to pitch in the big leagues right now. To me, you're talking about a number-two starter. I'm surprised this guy was not protected."

At the top of the Cubs list is a hard-throwing right-handed pitcher, but Gary Hughes doesn't like him. "I just want to go on record saying whatever his tools, I just don't think he's ever going to be a winner or a guy you can depend on." And after the pitcher, the catcher Joe Girardi.

"Could he be our catcher?" Dombrowski asks Rojas.

"Yeah, he could be our catcher. If we don't have anybody else."

"We're not talking about Bill Dickey?" says Hughes.

"No, absolutely not."

THE DODGERS are like the Mets used to be and the Blue Jays are today. They've always got a prospect or two somewhere in the organization who is already a legend by the time he makes it to the big leagues. Once there, maybe he pans out and maybe he doesn't. This year's hot Dodger prospect is Rudy Seanez, a 5-10 (maybe) right-hander who's been clocked at over 100 miles per hour. Seanez didn't pitch at all the previous year because of a bad back, but in 1991, at class AA Canton-Akron in the Eastern League, he struck out 73 in 38.1

innings, a ratio that reads like a typographical error. He once pitched a whole winter in Mexico without allowing an earned run. "There's nobody better I'd like to beat than the Los Angeles Dodgers," says Reid, introducing Seanez. "I just want to make sure we don't get caught up in all the hype."

"I saw him pitch four games," Egan remembers, "and Jesus Christ could not have hit him."

"Assuming he's healthy, he's got about as good an arm as you could find," says Dombrowski.

"No-brainer," says Hughes. "We're not talking about a pitching staff next year that's the '54 Indians [who had two 20-game winners, plus the league leader in shutouts and earned run average]. We'll take his fastball and live with him."

It takes more than an hour to get through Montreal, if only because everybody in the room is an expert. Calderon gets crossed off the list right away because he makes too much money. Cook, who scouted the Expos, then tries to make a case for catcher Rob Natal as number one, but is voted down ("He looks like Fred Flintstone," says Dombrowski). They'll gamble on Natal still being there after the first round. After the dust settles, Barberie—a converted second baseman who struggled last year at third base—winds up on top of the list. If they can get him, the Marlins will return him to his old position.

On to the Mets. If it were up to Rojas, the Marlins would take right-handed pitcher John Johnstone in the first round. But Alou gave such a good report Monday on Jose Martinez ("I never seen Jesus so excited about a player," says Vasquez) that Dombrowski wants to hear more. Egan and Cook, it turns out, agree with Alou.

"You both feel that Martinez's ceiling is higher?" Dombrowski asks.

"Yes."

"Well, then, that answers it for me."

Time before dinner to knock off the Phillies, who don't have too much to offer other than comic relief. "I'd like to take a shot on this bad-bodied fucker with a great arm," says Egan.

"I've never liked him," says Hughes. "I think if you put a

thousand dollars out there and asked him to throw a strike, he'd throw a ball."

"What if you put out a cheeseburger?"

DOMBROWSKI'S STRONG INTEREST in Bryan Harvey goes somewhat against conventional wisdom. In order to win a championship, you have to have a bullpen closer, that's a given these days. But what good is a closer unless you have a team capable of carrying a lead into the late innings? More often than not—*much* more—the 1993 Marlins will be losing by the time the ninth inning rolls around, Dombrowski knows that. All the more reason, the way he sees it, to have a guy in the bullpen who can nail down what few games the Marlins have a chance to win. There's a psychological factor, Dombrowski believes, especially for a young team. A closer is insurance against hopelessness.

Lee Smith is available, too, but on the Cardinal's roster the Marlins prefer Chuck Carr, a quick (71 steals in 1992) little (5 feet 10 inches) outfielder coming off what scouts consider a breakthrough year. If they get him, Carr should be the Marlins starting center fielder on opening day. Speaking on Carr's behalf, Egan cites what he says is Whitey Herzog's theory of how to build a winner—with defense, starting with fleet outfielders and a solid left side of the infield.

Joe Magrane is available, which pleases Hughes. "He's a big Jimmy Buffet fan," says Hughes, himself a loyal member of the fraternity of parrot heads. "Remember when they used to put those lists in *USA Today*? He had a list of his ten favorite Jimmy Buffet songs. I think we ought to take him."

It has taken most of two twelve-hour days, but by ten o'clock on Wednesday night, one part of the job, at least, is over. Complete on the side board are all twenty-six revised lists of available players, organized by team. Tomorrow they'll begin putting names up on the front board, best to worst, in overall order of preference. Time now for bed.

"Being from California, I worry about this stuff," says Freeman, watching the interns pull a sheet over the side board for the night. "Do we have this board written down somewhere in case there's an earthquake?"

THURSDAY'S *Fort Lauderdale Sun-Sentinel* published the complete list of protected players, courtesy of Jerome Holtzman of the *Chicago Tribune*, accurate in every detail. Which is why Dombrowski begins the session with a warning. "Please, don't comment on it," he says. "To anybody. This is very dangerous territory." When the phone rings, it's Bill Murray calling back, demanding the names of every Marlin employee who may have had access to the lists. Dombrowski hates being a suspect, but he's glad the list is out. "There may be a lot of ticked-off GMs out there," he says, "but in some ways this helps us."

Perhaps because the lists are public now, trade talks intensify. The phones in the back of the room are ringing all the time, and as the day wears on, deals begin to take shape. The Phillies are interested in the Pirates' Danny Jackson, which makes sense to the Marlins for two reasons. One, they're pretty sure he'll still be available in the third round, given Pittsburgh's determination to shed salaries, which means they won't have to spend a high pick on him. And two, the only players on the Phillies that they want are prospects too young to be eligible for the draft, and Jackson ought to be worth at least two of them. Besides Jackson, several clubs seem interested in the Cubs' Shawon Dunston, including Houston, Kansas City, and the Yankees.

Okay, on to the big board, and the question, finally: Which player do they like best of all? "I don't think there's any question that Harvey is the best guy up there," says Dombrowski. But Harvey is a special case. He probably makes too much money for the Rockies, which means the Marlins might be able to wait a while and still pick him up later in the first round. Besides, they're still waiting for the final medical report on Harvey from the Angels' team doctor, which is of critical importance. "This is a not a case where if we take a guy and he's hurt, he just goes on the DL. This is a ten-million-dollar decision." For now, Harvey moves down the list.

"So it comes down to Nigel Wilson or Nied," Dombrowski continues. "You know we're going to get one of these two guys. I'd be happy to get either one, but I want to get the *best* one. Anybody feel real strongly that we ought to take the hitter?"

Doug Rader is here today. Though he's the Marlins hitting coach, he votes for Nied. "Anytime you can get a starting pitcher as opposed to a center fielder or DH, you do it," he says.

Two days earlier, the consensus in the organization was in favor of the outfielder, on the theory that pitchers are a bigger gamble. But Nied is thought to be a special case. "I would like to get Wilson," Dombrowski says finally. "I hope we do. But I would also say there are very few chances to get a number-one or number-two starter." Nied it is.

One by one the names go up on the board. The struggle always is between serviceable veterans who can fill spots in the lineup and prospects who might one day become stars. "We've got to discuss our purpose here," says Hughes, unhappy with the way the list is shaping up. "I thought we were going to go for high-ceiling guys."

"Right," says Dombrowski, "but we have to get guys who are going to play."

"The time to get prospects is in the first round," says Hughes, thinking more like a scout than a general manager. "We can fill in during the later rounds."

"We have talked about high-ceiling guys all along," says Dombrowski. "And that's real important. But I can't discard having to have a major league club."

"We're trying to put together a team," says Freeman, taking Dombrowski's side.

"No, we're not," says Hughes. "We're putting together an organization."

"We're doing both," says Dombrowski. "You're approaching this like it's an amateur draft."

"No, I'm not," says Hughes.

"You are, in some respects. *We have to have a team.*"

"Then we're changing our philosophy."

SOME GUYS have "parachutes"—they start out high on the board, then they fall. Guys like the Rangers' Kevin Reimer.

"I like Reimer's bat," says Dombrowski. "How bad a left fielder is he?"

MARCEL LACHEMANN: "Real bad."

RICK WILLIAMS: "Every ball that's hit to him, you wonder if he's going to catch it."

EGAN: "I've seen him go back for a fly ball and not even know where it landed."

DOMBROWSKI: "He may be one of those guys who can't play left field. How about first base?"

LACHEMANN: "Worse."

RADER: "If we're really going to try to be top heavy on pitching, I don't know that we should violate that with a guy like this. I think you can work with him, but I don't think it's ever going to be enough."

At least he thinks he can work with him. Charlie Hayes, on the other hand. . . . "I don't like his attitude," says Rader. "I don't like him as a player. I don't like him as a person. I think he's a dog." (Hayes doesn't even get a parachute. "I hope I didn't sour you guys on him," Rader says later. "I mean, a bunch of guys liked him and now he's not even on the board.")

Basically, though, the mood is upbeat for most of the afternoon. There are plenty of exciting players at the top of the list, and as the names go up, it's possible to imagine the beginnings of a respectable lineup. "Carr's a switch hitter, bats leadoff, and plays center for us," says Dombrowski, smiling while he dreams. "Barberie's a switch hitter, bats second, plays second. Destrade's a switch hitter, plays first, bats cleanup. That's a hopeful situation for an expansion team."

But as afternoon turns to evening—as daylight fades behind the window curtains, and the list grows longer—a suspicion is growing among some of the Marlin scouts that maybe they let themselves get too excited. The fact is, most of the players they want they probably won't get. Colorado will get some, of course, and others will be pulled back after the first round, leaving Florida to mine the bottom of the list. And the bottom of the list is ugly. "We're at the point now," Dombrowski says after just seventy-two names, "where we're talking about guys that will probably never be everyday players. Unfortunately, we've got a whole bunch more names to go through."

"We're going to have a horse-shit team," Young says flatly at the end of the evening. "I didn't realize it was going to be this bad. We're going to have to regroup."

THE BAD NEWS in the Marlin room on Friday is that the Rockies won the coin toss the day before and will choose first. The Marlins are now 0-2 in coin flips, having also lost to the Rockies before the June free-agent draft. The good news is that Philadelphia seems ready to go ahead with a deal for Danny Jackson, offering in return a couple of left-handed pitchers the Marlins are at least hopeful about, Joel Adamson and Matt Whisenant. What's even more exciting, Kansas City wants Dunston, and is willing to give the Marlins Conine or Berumen—whoever is not chosen in the first round—plus pitcher Dan Miceci, a highly touted prospect too young to be eligible for the draft. "Kansas City's a hot one," Dombrowski says. "We're at the point where doctors are talking to doctors."

But as quickly as it came together, the Kansas City deal falls apart. Royals GM Herk Robinson tells Wren in a late-afternoon phone call to the draft room that he's still not convinced Dunston's back is healthy; and, in his words: "I don't want to be known as the guy who traded the next David Cone," meaning Miceci.

Then, at 8:15 on Friday night, Destrade's agent, Willie Sanchez, calls and asks to speak to Dombrowski. More bad news. After a ten-minute conversation, Dombrowski reports: "I told him I have to walk away. I'm offering over three million dollars now and I'm just not going to give him any more money. He's trying to screw me, is what it comes down to."

By nine there's a party happening on the terrace outside the window, complete with a metal-drum band that might as well be playing right here inside the Marlin Room, the music is that loud. Dombrowski calls it a night. There are now more than 250 names on the board.

SATURDAY MORNING. The bosses are here—Barger and Huizenga, back from Scottsdale—and Barger is fuming. Today's *Sun-Sentinel* ran a story by writer Gordon Edes, speculating on what the Marlins might do in the draft. Nothing unusual about that, except that Edes mentioned the Marlins' interest in Carl Everett of the Yankees, which is close enough to the truth to cause Barger to suspect foul play. Everett is indeed high on the Marlins' list—number six, though later he will drop to number fourteen—but he was hurt most of the past year and has never played higher than class A. The Marlins happen to know that the Rockies' class-A coverage was spotty at best. They were sort of hoping Everett could be their little draft-day secret.

"Both Dave and I were more troubled by the story that came out today than any other," Barger says, indicating that Dombrowski, at least, is above suspicion. "We just got too many goddamn leaks in this organization! If Gordon has any connections with any of us, he's going to exploit them. I just hope it wasn't a direct leak because in all honesty, direct leaks will not be tolerated."

THIS MORNING, Dombrowski and his staff will take one last look at the draft board and make last-minute corrections. This afternoon they'll hold a mock draft, mainly to get a feel of what conditions will be like on draft day, when they'll have only four and a half minutes between picks and forty-five minutes between rounds. They'll try to nail down another trade or two—without mentioning any names, of course. And the next day they'll fly to New York aboard one of Huizenga's private jets, in plenty of time for the draft on Tuesday.

"Overall quality I think is less than what a lot of people thought it would be," says Reid, scanning the whole board with the benefit of a good night's sleep. "I'm disappointed in the number of quality everyday starters available. As for power, the way it looks right now our grounds crew won't even have to rake the warning track. Second-line guys—guys who've had a taste, and may get better given the chance to play—there aren't a whole lot of those either. Middle-infield defense is going to be extremely important to supplement our pitching staff."

Or as Hughes says later, "Not much for ninety-five million."

"WITH THE FIRST SELECTION in the first round," says Bill White shortly after two o'clock in a seventh-floor ballroom at the Times Square Marriott, "the Colorado Rockies select right-handed pitcher from the Atlanta Braves, Dave Nied."

"Well, that's one need that's filled," says the television announcer from inside the ballroom, so loudly that White thinks he's talking to him.

"What's that?"

Seven hours it lasts. And after that there are trades to announce and interviews to do, so that when Huizenga finally toasts his troops with champagne and congratulates them on a job well done, it is late in the evening.

Of the twenty-seven players on page one of their final list, the Marlins end up with seventeen, and lose only two—Nied and Darren Holmes—to the Rockies. "It's incredible," Lockman says.

Not really. The Rockies feel exactly the same way. "We went right down the list in the order that we wanted," says assistant GM Randy Smith with a smile that's at least as bright as Lockman's.

So whose list was better? Good question. Play ball.

# Index